Rock: The Primary Text

Developing a Musicology of Rock

Allan F Moore

Open University Press
Buckingham · Philadelphia

Open University Press
Celtic Court
22 Ballmoor
Buckingham
MK18 1XW

and

1900 Frost Road, Suite 101
Bristol, PA 19007, USA

First Published 1993

A catalogue record of this book is available from
the British Library

Library of Congress Cataloging-in-Publication Data

Moore, Allan F.
    Rock, the primary text: developing a musicology of rock / Allan
F. Moore.
        p.   cm. – (Popular music in Britain)
    Includes bibliographical references and index.
    ISBN 0-335-09787-1. – ISBN 0-335-09786-3 (pbk.)
    1. Rock music – History and criticism. I. Title. II. Series.
ML3534.M66 1992
781.66 – dc20   92-12471
                                                          CIP
                                                           MN

Typeset by Best-set Typesetter Ltd., Hong Kong
Printed in Great Britain by St Edmundsbury Press Ltd,
Bury St Edmunds, Suffolk

*For Sarah and Eleanor, for Mum and Dad,
and as a memorial to Kevin,
I dedicate this book to the glory of God*

Contents

Editorial Preface

What *is* British popular music? Does such a thing exist? What makes certain music and songs popular? And who made the musical cultures of these islands? What did Scots, Welsh, Irish and North American people have to do with the process? What part did people in the English regions play – the Geordies, Cockneys, Midlanders and all the rest? Where did the Empire fit in? How did European 'high' culture affect what most people played and sang? And how did all these factors vary in significance over time? In the end, just how much do we know about the history of musical culture on these tiny patches of land? The truth is that we know very little, and this realization led to this series.

The history of British people and culture has been dominated by capitalism for centuries; and capitalism helped polarize people into classes not only economically, but culturally too. Music was never *simply* music: songs were never *simply* songs. Both were produced and used by particular people in particular historical periods for particular reasons, and we have recognized this in the way in which we have put this series together.

Every book in this series aims to exemplify and to foster inter-disciplinary research. Each volume studies not only 'texts' and performances, but institutions and technology as well, and the culture practices and sets of social relationships through which music and songs were produced, disseminated and consumed. Ideas, values, attitudes and what is generally referred to as ideology are taken into account, as are factors such as gender, age, geography and traditions. Nor is our series above the struggle. We do not pretend to have helped produce an objective record. We are, unrepentantly, on the side of the majority, and our main perspective is from 'below', even though the whole musical field needs to be in view. We hope that by clarifying the history of popular musical culture we can help clear the ground for a genuinely democratic musical culture of the future.

Dave Harker and Richard Middleton

Acknowledgements

This book would not be in your hands were it not for the constructive presence of a wide variety of very different people: that it bears only my name seems somewhat iniquitous, a feeling mitigated only by the observation that its errors and misjudgements remain my responsibility. It has been the onerous task of three people in particular to tempt me to improve what is written here: my thanks are therefore particularly due to Richard Middleton, to Dave Harker and to Charlie Ford, all of whom read entire drafts of my material and gave me the benefit of much well-considered experience.

Many others have been good enough to share ideas with me over the twenty or more years I have been concerned with rock, particularly Lucy Green, who made comments on the early chapters of the book, Colin Stevens and Bob Sandek, with whom I practised for many years, Chris Bull and Antony Warde-Jones. For help in obtaining material, I thank Bruce and Alison Thompson, Mike and Louise Cole, Brenda and Paul Rowley, Mark Green, Julie Avenell, Jason Kaye, the UK National Sound Archive, Slough public library and the library of Thames Valley University.

Students of any music learn from the process of trying to communicate their ideas. I must acknowledge not only the particular formative influences of my teachers, of Peter Maxwell Davies, Peter Evans, Sebastian Forbes, Eric Graebner and Jonathan Harvey, but also the many students from whom I have learnt, and who have not always put up with my ill-conceived flights, particularly Anthony Followell, Peter Grimm and John Quirke.

Introduction

The title of this book raises two fundamental questions: what is 'rock' and, with respect to studies of musical practices, what constitutes 'the primary text'? The first of these questions is highly problematic, and I shall begin by refusing to offer a definition, in the belief that all readers will bring with them commonsense, and highly diverse, understandings of what 'rock' is to them. The question will receive its first detailed treatment in subsequent paragraphs of this introduction. Let me deal initially with the second question. This book has been written in the conviction that, within 'rock' criticism and commentary in general, insufficient attention is paid to what I call the 'primary text', i.e. that constituted by the sounds themselves, as opposed to commentaries on them, which constitute the 'secondary text'. In its principal concern with the primary text, this book's emphasis differs from that of most of the books in this series. I do not believe that in-depth consideration of the primary text is necessarily the most important approach for every music, at every time of writing, but for rock, in the 1990s, it is surely necessary. Rock is now well into its third decade (the term was first coined around 1967) and is still, at the detailed level, largely unstudied.

This is not the first book in this series to challenge established assumptions: Derek Scott's *The Singing Bourgeois* argues that the 'Victorian parlour song', perceived as a distinct genre, does not exist, while Dave Harker's *Fakesong* undertakes a similar task for the 'folk song'. Although it is not my primary intention to argue that the hallowed 'rock' is a similarly valueless term, it will be found that the range of applications and musics the term covers is sufficiently wide to caution against the belief in an 'essence' that separates rock from other sorts of music.

What does serve to separate rock from other sorts of music is a degree of consistency which can be found within its musical rules and practices. This consistency can most clearly be discussed by invoking the concept of 'style'. This concept I have borrowed from conventional musicological discourse (its first significant application was that of Guido Adler writing in the early years of this century: see Bent 1987: 41–3). For some writers, such as LaRue (1970), 'style' has a high degree of conceptual autonomy. Others, such as Crocker (1987) see it as historically mediated, at least: my approach is closer to Crocker's than LaRue's. Writers have also applied the concept of 'style' to rock, and here there is some real confusion over its meaning: thus Fabbri (1982: 133), discussing music, describes as 'genres' what many musicologists would tend to term 'styles', including those of hard rock, progressive rock and jazz rock. For many cultural theorists, particularly those concerned with film and literature, categories of genre seem to have priority over those of style. Style for these writers is more generally associated with ways of playing, singing, writing, etc., i.e. the specific techniques employed by an individual or established group and through which their work can be recognized. Genre is often elided with what musicologists might term 'form' (that is, the surface patterning of musical events), although even here the matter is not always dealt with clearly. In discussions of music, I believe all three categories to be present and distinguishable, while it is through consideration of 'style' that we can most clearly approach 'rock'. Stefani (1987: 14) offers a simple definition: ' "Style" is a blend of technical features, a way of forming objects or events; but it is at the same time a trace in music of agents and processes and contexts of production.' This fuller definition by Byrnside may be clearer:

> The term style refers to various levels, from the very general to the very particular. For instance, on a very general level one can refer to a Western style of music (as opposed to a non-Western style), or to a Renaissance style (as opposed to, say, a baroque style) . . . On a more particular level one may speak of a dixieland jazz style, as distinct from jazz style in general. On a still more particular level one can deal with the style of a given composer [sic], or even a specific composition. On any level the term style usually involves a description of the technical elements of the music. But a more complete assessment of a style takes into account certain things in the music that are not readily illustrated, verbally or graphically – certain aspects of performance, for instance, that are associated with, but not notated [sic] in, the music. A full assessment of a style also includes information and sometimes even speculation about the various relationships among the composer, the music, and its audience.
>
> (Byrnside 1975: 159–60)

The notion of 'one way of playing/writing' being more similar to a second than to a third, implicit in both Byrnside's and Stefani's definitions, is important for at least two reasons. Not only do rock's listeners concern themselves with such questions implicitly (by aligning themselves with, for example, 'heavy metal' but against 'progressive rock'), but also serious analysis of any area is predicated upon the recognition of degrees of difference within it. None the less, Philip Tagg has recently called attention to the essentialism present in such terms as 'black', 'white', 'Afro-American', 'European' when they refer to musics, questioning at how 'deep' a level supposed descriptions of style can be meaningful (Tagg 1989). Although Tagg is right, there is a danger that this can blind us to degrees of similarity between items of music. Thus, I shall take Byrnside's model of style as a starting point here, noting that although there can be no static definition of a 'rock' style, there do seem to be ways of articulating musical sounds that are *common to* (rather than *of the essence of*) many of those songs which listeners call 'rock', and that within this there are further sets of stylistic practices which, although they differ musically, need not imply other differences in cultural practices. It is those common features which are found widely pertinent to a style's practitioners which are basic to definitions of it. Genres, on the other hand, cut right across styles, such that there will be genres that intersect both rock *and* other styles of popular music. Any performance of an individual song will necessarily exemplify both. Thus, a list of genres relevant to rock style might include the 'uptempo dance number'[1] (notes, which in all cases are intended to provide further information, will be found immediately following the body of the text), the 'anthem'[2] and the 'romantic ballad'.[3] A more complete categorization would surely want to differentiate, with this last example, between the positions taken by the singer (unrequited approaches, love lost, etc.). The distinction approximates to that between the 'what' of the meaning of the song (genre) and the 'how' it is articulated (style). In some cases, the link between a particular genre and a particular style has taken on a degree of autonomy, as in what is often called the 'folk protest' song.[4] Throughout, my concern tends towards style, rather than genre. I shall also be concerned with how styles are musically constituted, and shall argue that styles tend to operate relatively passively, whereby they are historically constituted through the practices of particular bands, which practices thereby set up discernible stylistic conventions. It is these conventions which contribute to the concrete form of the consistencies alluded to above.

I am now in a position to begin to suggest what 'rock' is considered to be. I shall first parade some tentative definitions offered in the literature. Clarke (1989), the nearest we have to a complete encyclopedia of popular music in western industrial society, suggests that rock was no more than rock 'n' roll which had grown up, going on to assert that 'the name of the music was shortened to "rock" c.'67 to differentiate it from manufactured pop that had briefly subverted rock 'n' roll' (Clarke 1989: 996). In this short note we find a formulation of the biggest problem surrounding the term 'rock', that it was the antithesis of 'pop'. Thus Street (1986: 5) chooses to discuss 'rock' in terms that distinguish it from 'pop', while Ward *et al.* (1987: 249) insist that 'rock was more than just a *musical* development; it was a way of seeing the world, a way of life', setting up the opposition of 'authentic' rock and 'commercial' pop, to which I shall return. Ryback (1990), in discussing the developments of the music in 'Eastern Europe and the Soviet Union' (developments with which I am not concerned here), uses the terms 'rock' and 'rock 'n' roll' interchangeably, while Rees and Crampton (1989), although offering no definition, include chronologies of artists as diverse as Marvin Gaye, Tina Turner, Willie Nelson, Grandmaster Flash and Barbra Streisand, suggesting that 'rock' is almost synonymous with 'popular music'. Rather than adopt a simple definition, a more constructive approach is to focus on stylistic practices, suggesting that listeners cognize distinctions between styles through recognizing differences in the articulation of musical sounds, even though most listeners may be unable to explain those differences of articulation. Thus, rock styles tend to be distinct from 'soul' and its later offshoots (such as 'funk') in their treatments particularly of instrumentation, syncopation and the voice (although as funk bandleader George Clinton observed: 'Who says a funk band can't play rock?'). Rock styles are distinct from rock 'n' roll with reference to the same musical elements, although that latter music is a major progenitor. Rock styles are distinct from 'disco' and more recent 'dance' styles again in their treatment of syncopation (at least until the music of James and Jesus Jones, for instance), and also in their preferred media of transmission and venues. But, distinctions between rock and 'pop' styles are made not in terms of stylistic practice but in terms of the observations that rock (as opposed to 'pop') musicians apparently have control over both their material and their music's production. Rock is therefore ideologically defended simply as 'authentic' rather than 'commercial'. This is the greatest problem in defining 'rock', but I have reserved particular discussion of it until the section 'Blues as Pretext' in Chapter 3, because my argument depends on the techniques I shall argue for in Chapter 1, and develop in Chapter 2.

Aside from these difficulties, we should note here that rock is both a recorded and a live music, although my focus will be on the former, since it is in that format that the majority of its listeners know the majority of it. It is also as indigenous to the UK as it is to the USA and, as Ryback (1990) has shown, it is not restricted to these two main centres. In the interests of economy and intelligibility, I have had to restrict this study to developments in UK rock. There are material differences between UK and US rock, not only in terms of cultural practices, but in terms of stylistic factors too. I shall briefly raise these differences under the heading 'An Insular Path' in Chapter 3. The final thing to note here about rock is that it changes. Styles are brought to the fore through the prominence both of particular artists and associated cultural practices. Many will then recede and some will even seem to die. The industry that constructs the music develops new ways of operating. All of this means that we are always in the process of defining rock, and that no formulation I shall offer can be considered definitive.

Not only are there problems defining 'rock', there are similar problems defining a type of music to which I shall have need to refer, that (largely Central and Western European) music often called 'classical music', or 'concert music', or 'art music', or 'serious music'. That so many synonyms are used is an indication that there is no single music being referred to. Popular understanding frequently lumps together under a single heading the work of Bach, of Mozart, of Beethoven, of Wagner and a multitude of other composers, as if the stylistic and cultural practices of which they are part are in some sense monolithic. Our contemporary practices (concert going, record buying, etc.) make them appear so, but only through placing them in these, altogether new, contexts. I shall make reference to 'classical' and 'concert' and 'art' music, but shall define the terms further if I intend to refer to the practices which brought the music about, leaving the terms alone if I refer to current practices.

Because my emphasis is on texts, it will be necessary for me to establish the grounds for conceptualizing and considering such texts, which I shall largely do in Chapters 1 and 2. Thus, I shall have recourse to existing musicological concepts, although I shall further argue that the wholesale application of a conventional academic musicology is both unwarranted and unhelpful. My argument here will take the form that, since the techniques of such a discipline were developed for the analysis of musical pieces from the European 'classical' tradition, their application towards a music (rock) that involves very different assumptions and practices leads to unsupportable conclusions. Richard Middleton has recently suggested:

> A musicologist of popular music . . . [is] drawn to the 'cultivated' side by his training, to the 'popular' side by his subject-matter. Rather than pulling to one side, with the traditional musicologists, or the other, with the 'total critics' of musicology, it will be better to *look both ways, living out the tension.*
>
> (Middleton 1990: 123)

Although I would not claim to have succeeded in such a programme here, this has been my intention. While I neither require nor expect you, the reader, to have prior musicological competence, a familiarity with some technical concepts may make some of my illustrations easier to follow. (I have provided a glossary of musicological terms and concepts.) Notation examples are in all cases illustrative rather than central, and I have not therefore included notes on how to read notation: any standard introductory text (e.g. Karolyi 1965) performs this task simply. Although I shall take up the matter of competence in more detail in Chapter 5, I should say here that I recognize different types and degrees of competence. An inability to explain the musical details of a song (explanatory competence) does *not* entail an inability to understand those details (cognitive competence). I shall also cite what some psychological literature calls the 'trained listener'. This refers specifically to a listener who has acquired a high degree of cognitive competence, but with reference to (some) examples of the European 'classical' tradition. This point is important, because I shall maintain that competence is style-dependent, and thus that the 'trained listener' is not in a privileged position with regard to rock.

My emphasis on the listener I regard as central. We are not all performers, writers, producers, critics, or followers of any of the other activities supported by rock, but we are all listeners. Nattiez (1990) codifies three levels of analysis with which one can be concerned: the immanent (what actually inheres in the music), the poietic (how that music looks from the view of the producer) and the esthesic (how it looks from the point of view of the receiver), and it is the third on which I concentrate. As such, I deviate from most conventional musicological texts, which focus on the first two of Nattiez' levels. The esthesic level is, however, a difficult matter, for it is simply impossible to find out from every listener what sense they make of their listening activity. Basic information can potentially be sought from within two sub-disciplines. Psychologists of music collect data from listeners (whether 'trained' or not) with respect to European 'classical' music or its models. Although I shall make use of its findings where relevant, these must be considered provisional until such workers choose to collect data more widely. Sociologists of music have a tendency to assume monolithic listening publics, perhaps a necessary device in order to enable the question of music's reception to be addressed at all. Yet, as Grossberg (1985: 225) has noted: '[Rock's] fans differ radically among themselves although they may listen to the same music. Different fans seem to use the music for very different purposes in very different ways.' Thus, failing the detailed statistical exercises that are a necessary prerequisite to an adequate handling of how rock is used, I shall resort to a structure laying out possible 'functions' in the section of Chapter 1 on 'Listening strategy, style and functions'. I shall also adopt those tools of conventional analytical musicology that are pertinent to this study, largely those relating to discussions of harmony, melody and rhythm, but I shall re-interpret them in the light of the practices of rock.

Although the techniques I use are musicological, that does not mean that I regard them as self-sufficient. I must acknowledge here my indebtedness to those other secondary texts that approach rock from differing angles (particularly Frith 1983, Chambers 1985, Street 1986), to which I intend this book to be complementary. Consideration not only of musicological, but also of historical, political and sociological approaches are necessary to acquire anything approaching a rounded picture of the music. The problem is that the importance of the sounds is too often ignored. I shall tend to downplay cultural formations because of the difficulties in determining the mechanism(s) by which social relationships and cultural practices are embodied in musical sounds, difficulties which are yet to be satisfactorily resolved (I shall deal with this in more detail in Chapter 5). Although the sounds of rock cannot, ultimately, be divorced from their setting, they must be loosely separated in the interim, if the listening act is to receive adequate attention in any discussion of the cultural practices of rock.

Much of the book explores what may be loosely called an 'aesthetic' position. Simon Frith (1983: 54–5) suggests that the aesthetic question ('how does the text achieve its effects?') is secondary to the interpretation of the text's generalized social meaning: 'Is it repressive or liberating? Corrupting or uplifting? Escapist or instructive?' I remain unconvinced by the implicit essentialism here, and would suggest that what Frith cites as *the* aesthetic question is secondary to at least two others, which are 'what precise effects can the text achieve?' and, even more fundamentally, 'what does the text consist of?' Although it must be recognized that effects achieved for one listener may well not be perceived by another, there tends to be a *range* of effects that a listener is likely to find within a text. Gibson (1979) suggests that features of the environment *afford* a range of meanings to the perceiver,[5] which is a useful concept because it throws the emphasis on the text rather than the perceiver, the text being by far the more accessible. Although, ultimately, I think we should be most interested in the perception of a text, feasible responses, centred on that text, must first be explored, and it is in this area that my work moves. Any writing on music that attempts to be more than just superficial does depend on prior familiarity with the music under discussion. Owing to the introduction of compact disc technology, and the policy of many record companies to re-issue old discs in this format, access to much of the rock that was unavailable a few years ago is now possible, and not only in the countries in which that music originated. Although the thrust of my arguments throughout does not require access to any music, following up my detailed points does require some such access. In the UK, this is facilitated by the presence in many local libraries of compact disc and cassette tape stocks. (The library of the National Sound Archive in Kensington, London, is also invaluable.) My examples are many and varied. One important reason for this comes from my attempt to subvert the growth of an accepted 'canon' of popular music (which already accepts the Beatles, 'punk' and Bob Dylan, at the very least). The study of European 'classical' music has been greatly hampered by an over-profusion of studies of 'the great composers' at the expense of those whose music is considered to be self-evidently of lesser value. Popular music studies must not be allowed to fall into the same trap.

So, the title of this book encapsulates both my subject matter and my approach to it. The argument it supports is diverse, and so I summarize its main elements here. Simple definitions of 'rock' are problematic, as I have shown. We can, however, evolve an understanding of what 'rock' is, in musical terms, by treating it as structured by a multiply-evolving but coherent set of rules and practices. In order to elucidate these, Chapter 1 argues for the development of a musicology particular to rock, which may share aspects of established musicology, but which acknowledges that rock differs in its purposes, publics and aims. The primary elements of such a musicology are then laid out in Chapter 2, chiefly exemplified by the beat and rhythm 'n' blues styles of the early 1960s, while further aspects are held back until later.

Like all musics, the rules of rock are culturally constructed. Meaning, feeling, expression and the like are always mediated. This leads me to critiques of rock myths of authenticity and unmediated expression. These are centred on the ideological appropriation of the ethos and techniques of the 'blues' in Chapter 3, and extend to discussions of a range of more recent rock styles in Chapter 4. It also leads me, in Chapter 3, to a critical rehabilitation of 'progressive rock' (which is often attacked as *too* constructed), through consideration of the sources of the styles which constitute it, and related issues such as the practices of improvisation. The internal consistencies of rock's rules and practices enable rock history to be explained in a relatively immanent way, and 'progressive' rock occupies a pivotal position in such an explanation.

The concept of *style* is crucial to an understanding of these rules and practices, since it is in this context that their consistencies are most clearly exhibited. This will be demonstrated throughout Chapters 2, 3 and 4. It is, moreover, the main mechanism of musical *meaning*. This issue forms the focus of Chapter 5 where I shall problematize other mechanisms, notably the concept of homologies and the semiotic interpretation of individual songs. I shall propose an alternative way of proceeding with the latter. Other meanings exist, and I do not deny the cultural and political power of much of rock, but my findings lead me to question the extent to which these meanings inhere in the music.

1   *Issues in Theory*

The opening sections of this chapter situate the activity of analytical musicology, and explore its use to date in discussions of 'rock'. The remainder of the chapter focuses on purported differences between 'classical' and 'popular' musics. 'Classical' in this sense refers to the musical tradition of Mozart and Beethoven, of Tchaikovsky, Stravinsky and Stockhausen, about whose products detailed musical theories have been constructed. 'Popular' refers here not only to 'rock', but in this discussion, it would be pedantic to insist on a separation of 'rock' from the more general 'popular'. After discussing the generalized differences which are supposed to distinguish these musics, I argue that conventional bourgeois musicology (those 'detailed musical theories') cannot simply be applied to rock. It will be the task of Chapter 2 to begin the necessary re-formulation.

The musicological background

As a musicologist practising in twentieth-century music, but with many years' experience and love of that music called 'rock', I find it as difficult as ever to understand the intransigence of the academic musical community in refusing to negotiate with what has recently been, according to Frith (1983: 137–50) and Wallis and Malm (1984: 74–85), the fastest growing industry in the world. Some initial reason[1] for this may be sought in the fact that most musicologists still labour under a notion of music as 'pure form, liberated from any object or from matter' (Schelling, writing in the eighteenth century, quoted in Street 1989: 86). This notion encourages a belief that music is somehow autonomous with respect to the culture in which it appears, a belief that has become an intrinsic aspect of most analytic musicology. As a set of techniques for dealing with musical texts, analytic musicology (or music analysis) can be traced back as far as the fifteenth century, where it was used to supply tools for composition. It only began to assume its present form in the early nineteenth century (see Bent 1987: 32–6), when musicologists became particularly concerned with the canonical 'masterpieces' of the western tradition (which they largely situated in what are now Austria and Germany). Their programme was to discover what made these works 'great'. In this century analytic musicology has come under the sway of positivism, such that it argues that the 'effects' of music, because they are unquantifiable, are not worthy of consideration. Although the activity of analysing music has, thus, treated the music as autonomous, that activity itself is clearly an expression of its culture. As the historian of analysis Ian Bent observes:

> Analysis is the means of answering directly the question 'How does it work?' . . . [but] the analyst works with the preconceptions of his [sic] culture, age and personality. Thus the preoccupation which the 19th century had with the nature of 'genius' led to the phrasing of the initial question not as 'how does it work?' but as 'What makes this great?', and this has remained the initial question for some analytical traditions late in the 20th century.
>
> (Bent 1987: 50)

The programme of Heinrich Schenker, the most notable of the early twentieth-century analysts, was designed to 'prove' that the music of Bach, Beethoven and Brahms was intrinsically better than the modernism of Stravinsky, Schoenberg *et al.* (see, for example, Schenker 1979). His methods remain paradigmatic. As will become plain, it is not this initial question (what makes this great?) that concerns me. Lucy Green, a writer who regards the wholesale assumption of autonomy as erroneous, none the less notes that styles of music are autonomous in the sense that their internal logic can be explored without reference to external matters (Green 1988: 82). This gives rise in the minds of musicologists to the belief that this internal logic somehow represents the essence of the music (an essence which is incommunicable), while extra-musical factors act to distract listeners from this and are thus dispensable (Green 1988: 100).[2]

Against this assumption of autonomy, sociologists in particular have recently begun to argue that musical structures are entirely socially determined (e.g. Willis 1978), a position with which the musicologist John Shepherd seems to have some sympathy. He notes that music in Western societies has been considered autonomous because of the marginal position it occupies: he notes that 'music is not seen as central to social processes' (Shepherd 1991: 215), a belief that is far less common in other societies. The oppositional views adopted by musicologists and sociologists arise because, whereas musicologists have assumed that the 'internal logic' constitutes the entire meaning of music, sociologists have argued that the 'social role' of music constitutes its entire meaning. Neither position, I think, is useful to adopt. Although in explaining the internal logic of a style it is not always necessary to refer to external factors, a style cannot appear *ex nihilo*. To take a gross example, 'rock' could not have arisen in sixteenth-century Florence, for its style is in part constituted by the use to which it puts electronic technology (see Chapter 4, first section). It is necessary, therefore, to regard musical styles as partially autonomous, whereby internal and external features inform each other.

Analytical approaches

Fortunately, over the past twenty years, a few musicologists have begun to focus their attention on rock and its related musics, and it is to them that I now turn. Although these writers have adopted a number of different approaches, they seek one of three goals. The first is to elucidate theoretical approaches pertinent to the music. This activity is best considered pre-analytical, since any analysis must be based on theoretical preconceptions, which too often remain implicit. Its most outstanding example is Middleton (1990). The remaining approaches are both strictly analytical. Of these, one aims to unearth the 'meaning' of individual songs, while the other aims to discover the characteristic features of particular styles.

To the specialist reader, probably the most familiar of the texts taking either of these latter approaches is Wilfrid Mellers's treatment of the Beatles (1973). It is also, perhaps, the most conventional, for Mellers writes from a position firmly within established musicology. He approaches the meaning of individual songs through examining music-theoretical constructs, particularly those of rhythm[3] and mode/key, referring these back to the content of the songs' lyrics. Speaking of the girl in 'Norwegian Wood', Mellers tells us that 'her polished archness is satirised in an arching waltz tune wearily fey, yet mildly surprising because in the mixolydian mode. Here the flat seventh gives to the comedy an undercurrent of wistfulness' (Mellers 1973: 59). Elsewhere, discussing Debussy's opera 'Pelléas et Mélisande', Mellers suggests that Pelléas' 'life-enhancing qualities are associated with a characteristically eager, syncopated rhythm, and with the "sharp" key of E. But his music . . . never "gets anywhere" harmonically' (Mellers 1968: 66). The terms of discussion are fundamentally the same: they support his general programme of 'starting from a . . . detailed description of what happens in musical terms, [and proceeding] to relate these musical events to their physiological and psychological consequences' (Mellers 1980: vii).

Mellers clearly does not believe that 'popular' and 'classical' musics need to be discussed in different terms; he straightforwardly applies the same types of criteria to the music of both Lennon and McCartney, and Debussy, although he avoids making value judgements between these musics on the basis of those criteria. In so doing, he assumes that mode/key, lyrics and basic rhythmic pattern are the fundamental aspects of the Beatles' music: they are what constitute the 'musical events'. All other factors, including those others we are able to hear, have secondary, articulative functions.[4] This assumption is taken over wholesale from the established musicological position relating to concert music (whether it is adequate to this music is not an issue I can raise here).

The music of Lennon and McCartney is also the subject of two articles by Walter Everett (1985, 1986) among the first on rock to appear in musicological journals. That neither seems to have attracted comment may be taken to mean that the Beatles have joined some established musical canon, although what other music that canon may include is unclear. Everett undertakes analyses of 'She's Leaving Home', 'Strawberry Fields Forever' and 'Julia', from the perspective of Schenkerian theory:[5] I shall restrict my own comments to the first article.

Schenkerian theory assumes (and undertakes to demonstrate) that any musical surface (foreground) is an elaboration of more middleground and background successions of sound-events. As such, it does not suggest that musical phenomena are in some way special: this theory of elaboration would correspond to established theories of generative linguistics, taking the spoken sentence as an elaboration of an underlying 'deep' structure: see Brown (1984: 117–20).[6] A Schenkerian theorist interested in Cream's 'Sunshine of Your Love' would demonstrate how the riff that underlies the first two-thirds of each stanza elaborates the chords of the blues progression that form its conceptual background. This is an unproblematic example, for there are direct correspondences between the notes of the blues chords and the notes of the riff, and between the I–IV–I succession[7] (A minor – D minor – A minor) which begins the blues progression and the transposition of the riff by the equivalent interval. In 'She's Leaving Home', Everett argues that the surface (the notes we actually hear) and the background (which, at its deepest level, is simply a I–V–V–I progression) are rather divorced from each other. Indeed, he suggests that this background actually becomes lost as the song progresses, and uses this observation to suggest that the music itself thereby enhances the psychological conflict between the parents and daughter that is the subject of the lyrics. As a demonstration of the interdependence of music and text it is both interesting and persuasive. In practice, it is a sophisticated attempt to carry out the same task Mellers set himself, to understand the meaning of the song (both words and music) through the application of established music-theoretical methodology. It is hard to argue that 'surface' and 'background' are inappropriate concepts for popular musics, but it cannot be unquestioningly assumed that those procedures for generating a surface from a middleground that are normative in tonal concert music will necessarily apply to these musics. As I shall later argue, they must be considered different 'languages', especially with regard to harmonic succession and rhythmic profile. Again, Everett assumes that *pitches* and the order in which they occur (the subject of Schenkerian theory) constitute the events of this music, articulated as they are by instrumentation, timbre, studio techniques and other musical features.

The most thoroughgoing attempt at providing an analytical model for the study of popular music is probably that of Philip Tagg (1979), a summary of which is reported in Tagg (1982). Part of the value of his work lies in its concern both with the sounds themselves, and with their transmission and mediation. The music-analytic part of his theory is explicit and detailed in its concern with the encoding of meaning within harmony and melody, a topic which has long exercised music theorists, and to which I shall return in

Chapter 5. Indeed, in this area his theory seems most reminiscent of that developed by Deryck Cooke (1959), who effectively offered a lexicon of melodic phrases and their range of associative meanings. Tagg (1982) analyses the Abba hit 'Fernando'. Part of his argument hinges on the interval of the tritone (six semitones), which he describes as 'a stereotype of longing'. Although this enables him to make a very powerful interpretation of the song, the link between 'longing' and the tritone is merely one hallowed by association. (I find the importance attached to such associative meanings unsatisfactory, and shall return to the question in Chapter 5). In the same article, we are offered a detailed 'generative' analysis of the opening of the signature tune to the 1970s TV show *Kojak*. This utilizes not only the Schenkerian notions of foreground and background, but also the somewhat anti-Schenkerian theories of melodic implication adapted from Gestalt psychology by Meyer (especially 1956) and Narmour (1977). Tagg argues that much popular music relies on a melody–accompaniment dualism, and there is the implication in this work that an explication of the melody can largely stand for an explication of the entire musical fabric. Thus, other features of the sound-surface can effectively be ignored. As far as the music-analytic part of his theory is concerned, his aim is reminiscent of those of both Mellers and Everett.

A rather different approach was adopted in Richard Middleton's early discussion of the relationship between the 'blues' and what was then just 'pop music' (Middleton 1972). Middleton's implicit concern is with style, and with the adoption of stylistic features of what was understood as 'the blues', and of its cultural position, by white youth in the 1950s and 1960s. Aside from providing a useful investigation into the cultural role of the style, for both its black originators and its more socially advantaged white adopters, Middleton defines the blues stylistically with reference primarily to rhythmic profiles, but also to harmonic usage, melodic patterns and vocal tone. In its refusal to make reference to criteria adopted from concert music, his treatment of pop is illuminating, and his discussion of how effects are achieved is not limited to the melodic and harmonic aspects of the music:

> In *Lucy in the Sky with Diamonds* . . . the visionary dream induced by the uninvolved, feelingless glare of the timbres (the brightness of hallucination), by the ostinato, the surrealist lyrics, the electronics and the vague, 'timeless' vocal tone is 'awakened' by a faster, simpler, more tonally obvious refrain, which each time it comes brings us back to 'reality'.
>
> (Middleton 1972: 233–4)

Although Hatch and Millward (1987) are also concerned to trace the stylistic development of blues into rock, they adopt an alternative approach in their 'analytic history of pop music' (to quote the book's subtitle). They offer definitions of the blues in terms of harmonic structure and rhythmic contour, which (like Middleton 1972: 34) they insist distorts the musical object, but their music-analytic content focuses on the concept of 'song families'. This derives from studies of so-called traditional song, wherein songs are considered to belong to the same family if their tunes share a putative common origin, or if one can be considered as derived from another by the 'normal' processes of transmission, both oral and written (see Bohlman 1988: 14–32). It is a concept far removed from those of conventional analytical musicology, which is interested in what makes individual pieces unique. Hatch and Millward's emphasis is likewise on mode/key, harmonic patterns and melodic structure, although they do attempt to incorporate the particular performance charac-teristics that are always so hard to notate: slides, vocally toying with the beat, non-tempered pitching and the like. This is important because the object, for analytical musicology, tends to be visual (the score) rather than aural (the performance). Thus, anything resistant to notation usually gets marginalized.

Thus far, two broad approaches can be discerned. Mellers and Everett make use of tools from conventional analytical musicology in making inter-pretations of individual songs. Middleton and Hatch and Millward demon-strate that it is possible to make some analytical comment on popular music without wholesale recourse to criteria derived from concert music. Ronald Byrnside's short essay on the formation of early rock 'n' roll style (1975) further develops the discussion of rhythmic, rather than pitch, patterns, but to a different end. His aim is to define the style through certain exemplars, rather than to interpret those examples themselves. He provides justification for his approach through noting that 'rhythm and blues was dance music,' where the accentual pattern he identifies in the music closely corresponds to the bodily movements made in dancing to it. Byrnside does not ignore other domains – indeed, he acknowledges the importance of the harmonic language and formal structure of the blues in the formation of rock 'n' roll style – but his concen-tration on rhythmic patterns leads one to believe that he would have the listener hear this as the style's defining element (as listeners may well do). Although this is hardly an approach one would find adopted by a concert music analyst, it would be possible to argue that other musical styles are equally rhythmically, rather than harmonically, determined. Reggae comes clearly to mind, as does the eighteenth-century classicism of Mozart and Haydn. The fact that such arguments are rarely proposed with reference to Western styles[8] probably tells us more about writers on such music, and their traditions of enquiry, than about the styles themselves. Byrnside's approach does have links with conventional musicology, for in his concentration on the formation of rock 'n' roll style, he draws analogies with stylistic change in Western art music at the beginning of the seventeenth and twentieth centuries. These links are wholly absent in Gary Burns's recent discussion of 'hooks' in popular music (Burns 1987).

Burns adopts an initial definition of a hook as 'a musical or lyrical phrase that stands out and is easily remembered' (Burns 1987: 1). His definition would seem to limit the 'hook' to the realm of melody, but he attempts to extend it to cover almost every conceivable realm, from rhythm, melody, harmony and lyrics through to improvisation, tempo, dynamics, effects, editing, mix etc. Although he actually argues that rhythm should be accorded priority, the implication in his analysis is that none of these domains is effectively prior, and that all can contribute independently. (It would be interesting to see the use of this typology pursued in practice.) Indeed, he defines his aim in terms of providing the basic elements for a musical analogue to the 'close analysis' of film criticism, in that he suggests the 'hook' to be the musical equivalent of the film 'frame', the 'smallest unit that has meaning in itself and is recognisable as belonging to a specific whole' (Burns 1987: 17). Thought of in this way, his 'hook' is remarkably similar to the 'chunk',[9] in terms of which, psychologists tell us, all perception seems to be organized. The article originating this notion was Miller (1956), and a great deal of work has recently been directed to it among researchers in the psychology of music. An explanation of its major use in this sphere appears in Lerdahl and Jackendoff (1985: 13–17), while Moore (1990) gives an overview of its use. The aim of Burns's analysis may be interpreted as enabling possibly more sophisticated analyses of meaning than those mentioned above.

Although this brief survey[10] would tend to suggest that a variety of *analytical* approaches has been adopted by musicologists, their aims are really only two-fold. Some are interested in individual songs, in which case the aim is to discover their meaning through the (adaption and) application of established musicological theories that treat the music as an established entity largely in isolation from its transmission, mediation and style (Tagg's work clearly stands out against this trend). Others are interested in the style constituted by individual songs, in which case the interpretation of the meaning of those individual songs is of far less importance. The criteria adopted tend to assume that the musical entities under discussion are formed from domains of different levels of importance. Pitch (melody and harmony) or rhythm are considered prior; texture, timbre, sound manipulation etc. are secondary. Nowhere does this position, which derives directly from the theoretical position adopted towards concert music, seem to be argued.

The aesthetic question

Because of the importance of rock to the leisure industry, with all that this entails, the majority of writers on it have not been musicologists. Aside from the mass of popular music journalism, we can find general histories of the styles of popular music (Ward *et al.* 1987) and histories of particular eras (Taylor 1987). We have myriad biographical studies, from those of individual artists (Sanders 1976), to those of individual record companies (Gillett 1975), to those of particular movements (Rimmer 1985). We have sociological over-views of the music's institutions (Frith 1983), its cultural meanings (Hebdige 1985) and its lack of them (Reynolds 1990), its political content (Harker 1980), its record companies (Gillett 1983) and its history (Chambers 1985). We can also find interpretations of purpose (Turner 1988), personal histories (Cohn 1970), involved backgrounds to individual projects (Braun *et al.* 1970) and studies that attempt to incorporate almost every possible approach (Eisen 1969). To the musicologist interested in popular music, this wide range of writings is extremely valuable for, as Tagg states, 'Studying popular music is an interdisciplinary matter. . . . The musicologist . . . can draw on sociological research to give his analysis proper perspective' (Tagg 1982: 40). Yet the general lack of concern in such writing with the primary text, with the sounds themselves, cannot go unchallenged. I would concur with Middleton (1990: 115ff.), who argues for the value of giving 'an independent account of what actually happens in the music', for reasons that I hope are worth exploring.

At the outset of Simon Frith's key work, in what seems to me a crucial passage, he states:

> Most rock musicians lack formal training, and so do all rock commentators. They lack the vocabulary and techniques of musical analysis, and even the descriptive words that critics and fans do use – harmony, melody, riff, beat – are only loosely understood and applied. I share this ignorance.
>
> (Frith 1983: 13)

In the face of such professed ignorance, it would seem foolhardy to attempt to come to terms with the sounds themselves. As we shall see below, Frith does not consider this a particularly important exercise although he, at least, is aware of the intoxicating effect of the sounds of the music (Frith 1987, 1988a). To exemplify the problem, note that he suggests that 'disco is a much richer musical genre than progressive rock' (Frith 1987: 134), a statement he does not pursue. Paolo Prato appears to disagree: 'Disco music can be viewed as a "senile disease" of rock and soul music' (Prato 1985: 381); this is a view he does something to support. At the very least, we would need to know how 'richness' and 'senility' are musically constituted, unless they are simply rhetorical disguise for 'like' and 'dislike'. The problem is that a commentary that does not have a sound theoretical underpinning is liable to be of uncertain quality at best. Certainly no sociologist would attempt to explain, say, the role of the record companies in the changing business of popular music without having an acceptable framework of cultural theory on which to base it (Frith has recently offered such a theory; see Frith 1990: 104–14). Such an explanation (as opposed to a description) would be impossible. The sounds, however, are frequently considered not to merit such a framework.

This in turn makes it vital to distinguish between the text and its interpretation, between cognition and aesthetic value.[11] The interpretative content of subsequent chapters, which follows on from textual description, is limited to the development of an acceptable framework for considering rock's sounds, and to discussions of style. Frith, on the other hand, emphasizes value, taking what Paul Willis cites as one extreme position, insisting 'that the "value" of the music is *totally* socially given' (Willis n.d.: 14). Frith considers value a function of use:

> What makes a work of mass culture good or bad? The problem is to decide the criteria of judgment. High art critics often write as if their terms of evaluation were purely aesthetic, but mass culture critics can't escape the fact that the bases for cultural evaluation are always social: what is at issue is the *effect* of a cultural product. . . . The aesthetic question – how does the text achieve its effects? – is secondary.
>
> (Frith 1983: 54–5)

It seems to me that our concern with the music includes, but does not begin from, the ways that it is used: in other words, the aesthetic question is primary, as I have suggested in the introduction. Our concern has to begin from the sounds, because *until we cognize the sounds*, until we have created an internal representation on the basis of their assimilation, *we have no musical entity to care about*, or to which to give value.[12] Once it has been produced, nobody is in a position to exclusively determine how it is to be taken (the appropriation by racist skinhead culture of millenarian reggae is a prime example). This does not mean that the musical text may be considered to arise *ex nihilo*. It is produced by groups of musicians working in social contexts, but they are not my primary concern. I am far less interested in uncovering the circumstances which produced the music than I am in exploring how listeners may respond to it. As listeners, although we must recognize and exteriorize our grounds for cognizing the text, this does not imply that we will all do it in the same way. This will depend on the style to which we assign that text, and our competence within that style, a matter I shall pursue in Chapter 5. I therefore make no apology for my emphasis throughout being on the sounds themselves, nor for attempting to provide for any interpretation of them a theoretical underpinning that does not assume one particular established musicological theory to be congruent to the music at all points (and thus correct), merely because of apparent surface similarities between the melody, chords or rhythm used by Schumann (say) and the Beatles (this hallowed comparison stems from the American composer Ned Rorem; see Rorem 1969). I shall 'draw on sociological research to give my analysis proper perspective' (Tagg 1982: 40) but, for me, the aesthetic question has primacy.

In order to propose answers to this question, quite a large amount of technical discussion will prove necessary. I would encourage you, from whatever background you come, to persevere with the discussions of styles that interest you. It seems to me important to explore any human activity as fully as possible, from any angle that may hold promise, especially since, with this activity (listening to rock), so many pairs of ears are involved. Any thought about music must be predicated upon the perception of differences and degrees of difference, and I intend subsequent chapters to develop something of a 'language' to permit this to take place for rock. Ultimately, I doubt that the value of any music analysis can actually be argued – it can only be demonstrated – but I hope to demonstrate that the criteria I explicitly put forward are of more use than those adopted by musicologists considered above.

The pop–classical split

I shall consider many of the supposed distinctions between 'popular' and 'classical' musics in detail later in this section. For now, let me focus just on the most blatant of these. Musicologists have tended to ignore popular musics through a mis-equation of complexity with profundity (see Blacking 1987: 1–27). Popular musics, with their apparently simplistic uses of the most banal harmonic and rhythmic material, have simply not been thought worthy of any effort. Excellent studies such as Whittall (1988), intended for the informed amateur, are thought to need no qualification as to the sort of music they are concerned with. The one area where musicologists have been unable to avoid the confrontation is in the use of electronics in music. Most of the standard texts on the development of electronic concert music include a chapter or so on rock, and their treatment can be poor and uncomprehending. For example, Peter Manning's introduction to the area praises the dexterity of Rick Waterman [*sic*] of Yes, and Brian Eno in his album '*Roxy Music* (1972)'. His understanding of the electric guitar also seems suspect, resulting in some confusion between vibrato (frequency modulation) and tremolo (amplitude modulation):

> Tremolo . . . found early favour. . . . Pitch vibrato could not be generated elec-
> tronically except with extreme difficulty . . . the presence of frets on the finger-
> board restricted the performer's ability to produce such an effect himself.
>
> (Manning 1985: 202)

Manning is an acknowledged expert in the field of electronic avant-garde music, but no rock writer considering the importance to the classical style of, say, 'Bathoven'[13] could expect to be taken seriously. (I have found the best cursory survey of this type to be that in Griffiths 1979: 60–5.)

Clearly, any attempt at evaluation has to be made against the background of a (stylistic) norm. The issue for any critic is one of choosing a valid norm. The cultural practices of rock not being those of most musicologists, such critics tend to use the norms of music familiar to them that hold the greatest surface similarity to that of writers like McCartney, for instance, i.e. songs and other miniatures of late eighteenth- and nineteenth-century concert music. Where this concert music tradition can be shown to have a direct influence, such an approach is justified. But, the norms of this tradition leave untouched those very factors where rock can be at its most interesting (and complex and profound): timbre, texture, sound manipulation, performance practice etc. Thus, whatever criteria are proposed, they must relate explicitly to the music under discussion, rather than be imported unaltered from some distantly related tradition. (Much of my purpose in the ensuing chapters will be to try to map out certain normative aspects.) This point cannot be over-stressed. It explains many of the difficulties that have marked the inclusion of pop music in the school music curriculum, and also the misunderstandings of classical music perpetrated by pop educators.[14] This brings me to explicit consideration of the supposed distinctions between 'popular' and 'classical' musics, or the 'pop–classical split', which, although less vehemently argued than it was ten or fifteen years ago, is still a matter of some import.

The historical basis of the demarcation between 'popular' and 'classical' musics in Europe is well attested, and can be located in the decline of artistic patronage and the attendant rise of a bourgeois market in the late eighteenth century. (I am inclined to agree with Harker (1985), who argues that the third strand, the music of the so-called 'folk', was effectively a creation of the leisured audience.) The division is not as straightforward as it is sometimes made out to be. Richard Middleton (1990: 12–15) argues for three periods of momentous change in the relationship between the two musics, citing (with respect to Britain) the 1790s to 1840s, the 1890s to 1920s, and possibly the 1950s. After each period, the lines of demarcation have been redrawn. Thus, for example, in the second half of the previous century, composers such as Grieg and Brahms would produce music that often straddled the divide. In the early years of this century, classical composers were recognized as either more 'serious' (e.g. Schoenberg) or more 'popular' (e.g. Léhar). In recent years, partly owing to apparently declining audiences for classical musics, the split has become properly worthy of debate (see Tegen 1985).

Although those who have taken part in this debate have come from a variety of intellectual traditions, they seem to have taken up one of three basic positions. The first of these, to *deny the split*, and the second, to use it to *argue the concomitant superiority of one or the other music*, will be explored now. The third, to deny that the split enables *judgements of comparative value* to be made, will be approached below.

Many writers have denied the pop–classical split, frequently implying in the process that 'good' music is self-evident, no matter what the style. This is the approach adopted by those who have tended to argue that the Beatles were in a direct line of descent from the *lieder* composers of the nineteenth century, a position exemplified by Mellers and Everett (see above), who apply to rock techniques developed from, and for, classical styles. Graham Vulliamy (1975) has argued that this denial of the split is a result of the increasing legitimation gained by rock, as it has approached the status of a canonical music. With the work of the Beatles and, later, progressive rock groups, this came about both through their appeal to higher status social groups, and through the changing content of the music. Such musics are thus opposed to reggae, for example, which in its appeal to ethnic, religious and sub-cultural minorities (Rastafarians and skinheads) has never been burdened with the same charges. Vulliamy does not suggest that the rock musicians involved have consciously striven for this legitimation, although he does argue a parallel case for the 'third stream' jazz that arose in the 1950s. He further points out that the 'legitimations of rock music which incorporate "high culture" terminology serve merely to reinforce the acceptance of a set of assumptions which have been shown to be highly questionable' (Vulliamy 1975: 147).

A further legitimation has been sought by those apologists for classical music who have felt their position to be beleaguered, and who attempt to accommodate the 'best' rock into their canon on the basis of certain observed similarities with classical styles. They frequently seem to be involved in education (see Green 1988: 116–18). Middleton has argued that this position is unnecessarily simplistic, insisting that 'there is no longer a basic division in the musical field between "pop" and "classics". Instead the lines of contradiction cross *all* genres and practices' (Middleton 1985b: 41; see also 1990: 248). Thus, the most generous formulation of this position holds that differences cannot be adequately accounted for along the lines of a simple 'pop–classical' split.

Both the remaining positions involve acceptance of a split, but disagree over its consequences: writers have argued the necessary superiority of both classical and popular styles. Arguments in favour of classical music ultimately depend either on its continued existence through historical time, or on its aesthetic autonomy (a concise summary of these is given by Vulliamy 1975: 133–4). The ideology of musical autonomy, which has held sway since the Enlightenment, has been discussed above. In this context, its most important assertion is that European 'classical' music is functionless: the music is therefore divorced from the more mundane concerns of living. Consequently, it somehow transcends these and is thus 'superior' to musics that are clearly functional. (Oddly, arguments proposing lack of functionality tend not to be levelled at the 'classical' musics of South-East Asia.) I shall argue below that this apparent lack of function is not actually the case.

Arguments in favour of popular musics are mostly of more recent origin, and tend to focus on the belief that classical music is elitist, both because it considers itself autonomous and because its 'language' needs to be learnt (unlike the 'languages' of 'popular' musics). Such arguments stretch from consideration of the availability of musical training, through the sound of the music itself, to access to its institutions (including financial access). Again, I shall argue that the 'language' argument fails. All musics require learning.

The most persuasive arguments in favour of popular musics in this context have tended to be put forward by John Shepherd (e.g. 1976, 1987a, 1991). They seem to hinge on a basic claim, which follows from an important distinction offered by Andrew Chester (1970). Although Chester does not actually argue for the superiority of either classical or pupular musics, he suggests that

> Western classical music is the apodigm of the *extensional* form of musical composition. [Its forms] build diachronically and synchronically outwards from basic musical atoms. The complex is created by a combination of the simple, which remains discrete and unchanged in the complex unity. . . . Rock however follows . . . the path of *intensional* development. . . . The simple entity is constituted by the parameters of melody, harmony and beat, while the complex is built up by modulation [*sic*] of the basic notes, and by inflexion of the basic beat.
>
> (Chester 1970: 78–9)

For Shepherd, Chester's argument would be a little simplistic: the classical tradition never actually espoused perfect intonation and mathematically precise rhythms. Shepherd is correct when he claims that 'Good performances in the "classical" tradition *depend* on subtle deviations from the notational norms of pitch and rhythm' (Shepherd 1987b: 159), although our sure evidence of this dates only from the advent of recordings. He cites classical ('analytic') notational practice as the cause of the misunderstanding, suggesting that the very repeatability built into the tonal system means that its logic is clear and self-evident, and that therefore 'people hear only the external surface of notes in the "classical" tradition, not the interior richness that remains even after analytic notation has done its work' (Shepherd 1987b: 161). His argument then follows the path that 'classical' music thus engenders alienation between the minority with and the majority without 'power and influence'. 'Classical' music is thus of negative value to that majority. The chief problem is not only that his prior claim, that classical logic *seems* 'clear and transparent' and that listeners can then hear only the 'external surface', is unsubstantiated, but also that it is difficult to see how it could properly be determined (that a wide range of listeners can *learn* to hear the 'interior richness' is demonstrable).

Shepherd has gone further in his attack on classical styles, arguing that the alienation from the music felt by listeners corresponds to their lack of power in Western industrial society. He bases his argument on a supposed homological relation that exists between 'classical' music and Western industrialized society (Shepherd 1977c), with the unfortunate conclusion that a liking for classical music implies membership of the minority with 'power and influence', rather than the reverse.[15]

The third position is taken by writers who acknowledge the existence of distinctions between popular and classical musics, but for whom there are no objective grounds for attempting any value judgements between popular and classical styles. I shall investigate this position through discussion of two sets of features: firstly, through the dichotomy 'intensional/extensional' introduced in Chester (1970); and secondly, through the notions of listening strategy, style and function.

Intensional/extensional

This pair of terms, which I have introduced above, is widely used by critics, from Vulliamy (1977) through to Chambers (1985) and Frith (1987). However, as intimated above, at the heart of Chester's discussion there seems to me to be a fundamental misunderstanding, which invalidates many of the conclusions others draw from him.

Chester does not provide a fixed definition for his term *intensional*, preferring to illustrate its range of reference by example, but it would appear to denote a music taking place within relatively rigid harmonic, melodic and perhaps rhythmic archetypes (almost in the sense of an external skeleton), within which performers can utilize a great degree of freedom, particularly with respect to aspects of sound production that defy analysis by notation. In contrast, *extensional* appears to denote a music built up from 'basic musical atoms' (the discrete pitch, the discrete duration, the individual chord etc.), and in which the performer is constrained by the notion of fidelity to the score (the composer's instructions).

Chester describes what he terms 'Western classical music' as the 'apodigm of the *extensional* form of musical construction' (Chester 1970: 78) and in a footnote states that this is most strictly true of the classical era (i.e. c.1750–1820), but that '"serious" music only marginally departed from the extensional principle until the post-1945 era of electronic experimentation.' It must be asserted here that the terms Chester is using refer to music as seen from the *performer's* point of view, since the difference in constraint between the blues composer and the composer of minuets, such as Mozart, is a *difference of degree, not of kind*. I shall argue below that reference from the point of view of the *listener* seems a more useful approach. Both this blues composer and this Mozart have recourse to harmonic, melodic and rhythmic formulae 'received from tradition' and do not, in any sense, begin from 'basic musical atoms', where the inference is that the rules of combination reside inside, rather than outside, the composer. Schenker's conception of tonal structure as the elaboration of a background supports this notion as far as Mozart is concerned. Chester's own example of the Band[16] as a group working 'at a purely intensional development' (Chester 1970: 80) is instructive – a track like 'Lonesome Suzie' is no less harmonically elaborate, although it is formally more concise, than the minuet of Mozart's 'Eine kleine Nachtmusik'. Even treating the 'blues' as monolithically intensional is fraught with difficulty. If Robert Johnson's 'Crossroads' is a conventional example of Chester's 'almost purely intensional form of the rural blues' (Chester 1970: 79), Howlin' Wolf's 'Little Red Rooster', with its use of substitute harmonies, has surely resulted from some extensional development.

The difference in constraint between the Mozart minuet and the music of Boulez (or even the development section of a late Mozart symphony) is more nearly qualitative: in the latter the 'rules of combination' are much more particular to the individual work. Ligeti (1958) effectively shows that Boulez redefines these for each new work: they are minimally received from the art music tradition. Virden and Wishart (1977), in employing Chester's concepts, argue that they form either end of a continuum, a notion we certainly need in discussing examples of the blues. Chester would appear to me to be in agreement, although in talking of the ubiquity of 'combined intensional and extensional development' in Afro-American musics (Chester 1970: 79), as if they were separate entities, he may be a little ambiguous. Barton McLean, in an article which argues in a similar fashion to Chester's but from the other side of the fence, chooses fundamentally to compare 'a contemporary abstract piano sonata (externalized) with an improvised piano jazz solo (internalized)' (McLean 1981–2: 333). It is surely no accident that McLean's and Chester's terminologies correspond, although they derive from radically different sources.

For the performer, then, an intensional music permits a great degree of 'modulation [*sic*] of the basic notes, and . . . inflexion of the basic beat' (Chester 1970: 79). (By 'modulation', Chester seems to be referring to microtonal modifications of pitch, rather than implying a change of key: see glossary entry.) In the wording of Virden and Wishart (1977: 162), who use Chester's terminology: 'The idiosyncratic *sounds* of the different blues artists, rather than the specifiable *notes* they play and sing, are the heart of the artform.' As I have argued above, this extends to far more than just the blues. An extensional music, on the other hand, exhibits 'rigorous adherence to standard timbres . . . even for the most flexible of all instruments, the human voice. Room for interpretation of the written notation is in fact marginal' (Chester 1970: 78).

The distinction between intensional and extensional hinges, then, on the degree of marginality of the 'room for interpretation' of the classical performer and the blues singer. However, from the point of view of the performer (from where the distinction comes), surely Virden and Wishart's statement, quoted above, would be liable to be appropriated by any performer of Mozart. In the overriding desire for self-expression, tempo, dynamic level, rhythm and even pitch will not necessarily correspond to the score (especially in such an ensemble as the string quartet[17]). These are precisely the devices a performer of intensional music will utilize, although without doubt to a far greater extent. It tends only to be in more recent music, where the attempt is made to notate all such idiosyncrasies, that faithful execution is requested (even though it is frequently impossible!). The intensional component of much popular 'classical' music is overlooked in Chester's formulation.[18] A reading of Tagg (1989) suggests that any attempt strictly to demarcate 'Afro-American' and even 'blues' musics and such things as 'Western classical music' is no longer satisfactory, as this discussion demonstrates. Although the terms will retain a certain conversational value, it will be of more value to look at how listeners may approach these various musics, in order to construct them for themselves.

Listening strategy, style and function

In this section, I shall outline three further ways to consider the difference between rock and classical musics, none of which necessitates the assertion of the superiority of either. In his *Introduction to the Sociology of Music* (Adorno 1976: 3–14), Adorno identifies six types of listener.[19] The *expert* is a profoundly competent listener, able to comprehend the multiple interrelationships present in the music during the act of listening, and is therefore exceedingly rare. The *good listener* is also competent, but with a mastery that is unconscious, being 'not, or not fully, aware of the technical and structural implications.' The *culture consumer* treats music as a cultural asset, valuing it for the 'joy of consumption' it gives, rather than for the demands it makes. The *emotional listener* uses music as a trigger for personal feelings. The *resentment listener* does likewise, but the feelings here are directed against some musical establishment. Finally, the *entertainment listener* uses music only as the provision of a passive background to other activities. It is clear that Adorno's list is culture-specific, i.e. experts are those capable of comprehending syntactical relationships. I shall suggest below that such a discrete categorization of listeners is far less helpful than considering similar attitudes to be listening strategies. Adorno identifies his typology as resting 'upon the adequacy or inadequacy of the act of listening to that which is heard,' a distinction that depends not only on competence, but also on attention. The distinction is reminiscent of the common usage of 'listening to' and 'hearing', themselves akin to the difference between 'looking at' and 'seeing' in the visual realm.

We are in a constant state of hearing sounds and, perhaps because the ear accepts stimuli from all directions and has no 'earlid', we may assume that we take everything in, without having to make any conscious effort. Yet, as we know from the difficulty we have in picking out a particular voice in a crowd, in order to listen to a set of sounds more is required of us. Indeed, in order to give a musical work existence, the conjunction of the sound and the listening mind is required: as listeners, we need to internalize the music. This means that the act of listening is actually a creative act. What the ears register are only vibrations. The brain has to interpret these vibrations as sounds, and then bring into play prior (learnt) experience in order to perceive relationships between these sounds. Only after these relationships have been acknowledged (and, strictly speaking, created for the experience of listening to each new piece) can the music be created, in the listener's ear, for the music is nothing less than the relationships thrown up, however 'inadequately', by the sounds. In his exploration of Adorno's position, Dick Bradley argues similarly at some length, concluding that

> Listening to music is always a *creative* process, and this is always *mediated* by the listener's *knowledge*, or lack of knowledge of musical conventions. . . . It is always *'placed'* by the social practices surrounding that act of listening.
>
> (Bradley n.d.: 51)

Antoine Hennion (1983) goes as far as to argue that popular music can *only* be analysed 'as received', i.e. in the context of its social consumption. While this represents the ideal, in that I would want to know exactly what a listener *does* make of what he or she hears, taking into full account who that listener is, none the less a prior task is to determine the possible interpretations that a song or piece of music *affords*, i.e. what it is possible for a listener to make of it, and that will require a detailed investigation of the sound-constructs themselves.

In practice, a simple hearing/listening dichotomy is unsatisfactory, if only because we can experience the recall of sounds we were not aware of listening to: thus Adorno's expansion of this simple position. The static analysis that results is similarly unsatisfactory, however, in its suggestion that an individual has a direct and permanent relationship with a particular mode of listening. An alternative analysis is suggested by David Lincicome, who argues for

> four different degrees of semantic involvement, or semiotic status, that . . . heard music, can have. These four are (a) music as a purely formal entity with no semantic dimension at all; (b) music as a formal entity with what, to use Langer's vocabulary, might be called 'virtual meaning'; (c) music as a symbolic entity with an equivocal semantic dimension; and (d) music as a symbolic entity with a univocal semantic dimension.
>
> (Lincicome 1972: 192)

Although this list, which Lincicome subsequently expounds in greater detail, is not totally congruent with Adorno's, there are clear points of contact.

Moreover, although listening with certain degrees of semantic involvement to any particular style requires learning, Lincicome's suggestion that modes of listening are techniques (strategies) to be employed seems more valuable. Such assertions are frequently met with the comment that certain musics are more amenable to certain degrees of semantic involvement, 'extensional' musics requiring less, 'intensional' musics requiring more; hence the greater value in classical musics.

As most of the remainder of this book is intended to demonstrate, such is not the case. It is the mode adopted by the listener that determines what the music will yield. Although it must be acknowledged that the means for acquiring competence in certain listening strategies may not be available to all listeners, it cannot be argued that some listeners are inherently incapable of acquiring that competence. The matter clearly troubles Simon Frith: 'Can it really be the case that my pleasure in a song by Abba carries the same aesthetic weight as someone else's pleasure in Mozart? Even to pose such a question is to invite ridicule' (Frith 1987: 134). While acknowledging that the pleasures offered by the musics of Abba and Mozart differ, he notes that they are both subject to social determination, but that academic sociological writing tends to equate aesthetic and commercial judgements. He rightly states that such analysis cannot explain the basis for value judgements made about the music. Although this is not the place to argue the relative aesthetic and social values of these musics (that *some* Abba has greater aesthetic viability than *some* Mozart will be self-evident), any such argument must be based not only on a sure knowledge of what constitutes their musical practices, both social and aesthetic, but also upon the listening strategy adopted.

In order to provide a closer focus for the differences in listening strategies, I shall invoke the term 'style', which ultimately contributes to more precise distinctions than just those of 'popular' and 'classical'. Musical competence, in the abstract is a meaningless concept. To take an extreme example, the ability to comprehend the musical relationships present in a work of Mozart is of no help in comprehending the relationships present in the songs of the Aborigines of Arnhem Land (see Jones 1980). Competence is only gained in terms of a style, where it tends to entail the ability to recognize normative from unusual exemplars, and to make predictions of the likelihood of certain events in real-time listening, on the basis of past events within the example under consideration. (This is a simplified account of the conventional position. See Green (1988: 17–25) for further comment.) To be sure, competence in one style may make it easier to acquire competence in another, particularly if they are related, and particularly if the first style has been acquired at an early age, but no more (see Green 1988: 102ff.). Thus, competence in a 'classical' style does not ensure competence in a 'popular' style, nor vice versa: competence within any style is learnt. This point frequently causes difficulty for those listeners who believe their 'native' style to be somehow 'natural', in opposition to others, which are somehow 'constructed', 'artificial' and even 'contrived'. The observation that we learn a style through familiarity and constant exposure (in the same way that we learn our native tongue) rather than through methodical exposition, does not mean that it was not, at some historical juncture, invented. And, to reiterate, we do learn styles through familiarity and constant exposure, and it is this that I mean here by competence. It is not necessary to be able to explain a style (to be trained in it, perhaps as a performer) in order to have a cognitive competence in it. That competence is demonstrated by being comfortable with particular styles. I shall return to matters of competence and style, as issues, in Chapter 5.

We can invoke a third way to discuss the differences between popular and classical styles by focusing on the musics' functions. The ethnomusicologist Alan Merriam draws upon a long line of thought in both ethnomusicology and cultural anthropology in making a distinction between the use of a cultural practice (see Merriam 1964: 217–18) and the function(s) it serves. Merriam suggests that uses tend to be overt. Parallel to them, he proposes some ten categories of function, stressing that they concern what he calls 'analytical' rather than 'folk' evaluations. Not all these functions will be relevant to every culture, but they do offer a global perspective.

Merriam's first four categories, although problematic, are probably familiar. The first, 'emotional expression', includes music as a means of emotional release and of evoking specific emotional states. Concerning the second, 'aesthetic enjoyment', he attempts to analyse the Western concept of 'aesthetic', comparing its constituent aspects with views from other literate cultures. He argues that it may not be relevant to non-literate cultures on the grounds that the function of aesthetic enjoyment is predicated upon the existence of a philosophy of the aesthetic (which is not, of course, the way I have used the term above). His third category, entertainment, he treats as self-evident. The function of communication, his fourth, is beset with problems, to which I shall return in Chapter 5. Merriam's next two functions are also fairly self-evident. Symbolic representation refers to the practice of mimesis, the representation (rather than the evocation) of emotional states, and perhaps the existence of homologies. Physical response includes dance, the encouragement of the reactions of warrior and hunter, practices of possession and the excitation and control of crowd behaviour. His last group of four are less transparent, and less easy to differentiate. He terms them the functions of

> enforcing conformity to social norms ... validation of social institutions and religious rituals ... contribution to the continuity and stability of culture [and] ... contribution to the integration of society.
>
> (Merriam 1964: 224–7)

Merriam's distinction between use and function, and his stress on the difference between 'analytic' and 'folk' evaluations, seems close to arguing that 'use' refers to a folk evaluation (an 'emic' understanding), while 'function' represents the analytic evaluation (an "etic" understanding). This reading of the situation has been criticized by another leading ethnomusicologist, Bruno Nettl. Nettl argues, with reference to particular cultures, that we need to take account not only of etic statements of function and emic statements of use, but also of etic statements of use and emic statements of function: 'in field research it turns out that informants are quite capable of making "etic" statements, that is, of describing their own culture in "objective" ways that do not give the culture's primary evaluations' (Nettl 1983: 154–5). Nettl subscribes to an alternative ethnomusicological position which claims that music has only one function, which for him

> is to control humanity's relationship to the supernatural, mediating between people and other beings, and to support the integrity of individual social groups. It does this by expressing the relevant central values of culture in abstracted form.
>
> (Nettl 1983: 159)

Although Nettl's position often finds greater favour (it espouses the 'homological' model, to which I shall return in Chapter 5), Merriam's further distinctions are fruitful in the case of the pop–classical split. To exemplify this, I shall use 'popular classics' (the 'Mozart's Greatest Hits' phenomenon), the post-war 'avant-garde' (Stockhausen, Boulez, Xenakis *et al.*) and 'pop dance' (what used to be simply disco).

Pop dance music clearly calls forth physical responses (Merriam's sixth function): the explicit nature of the beat and, more particularly, the syncopations in the bass of a song like Cameo's 'Word Up' make it hard not to move some part of the body in time. The physical response called up by some Mozart will depend far more on its performance situation, and is thus a reaction to the performers rather than the music. The applause given it in a concert hall would normally be out of place when listening at home to the recording. On the one hand, the addition of a bass and drums line with a strong rhythmic profile may have turned it into acceptable disco. On the other, it may be hard for such dance music to provide aesthetic enjoyment (Merriam's second function). Both Mozart and Stockhausen are found by some to do this. Stockhausen, however, may only rarely be listened to for entertainment (Merriam's third function), for his music makes strenuous demands on any listener. And so on.

I would suggest that many of the arguments concerning the relative merits of different musics can be resolved into arguments concerning the relative merits of different functions, which thus becomes an ethical rather than an explicitly musical issue. I, for one, have a rather extreme dislike of being 'entertained'; I would always try to argue that the music I use is serving some other function. Thus, an evaluation is more useful if it asks how well a particular function is served. (Stockhausen's music cannot be described as bad merely on the grounds that we cannot dance to it. Nor do we devalue the music of the Clash in noting that it is not used for quiet contemplation.) Even this can depend on other factors: time, place, mood, will. The function a music serves is not an attribute of that music, but is dependent on both the music itself and the user. Two evenings before writing this, I spent time on Tears for Fears' 'Sowing the Seeds of Love', primarily for the teasing reminiscences of the Beatles' 'All You Need Is Love', 'I Am the Walrus' and 'Hello, Goodbye' it contains. The previous day, I had spent time with the third movement of Tchaikovsky's Fourth Symphony, in order to experience the composer's virtuosic control of orchestral sonority. In both cases, the music functioned aesthetically for me, because of the listening strategy I decided to adopt (I could have used Tears for Fears to dance to, or the Tchaikovsky as a means of emotional catharsis). Neither could have served me as well on the next day. Thus, to acknowledge that we cannot just talk about 'music', that it is necessary to be particular about which music, does not demean any particular style. It is merely a way of acknowledging that no music is suitable in all circumstances, by recognizing that differences in listening strategies and differences of function are not directly congruent to differences of style.

Analytical language

In 1956, the influential musicologist Leonard B. Meyer described two modes by which meaning can be considered to be conveyed in music. The first he termed 'absolutist': it describes the belief that 'musical meaning lies exclusively within the context of the work itself, in the perception of the relationships set forth within the musical work of art. The second, the 'referentialist' mode, asserts that 'in addition to these abstract, intellectual meanings, music also communicates meanings which in some way refer to the extramusical world of concepts, actions, emotional states and character' (Meyer 1956: 1). Although this is a looser discussion than that offered by Lincicome, his positing of just two terms allows us to focus on a vital issue. Note that the referentialist mode contains the absolutist in this definition, despite the fact that he subsequently treats them as direct opposites; in this, he is followed by other writers.

An alternative terminology might therefore be helpful: I shall adopt 'syntactical' for his 'absolutist', 'holistic' for his 'referentialist', and 'analogue' for that portion of 'referentialist' which deals with extramusical things. Thus, 'holistic' admits the relevance, but the necessary incompleteness, of both 'syntactical' and 'analogue' modes of understanding. This is not dissimilar to the extended argument put forward by Lucy Green, who adopts the terms 'inherent' and 'delineated' musical meanings, with similar ranges of reference to my 'syntactical' and 'analogue'.[20] Yet there is far more to her discussion: the distinction between her terms can only be made in reflection on the music. The two concepts are so intertwined as to make any distinction between them impossible during the listening process. Thus, we are in the realm of 'holistic' meaning at the moment of experience. So much musicological writing on 'classical' musics that purports to be serious in intent, and that does not concern itself with aesthetics *per se*, ignores the 'analogue' mode. As I have suggested above, not only does non-musicological writing on popular musics try to concentrate solely on this mode, but even musicological writing that takes an individual song as its focus has a tendency to do the same. Both 'syntactical' and 'analogue' meanings are concerned with relationships, whether these are the relationships between sound-events within the music, or analogous patterns between these relationships and 'concepts, actions, emotional states and character' (Meyer 1956: 1) outside the music.

It is often believed that discussions of the 'syntactical' aspect of music are value-free, since they only deal with sound data, on whose existence all listeners must agree. The musical text has an objective existence (see Green 1988: 12–16), but it is an existence not founded upon words. Any discussion of it in words cannot, therefore, avoid interposing itself between the text and its listeners: one thing that can be said with some confidence is that no discussion of music is totally value-free. I have already argued that Walter Everett, in applying an established music-analytic methodology to music for which it was not developed, is effectively making unsubstantiated assertions about the music of the Beatles.

A further example of this is provided by the music and concepts of the Hopi people. They are unusual to us to the extent that they do not seem to accept pitches as discrete sound concepts (see List 1985). Given two performances of songs with the same melodic contour, an experienced Western listener would require the two melodies' notes to be identical (or virtually so) in order to call them the same song. For the Hopi, the equivalence of the contours appears to be sufficient. Thus, an etic description of their music would make distinctions of which they were seemingly unaware, and about which they did not care. Who would dare argue that it was, therefore, more complete or correct? Indeed, psychologists such as Dowling (1978) and Edworthy (1985) have discovered that, for listeners, the identity of a musical line is conveyed more by general contour outline than by precise intervallic content. Edworthy's conclusion states: 'A theme can therefore be more clearly conveyed through its rhythm and contour than through its interval relationships.' However, these results refer to the practice of listening, which is subject to many changing factors, rather than underlying concepts, with which it is necessary to deal first.

A concrete example is provided by a song recorded by Samuel Charters on his search for the roots of the blues in West Africa (reported in Charters 1982). Jali Nyama Suso sings the ancient praise song 'Kelefa Ba', to the accompaniment of his kora. At first hearing, the song seems to be in the key of G major. The kora is tuned to the diatonic scale of G, Suso begins with alternating chords of I and V, while alternating chords of I and II^7 underpin the opening stanza or so. Although this is a correct objective description, it brings with it other assumptions about the use of diatonic scales, which are not supported by the style of which this song forms a part, and which cannot be accepted without some supporting evidence referring to the export of a European musical system to West Africa at some period in the extreme past, 'Kelefa Ba' being a song which appears to have had a long life. Conclusive evidence being unavailable, this 'accurate' description is misleading – the song happens to employ pitches that share the same frequencies as those of the European diatonic scale of G, and that is as far as it goes.

The problem of the emic/etic dichotomy surfaces throughout ethnomusicological writings, and is well treated by Nettl (1983). With reference to the subject of this book, however, the issue of value-free discussions is different. I would claim to be a member of that cultural group to whom rock music 'belongs', even if, in reflecting on it, I put various feet in other camps. Thus, I shall not make the error of applying concepts taken from outside the culture to a music of which I have only an outsider's knowledge. And yet, even when discussion is undertaken by knowledgeable insiders, its value-free status must be problematic. Janet Levy has recently argued that the values of economy, simplification-cum-concentration, individuality and other factors are frequently smuggled into the writings of conventional musicologists through injudicious use of vocabulary, although she does not argue concomitantly for a more clinical use of language. She concludes that

> by forcing both the sources and the nature of such values into the open, and by challenging the cherished absoluteness that many seem to have acquired, we may move toward replacing slogans with explicit reasons for judgements.
>
> (Levy 1987: 27)

Even from within the rather positivist field that is music theory, Thomas Clifton warns us that 'a theory, ultimately, represents a decision to regard objects from a particular point of view ... our judgements and conclusions about them [the objects] are purely of our own making' (Clifton 1969: 63), by which he seems to me to be saying that the responsibility for the judgements is individually ours, resulting as it does from the initial decision. This truth needs to be set alongside the fact that we can have no perceptions in any field unless they are based on prior theories about the world (see Middleton 1990: 123–4). From a musical standpoint, evidence for the involvement of inter-pretation in the act of perception is offered by Barney Childs, who goes further and suggests that certain culturally defined models are ours by necessity rather than choice: 'as long as a model of living seems natural to us ... we will approach perception of ... works of time art in terms of this model' (Childs 1977: 196).

Care, therefore, is needed. Although I can state that the terminology I use is to be regarded as value-free (I am not necessarily praising a song I describe as 'economical', although I would claim for it a European inheritance were I to describe it as being 'in G major'), I can never be totally sure that it does not carry residual values for me as analyst, nor for you as reader or listener. Although I can claim that 'this song is economical in that it tends to repeat the same rhythmic pattern throughout' is an objective description, it pre-supposes that you will recognize its subtle variations as variations, like I do, and not as new patterns. Even from psychologists, we only have very vague data as to whether listeners who share the same cultural background and environment create similar internal representations of examples of their music. Thus, although these matters may rarely hinder, let alone prevent, my attempt to communicate my findings to you, there will be moments when we cannot avoid inhabiting this tension.

2 Elements of an Analytical Musicology of Rock

One of the major difficulties in discussing music lies in its multi-dimensionality. The stream of sounds a listener hears is composed of rhythm *and* harmony *and* melody *and* instrumental timbre *and* lyrics and, quite possibly, other elements as well. These basic elements are distinguishable one from another in the abstract, and on reflection (listeners can frequently clap to the beat without having to focus on where the melody is going), but they conspire together to produce the music we hear. In this chapter, it will be necessary to focus on them in turn, in order to ascertain how they interact in rock styles. I shall exemplify this chiefly, but not exclusively, through the music of 1963–7. It is at this time that the interaction of these elements, or domains, is reasonably unproblematic. This process of analytical reduction is only valid if it is completed by putting the elements together again, which I shall do in subsequent chapters.

Throughout this and subsequent discussion, I shall make use of a model which suggests that the instruments and voices of rock are stratified into relatively discrete layers. This model is by no means the sole preserve of rock, although there are many styles where it does not operate. A list of these would stretch from Flemish Renaissance polyphony through Wagnerian opera to the music of Stockhausen, and would include styles which have no use for European harmony (those of much of Indonesia, for example).

The model stratifies sound-sources into four layers. The first is an explicit rhythmic layer, where precise pitch is irrelevant. This layer is the preserve of the drum kit and other percussion. The second layer is formed by the music's deepest notes (those with lowest frequency), and which can be thought of as a low register melody. This layer is normally restricted to the bass guitar. A third layer is formed from higher frequency melodies, whether sung or played by a variety of instruments. This layer corresponds to the commonsense understanding of 'tune'. The fourth layer fills the registral gap between the second and third by supplying harmonies congruent to each of these (I shall tend to refer to the function of this layer as that of 'harmonic filler'). Again, the instruments used here can vary, and can include voices. I shall further develop this model, in terms of the way these layers function in the heard experience, at the beginning of Chapter 4. I shall have recourse to a related pair of concepts, those of perceived foreground and background, where the latter accompanies (in the sense of being subsidiary to) the former. Most commonly, it is the third layer above (the 'tune') which is accompanied in the other layers. In attempting to communicate the memory of a song, it is always the tune which seems to be the prime carrier of the song's identity.

One important problem requires indicating at this point. The technical terms that musicologists use have a number of sources, of which two of the most important are purely conversational words, and words developed by musicians themselves. Such words do not become technical terms instantaneously. An interesting example is the word 'groove'. In conversation among fans, music with a good groove tends to be music users can relate to easily. For musicians, the groove is more particularly the pattern laid down by the bass and drum kit. As such, it is beginning to be used in this way as a technical term. 'Beat' is a similar, but more difficult example. Technically, it has a very precise meaning, beats being identified as a series of accents formed from the perception of a (normally) regular pulse within the music's rhythm. Colloquially, 'beat' is often indistinguishable from 'groove'. We are inevitably in the midst of a historical process wherein the meanings of various conversational words become more rigid as they begin to assume the status of technical terms. This problem cannot be circumvented – I signal it here in the hope that it may prevent misunderstandings at a later stage, and I have endeavoured to be sensitive.

There are many ways to try to define a musical style. The commonest approach in the musicological literature is to start with harmonic/melodic formulae and formal patterns, for which musicologists refer solely to musical scores. With aurally transmitted musics, however, approaches which pay heed to what is aurally most evident are more helpful places to start. Hence, in determining the stylistic norms of the early stages of rock, I shall begin by looking at instrumentation, and the roles fulfilled by those instruments within the 'layer' model cited above, before moving on to discuss relevant aspects of rhythm, the use of the voice, and finally various harmonic strategies. Because it is unhelpful to resort solely to musical scores when discussing rock, I shall first briefly deal with the problem that is notation.

Notation

The primary medium of transmission of music throughout the European art tradition is and always has been stave notation. The primary medium of transmission of rock, since at least mid-1950s rock 'n' roll, has been the recording. This distinction is fundamental. European art music is performed with reference to a pre-existent score, which is accepted as an encoded version of the sounds intended by the composer. The rock score, where one exists, is actually a transcription of what has already been performed and produced. Therefore, although the analysis of art music *is*, normally, the analysis of the score, an analysis of rock *cannot* follow the same procedure. It must refer to the primary text, which is, in this case, what is heard. And yet, we cannot ignore notation altogether, since it does play a role (sheet music remains available), and can be valuable if its use is carefully considered.[1]

As we shall see, one of the problems in discussing vocal quality, indeed in discussing the timbral qualities of any instrument, is the absence of a standard, easy visual representation. Conventional music notation is helpless here. Indeed, the main problem with notation is that it was developed for music where pitch and duration were the prime carriers of musical 'meaning'. Timbre was initially secondary (in the seventeenth century, the comment 'apt for voyces or viols' would be used[2]) and was only later standardized.

For listeners who have learnt the code, notation can act as a memory aid, enabling the aural experience to be (re-)constructed. With standard instruments, the timbre is recreatable from visual clues. With the non-standard timbres that can be synthesized in the studio, this is a great problem. Stroppa (1984) cites this in explanation of the general absence of scores of electronic music. With rock this is a little less of a problem, since discrete pitches and rhythms are usually present, even though they are not as 'exact' as notation tends to imply. None the less, careful transcriptions, such as those found in many guitarists' magazines, require numerous additional signs in order to try to convey the intricacies of particular players' techniques. The simple descriptions 'electric guitar', or even 'Hammond organ' are wholly inadequate as ways of conveying the sound to be heard. Although most publications of rock songs give just standard notation, relying on the player's ear to recreate the sound heard, as far as possible,[3] this still suggests that transmission is taking place primarily via the eye. This carries with it the implication that one *should* re-create others' performances rather than develop one's own, a process that is difficult no matter how accurate the transcription.

Small (1977: 31) argues that the very development of notation permitted the bringing into existence of 'classics', which can be repeated at will no matter who the musicians and what the circumstance, and notation used as a means of transmission for rock songs encourages the same situation. This is not to argue that notation is useless. In order to convey or dissect a simple harmonic sequence, a basic rhythmic pattern or a simple melodic shape, it remains the most economical method, but it can at no point *stand for* the music as heard. While analysis of the score is considered appropriate for notated music, it cannot be appropriate for rock.

Instrumental roles

The instrumentation of British beat groups, and the majority of rhythm 'n' blues based bands, was simple and quite static, consisting of voice(s), two guitars (i.e. lead and rhythm), bass guitar and kit (drums, cymbals and other *ad hoc* percussion). If rock in Britain is considered to have developed as an *import* of styles established within the USA (i.e. rock 'n' roll and urban blues), then the model for this line-up was the Chicago-based rhythm 'n' blues of Howlin' Wolf, Muddy Waters and (later) Chuck Berry, rather than the New Orleans sound of Fats Domino and Little Richard with its emphasis on piano and saxophone rather at the expense of the guitar. In fact, many of the early British rock 'n' roll and beat groups began as skiffle groups (the Shadows and the Beatles, for instance), who also emphasized guitar at the expense of keyboards and saxophones. Wolf commonly used two electric guitars, bass and drums: this pattern seems first to have been successfully adopted in England by the Shadows, and was later followed right across the early beat/rhythm 'n' blues divide from the Searchers through the Beatles to the Yardbirds and the Rolling Stones. One of the consequences of an instrumentation as minimal as this is that the function of each instrument (and, by extension, that of each player) within the whole is fairly closely defined.

It is often found convenient to observe a three-way split in this early style: beat music (essentially Liverpool Scene: see Cohen 1991: 12–14), the harder edge of rhythm 'n' blues-influenced music with blues harp prominent (frequently based in London) and the soul-tinged music associated with the mods and with rhythm organ rather than guitar. Hard-and-fast distinctions are not helpful, however. Shapiro suggests that the mod image of the Who (who did not use organ) was 'constructed' rather than 'genuine' (Shapiro 1990: 113–15), while the 'harder' edge of some rhythm 'n' blues-influenced bands was also sometimes a function of the use of the organ (the Animals, the Spencer Davis Group). The very question of defining what 'mod' entailed, or indeed entails, must be hedged about with qualifications (see Weller 1981). That mods formed a distinct sub-cultural grouping is generally agreed (although Shapiro (1990: 108) sees the term as a catch-all for 'Swinging London'), but that they adopted only limited styles is not: George Melly's contemporary account (1970) tends to ignore the 'soul' influence entirely, tentatively identifying the music of the early mods as modern jazz. This exemplifies the problem of the appropriation of cultural labels to define musical styles. For Melly, Weller (1981) and Wicke (1990), for example, mods were more strongly associated with life-style and accessories (parkas and scooters etc.) than music: the term 'mod' is certainly best ignored as a musical style label. Indeed, the *roles* of organ and rhythm guitar, as distinct from their sound, are very similar. One of the things that so clearly defines this early rock style is the roles it assigns to its instruments: bass and treble parts are prioritized and given separate timbres (bass guitar, voice and/or lead guitar), while the rhythm guitar or keyboard fills in the remainder, the entire ensemble being held together by the kit, which lays down the principle of pattern repetition.

As the urban blues grew in the USA, the rhythmic function originally fulfilled by the guitar of a singer like Robert Johnson was retrieved by 'unpitched' percussion instruments, becoming the nucleus of the rock kit. It has always been the function of the kit to provide a basic pattern of stresses that underpin, and sometimes counterpoint, that of the pitched instruments. It is of the essence of this pattern that it is repeated. *Variations* will be found, particularly at important structural points such as beginnings and endings of phrases and verses, but at no time will they challenge the *identity* of the pattern. It is this constant repetition that seems to present the greatest initial barrier to those unfamiliar with the music. Justifications for it can vary from the pragmatic (the music is easier to dance to) to the theoretic (repetition permits perception of subtler surface variations, as opposed to the impoverished surface rhythm of much Mendelssohn, Tchaikovsky or Stockhausen), but it is arguably the most important musical feature.

Repetition is not restricted to the kit: it is present in all layers of the musical fabric at some point. Middleton (1990: 269–90) distinguishes between what he terms *discursive* and *musematic* modes of repetition in popular musics generally: discursive repetition refers to repetition at the level of the phrase or larger, while musematic repetition involves the repetition of tiny melodic or rhythmic cells, or short harmonic patterns. Both types are found in rock songs. The Who's 'My Generation' typifies musematic repetition in the repeated responses that follow each line of verse. David Bowie's 'Life on Mars' is more complicated here. It uses *sequence*, a standard discursive technique, to which Middleton (1990: 272) refers: 'In bourgeois song in general, sequence is a way of holding on to at least some of the power of repetition while . . . *stitching it into* other structural processes.' In this case, the 'other' process is one of growth from the first (harmonically static) phase of the verse to the second (harmonically modulatory) phase. Bowie employs sequence through the verse's first eight bars: the first, third, fifth and seventh have the same melodic rhythm and contour, but raised one step higher on each occasion, introducing motion towards the second phase (see example 2.1). The Boomtown Rats' 'Rat Trap' uses a more extreme form of discursive repetition, whereby the

Example 2.1 David Bowie: 'Life on Mars'

song's entire pattern – introduction; verse; verse; repeat of introduction to fade – interposes two separate stretches of music after each verse. Finally, King Crimson's 'Larks' Tongues in Aspic (Part I)' goes to the limit in its eschewal of discursive repetition altogether.

Normally, then, the kit repeats at the musematic level. The early kit was a simple affair: hihat and ride cymbals, snare and bass drums, with an occasional tomtom, tambourine and cowbell. A comparison of the first four tracks on the Beatles' *Hard Day's Night* demonstrates the importance of the kit in setting not only speed, but also intensity. The underlying rhythmic pattern is the same for all four songs. The snare sounds on the off- or back-beat, a cymbal sounds even quavers (twice per beat) and the bass drum (which tends to be less audible on recordings of this period) plays on beats one and three, and sometimes in between. The beginnings and ends of verses and refrains are frequently marked by greater density of events (fills), particularly on the snare. I shall call this pattern the 'standard rock beat'. By this, I do not intend to suggest that its presence is a prerequisite for a song to be identified as 'rock', although I do suggest that it is has become a fundamental technique for the rock drummer (see Feldstein 1978, Finkelstein 1979, Michaels 1990 etc.). I cannot recall hearing any rock drummer who did not have recourse to it, although subtle variations on it are also basic aspects of the technique.

The gentlest of these four songs is 'If I Fell', where the even quavers are on a closed hihat, while the backbeat is played very close to the edge of the snare's skin, giving a sound that barely resonates. 'I Should Have Known Better' maintains the same disposition at a slightly faster tempo, but with more resonance on the snare. For 'I'm Happy Just to Dance with You', the even quavers have moved on to the ride cymbal, creating a haze of sound surrounding the whole. On 'A Hard Day's Night' itself, the snare adds semiquaver infills, giving many bars an extended (two-beat) upbeat, while the cowbell, which was to become such a characteristic sound in hard rock by the end of the decade, is added. Although tempo setting remains the kit's most important function, a drummer as subtle as Ringo Starr shows its potential richness.

Some varied versions of the standard rock beat are common, as in the Rolling Stones' 'Satisfaction', where the tougher stance of the lyrics is reinforced particularly by the near inaudibility of the hihat quaver rhythm and a more audible bass drum. This results in the kit emphasizing four nearly even beats, as it will come to do far more with the onset of hard rock. Although rock is subject to a general stylistic evolution, the standard rock beat remained dominant in the 1980s in various styles that grew from the fragments of beat and rhythm 'n' blues. At random, Fleetwood Mac's *Tango in the Night*, Madness' *Keep Moving* and Big Country's *Steeltown* exemplify its remaining influence, although by this time the attitude to timbre and rhythm of the remaining instruments has often changed almost out of recognition.

In the mid-1960s, the kit primarily acts to provide a separable rhythm layer, that rhythm being stratified through different timbres. Its nearest neighbour in this respect is the bass: one aspect of the bass's role is to reinforce certain elements of the kit's basic pattern, for bass and kit will normally meet on stressed beats. In most of the bands of this period, the bass tends to be perceived much more as a 'presence', owing to its lack of treble frequencies. Like the bass drum, at high volume it was felt as much as heard: this timbre was to remain popular well into the 1970s, for example on Led Zeppelin's *Houses of the Holy*. On the Rolling Stones' 'It's All Over Now', the bass line emphasizes the bass drum's first and third beats, leaving the backbeats to stand alone. This is particularly clear throughout the instru-

mental, where the rhythm ♩ ♫ ♩ ♫ is shared by bass and bass drum.

This is the most common, but not the only, link. For instance, on the Beatles' 'Drive My Car', the bass joins the hihat pedal pattern for the extended upbeat

♪ ♬ ♪, which helps to give the song its sense of drive.

The other main aspect of the work of the bass is harmonic. Among the more widely known groups, most bass lines of this period are not content to sit on the root of each harmony as played by the guitar or keyboard, but construct an independent melodic line (a technique that has rather fallen out of fashion in more recent times). Unless it acts as a 'hook', what line the bass constructs is relatively unimportant: other bass players may construct a different line without destroying the identity of the song. Such melodic lines are most simply formed by inserting passing and auxiliary notes between the roots of successive chords, while the sense of line is rarely sufficiently important to replace the root by a different pitch from any chord. As has frequently been noted, the invention apparent in Paul McCartney's bass lines stands out: on 'With a Little Help from My Friends', for instance, he finds a variety of alternative lines to underpin a single harmonic pattern.

The original role of the guitar was to flesh out the harmony: as early as 1964, it was fulfilling this function in two distinct ways, the first making the song's harmonies explicit, the second leaving them implicit. The clearest way to make harmonies explicit was simply to strum the chords to a rhythm, which might either reinforce or counterpoint that of the bass and drums; hence 'rhythm guitar'. In the Who's 'Substitute', the guitar functions purely as a rhythm guitar, playing the harmonic outline in a rhythm it shares with

various parts of the kit: ♩ ♩ ♩. ♩♫ ♩ ♩. Indeed, throughout the

rest of the song, the sound from the bass and kit fills the texture so completely that the sound of the rhythm guitar is almost superfluous. It was, however, normative for an instrumental line-up to remain static throughout a song, and for a 'filler' part to be found where necessary, as in this case and that of 'Somebody Help Me Now' (see below). The guitar plays in the same way on the Beatles' 'Nowhere Man', but in this case it is not drowned and therefore helps to fill out the texture.

An alternative way to make the harmonies explicit is to use a fuller guitar sound and make its rhythmic profile simpler, the guitar here carrying the inchoate connotations of primitiveness used so fully in hard rock. On the Beatles' 'You Won't See Me' the guitar is hardly in the foreground: it joins the snare drum on the backbeats. On the Spencer Davis Group's 'Keep on Running', it plays a simple barre chord, without sustain, on every beat. Although the kit has the standard rock beat, the guitar encourages the beats to be heard as undifferentiated. A third way, the use of sustained 'power' chords (generally a bare open fifth) epitomized by Pete Townshend, can be seen as an outgrowth of this. As early as 'My Generation' (1965), the guitar holds a sustained chord throughout each bar, breaking into occasional quasi-soloistic fills, built around the chordal shapes held by the left hand. Each of these three ways makes the harmonies explicit, and can lead to the only instrumental melodic line being the preserve of the bass, particularly in the hands of the Who's John Entwistle, whose highly inventive lines carry jazz overtones.

The use of the guitar to leave harmonies implicit is also present early, being well exemplified by the Kinks' first hit 'You Really Got Me' (1964). Here, the guitar is content to outline the harmony via a riff. This word has two connotations. For many rock musicians, it has become synonymous with 'musical idea', particularly in the realm of melody. Here, however, it retains its earlier, jazz, sense of being an idea that is repeated, and that can often be used over different harmonies with minimal alteration. This is the technique from which much hard rock develops. The bass doubles (i.e. plays the same as) the guitar here, as it does in some of the tougher early Beatles material (such as 'Drive My Car'), and as it will later in Led Zeppelin's 'Immigrant Song', much of Deep Purple and other early 1970s hard rock. A similar though subtler riff is present in the Spencer Davis Group's 'Somebody Help Me Now'. This marked the first widely known use of distorted ('fuzz') guitar, which both plays the riff in response to the vocal calls, and elsewhere breaks into chords on the backbeat. (A neat summary of these uses of guitar is the Rolling Stone's 'Satisfaction'.)

There is, of course, a further role played by the guitar, that of soloing. However, until the advent of Eric Clapton,[4] such solos tend to remain secondary to the song itself. This is clear with George Harrison's solo on 'Nowhere Man', a solo that is clearly based on the acoustic guitar practice of holding the relevant chord and arpeggiating it in some way, making use of passing and auxiliary notes.

Other instruments can be found in many songs of 1963–7, but they tend to be imported for particular effects on particular songs, rather than functioning as intrinsic members of the ensemble. For instance, the role of the piano on the Kinks' 'You Really Got Me' is rhythmic (playing on even quavers as a replacement for the hihat) and timbral (adding high frequencies and consequently 'bright' timbre to complement the low range and nasal tone of the rest of the band). The other main use of the piano was as the focus for a song, as on the Beatles' 'You Won't See Me', where it tends to replace the rhythm guitar. This is frequently an indication that the song was written at the piano rather than at the guitar, an important matter that I shall take up below. Additionally, harpsichords, recorders, orchestral and even less familiar instruments would find their way into ensembles in the studio.

An important exception to the 'importation' thesis is the use of the organ by such bands as the Spencer Davis Group, Manfred Mann and the Small Faces. They tend to use it, particularly in evocation of performers like Ray Charles. (Such appropriations will come under examination in Chapter 3.) This use will ultimately develop into the line-up adopted by Deep Purple. A similar history, but with a different slant, is developed by Loewenthal (1988).

Rhythmic organization

In the previous section, I have had occasion to refer to the kit as the provider of a separate 'rhythm' layer, but it must not be overlooked that all the instrumental forces are involved in playing rhythms. Here, I shall concentrate on the rhythm that results from this totality. The presence of rhythm in any music depends in part upon the perception of a series of stresses, which are identified in theory as *beats*. Almost all rock music organizes these beats in groups of four: quadruple metre (four beats per bar) therefore acts as a stylistic norm. Beats will appear either *straight*, in which case each beat will in practice be divisible in half, or *shuffle*, in which case it will be divisible into three.

Metre is organized hierarchically. Just as groups of beats (normally four) are grouped to yield metre, groups of bars (normally four) are grouped to yield hypermetre. Example 2.2 explores this in diagrammatic fashion: sixteen bars yield four groups at the hypermetric level. The verse of the Kinks' 'Waterloo Sunset' illustrates this clearly: each line of lyric consists of four bars with a two-bar upbeat, such that the hypermetre of the verse can be

Example 2.2 Sixteen bars grouped as four 4-bar units

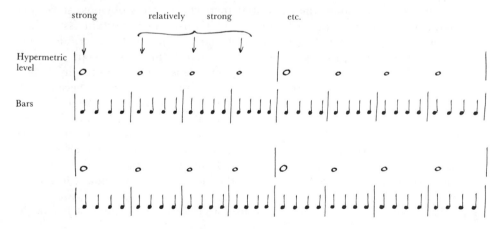

Example 2.3 Kinks: 'Waterloo Sunset'

represented as 4 bars + 4 bars + 4 bars + 4 bars, or 4 + 4 + 4 + 4. The hypermetric groups are numbered beneath the melody in example 2.3.[5] There are common variants on this pattern, formed by extending or compressing one of the groups: indeed, Berry (1987: 318–19) goes so far as to suggest that, in the Western art tradition, fluctuating metres are so common that they cannot be regarded as aberrant, a view which I think holds for rock. The verse of Jimi Hendrix's 'She's So Fine' groups 3 + 4 + 4 at the hypermetric level, while the Casuals' 'Jesamine' works constantly in groups of 3 + 4. The verse of Eric Clapton's 'Let It Grow' is similar, grouping as 6 + 8 at the hypermetric level. The proportions remain the same, but their effect is less obvious, since they take about twice as long to be heard. This raises an important issue. In a music that is not notated, how long is a 'bar' (or, for that matter, any other transferable unit)? Ultimately, of course, it hardly matters, except to enable communication about rhythm to take place. This is one reason why I have emphasized the 'standard rock beat' in the previous section, because the consistent appearance of a snare drum on the second and fourth beats of a bar allows this length to be standardized. As a result, we will find that rock songs *tend* to change harmony every bar. Other songs reverse the above '3 + 4 + . . .' pattern. A standard example is 'Substitute', which ends its refrain 2 + 2 + 2 + 1½ (i.e. 4 + 4 + 4 + 3 but at twice the speed), so that the emphasis comes on the first beat of the next group: 'I think I'll get my washing *done*'.[6]

These songs have exemplified the use of elisions, where the last bar of the shortened group is also heard as the first bar of the subsequent group. We can find extensions too, the verse of 'Substitute' exemplifying a common pattern. The first two lines of lyrics each take up four bars and the next four each take up two bars, giving the standard 4 + 4 + 4 + 4 grouping. But, an extra two bars (no lyrics) are inserted before the refrain.[7] As a feature of technique, which may well have limited style specificity, Cooper and Meyer (1960: 148) suggest that elisions heighten the sense of immediate continuity (try substituting 4 + 4 in the relevant places in 'Jesamine' or 'Substitute'), while extensions often appear at formal divisions (ends of verses, refrains, introductions), those moments where immediate continuity needs to be suspended.

Grouping elisions and extensions afford the perception of rhythmic tension between a perfectly regular metre and a heard pattern whose metre fluctuates. In rock, a more immediately perceived rhythmic tension will also be found between two heard aspects: the song's 'persona' (represented by the third layer, the 'tune', whether invested in voice or solo instrument) and its accompanimental background (represented by kit and bass). This tension is actualized in terms of strictness and waywardness with relation to the beat. The notion of 'feel', so beloved of commentators and players (see particularly Chapter 3) but so resistant to analysis, seems to concern 'playing around with' the beat. This practice can only be possible where the beat is rigidly enforced, because otherwise awareness of the degree of latitude involved cannot arise. The tension between 'wayward' voice or guitar and 'strict' kit and bass is clearly illustrated throughout Led Zeppelin's first album, while on the unaccompanied guitar solo on 'Heartbreaker' (on their second album), the tension is totally (and intentionally) lost. Few singers of rock fail to avail themselves of this facility, and it is thus to consideration of the voice that I now turn.

The voice

The fact that most popular music is vocal music means that we must take account of the voice rather closely. In Chapter 5 I shall broach the issue of communication between singer and listener. Here, I shall begin by looking at the strategies employed to discuss now the voice is *used* in rock: I should point out immediately that none of them seems adequate to me, but in order to suggest why this is, we need to look at what these strategies are. I shall then propose an alternative set of criteria whose inadequacies are, I hope, less marked. The fact that all the voices I refer to are male is not without significance, for two reasons. Firstly, rock singing has largely been constructed as a male preserve; secondly, I do not and cannot know what it feels like to produce the sounds of a female voice (informal discussion suggests that there are distinct, if hard-to-verbalize, differences between female and male vocal production), nor would I presume to do so. I would be very interested to learn the precise limitations of my criteria from that point of view.

The most widely used basic paradigm in the discussion of the rock 'voice' is to distinguish between what critics have called 'black' and 'white' voices. In talking of James Taylor's vocal style, which derives from styles of singing common in the rural southern USA, Dave Laing argues that:

> The criticisms of his singing tend to be based on a notion that the rock voice has to follow the ways of black music, where the range of vocal intonation and embellishment is crucial to the formation of a musical identity. [Taylor's voice tends to have] the 'high, lonesome quality of Appalachian music...a flat undemonstrative style which, nevertheless, bespeaks great emotion'.
> (Laing 1975: 68, quoting the reviewer Ben Gerson)

According to this analysis, the 'black' voice is demonstrative and communicates directly through the use of a wide variety of intonational and embellishing techniques. The 'white' voice, on the other hand, is restrained, gesturally restricted and *apparently* uninvolved.

An alternative distinction is that between the 'trained' and the 'untrained' voice. The 'trained' voice is apt to sing tempered pitches precisely 'in tune', to employ an even, full-throated tone with rich vibrato, and to have little use for other intonational and embellishing techniques. Although found in a range of older popular musics, it is not commonly found in rock, for its strongest connotations are those of legitimized music. And, notwithstanding the example of Willard White and other opera singers of black descent, it is considered a 'white' voice. Against this norm, the 'untrained' ('natural') voice (which is not clearly aligned with 'white/black') is important in the ideology of rock as signifying 'authenticity', since the trained voice is clearly held to have been tampered with.

Other writers have attempted to see some vocal norms as approaching the status of genres, through the construction of sets of conventions. An early manifestation of this was the categorization by Frith and McRobbie (1978) of 'cock rock' and 'teenybop'. Frith (1989) is more particular in suggesting that intimacy in rock has usually been represented both by 'the female voice' and by the use of the high-pitched, strained male voice. Shepherd (1987b: 166–7) adds further suggestions. He notes that the hard, rasping sound typical of 'cock' rock is 'produced overwhelmingly in the throat and mouth, with a minimum of recourse to the formants of the chest and head'; contrasting this with the rich chest formants[8] of the *woman-as-nurturer*, which speak to him of a person 'more fully aware of her inner, experiential being,' and the similar warmth of the *boy next door*. Here, however, the warmth comes from head tones, which still indicate 'an experiential emptiness in avoiding the formants of the chest cavity,' suggesting a vulnerability in the face of the warm female voice. Shepherd gives other examples, which seem to me equally unsatisfactory if only because of their essentialist assumptions.

None of these generalizing strategies seems to be particularly productive, primarily because they emphasize only one aspect of vocal production, and attempt to read meaning into the voice's presence on the basis of that single aspect. They ignore the fact that a multitude of factors characterizes a vocal style. There are four, I think, that represent the minimum that needs to be borne in mind in any analysis, and that I shall elaborate in turn. The first is the register and range which any particular voice achieves; the second focuses on its degree of resonance; the third concerns the singer's heard attitude to pitch; and the fourth the singer's heard attitude to rhythm.

Register and range describe simply the relative height and the spread of the pitches used in a song. Writers thus talk of 'high', 'medium' and 'low' register, and of 'large' and 'narrow' range. Precise determinations of these are unnecessary here. 'High', 'medium' and 'low' entered technical terminology as metaphors relating to notated sounds: high sounds appeared high on the page in relation to the staff, likewise with medium and low sounds. In fact, the terms are less ethnocentric, and less visually related than they seem, for high sounds are those whose fundamentals vibrate at high frequencies, and medium and low sounds likewise. Resonance can be thought of as distance from what is often called a 'colourless' tone, that which is produced electronically as a sine wave, and which cannot actually be achieved by the voice. The adjective 'colourless' comes from the tone's total lack of overtones. Discussion of resonance will therefore include such aspects as vibrato, changes of richness of voice with respect to register, whether the sound resonates in the nasal cavity (producing a thin tone) or in the chest (a fuller tone) and whether the sound seems to originate in the throat or is pushed from the diaphragm. This is, I think, the best way to take account of what Barthes (1979) calls the '*grain* of the voice'. The remaining two factors are best envisaged as 'deviations' from 'virtual' norms. Attitude to pitch is best considered against an abstract norm of tempered pitches (the only ones an in-tune piano can sound), while attitude to rhythm is a factor of both syncopation (anticipation of and delaying behind the beat) and the ways the beat is subdivided. The rhythmic tension between a (wayward) voice and (strict) rhythm section, mentioned above, is an aspect of this factor. I shall illustrate these factors initially through consideration of four 'standard' US voices that are frequently idealized as precursors of rock.

Bill Haley's singing of 'Rock around the Clock' will stand for the style of a number of white singers of early rock 'n' roll. As example 2.4 shows, his rhythm tends to coincide precisely with every strong beat (and, at this point, with every beat) – example 2.5 shows him slightly anticipating the third beat of the second bar of this example. It tends only to be this beat that is ever anticipated. The least important syllable, 'a-', is given the shortest possible space, not intruding on the most important 'rock'. Nowhere does he slip between the shuffle divisions of the beat. Other factors in his style are no less important. He sings strictly *on* the tempered pitch, hitting notes precisely, and anticipating stressed pitches that coincide with a change of harmony (as in the last three notes of example 2.5). His register is high, with no resonance from the chest cavity (he sings with a slightly 'strained' voice), and a narrow range.

Situating Bill Haley's singing at one end of a continuum, Little Richard's on 'Tutti Frutti' is located at the opposite end. A rhythmic norm is to anticipate the beat, as in example 2.6. The song has a shuffle beat and, although he is clearly toying with it, once he has coincided with the beat at the end

Example 2.4 Bill Haley: 'Rock around the Clock'

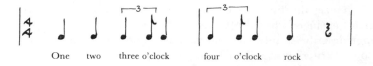

Example 2.5 Bill Haley: 'Rock around the Clock'

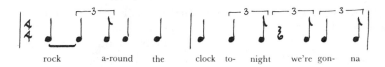

Example 2.6 Little Richard: 'Tutti Frutti'

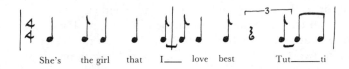

of a phrase or at intermediate points, he will then slip between the shuffle divisions (as here). Whereas my transcriptions or examples 2.4 and 2.5 are fully accurate with respect to rhythms, example 2.6 is an idealized version. A strict transcription would be almost illegible, because of Richard's very subtle rhythmic nuances. As if to complement these, he frequently adds melismas after attacking a note, as on the second occurrence of 'gotta *girl* named Sue'. *Girl* appears on the beat, but he then continues through three further notes to land on a consonance. He will also end a pitch either slightly sharp or flat with respect to the tempered scale, depending on circumstances. Again, his register is high, with little resonance and a narrow range, but his inflections seem less to do with carving out a particular melody than with equivalents to spoken emphasis ('rock to the *east*, rock to the *west*').

Fats Domino's 'Blueberry Hill' indicates a different approach, more in keeping with his laid-back style. Although he sticks with the beat and its subdivisions more readily than does Richard, he undermines its regularity by introducing abnormal stresses, as in example 2.7 (emphasizing *-dom* and *-ry*), which comes from the very opening to the song. His pitching is more regularly tempered than Richard's but, having attacked an important note, he too will frequently allow that pitch to slip or slide. Although his pace is generally slower, anticipations of the beat are no less common. His register tends to be lower, which, together with his slightly swallowed vocal production, gives an

Example 2.7 Fats Domino: 'Blueberry Hill'

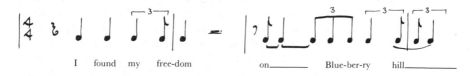

I found my free-dom   on____ Blue-ber-ry hill____

Example 2.8 Elvis Presley: 'Heartbreak Hotel'

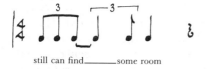

still can find____some room

impression of less energy and greater comfort. Again, his voice has little resonance.

Elvis Presley is frequently held to be the singer who pulled both 'white country' and 'black blues' voices together. As with all generalizations, this is a little over-generous, although he certainly made use of a number of the features already seen. As example 2.8 from 'Heartbreak Hotel' shows, he follows both Domino and Richard in making an anticipation play with our sense of normal stress. Although his register tends to be high, his wider range allows him to contrast his upper voice with a lower voice whose emotive content is more demonstrative. Moreover, he favours vibrato on held notes, which gives his voice greater resonance. He tends to sing tempered pitches, but will frequently begin a note from slightly below, sliding up to the required pitch within a matter of microseconds. Most importantly, both sighs and intakes of breath are frequently heard, making him relate to his audience with an immediacy that was new to many of those brought up on big band singers and crooners. Consideration of just these four singers, then, indicates something of the range and subtlety of vocal styles available to singers desirous of appropriating an 'American' sound.

As I shall discuss in Chapter 3, early beat and rhythm 'n' blues bands were frequently quite explicit in their endeavours to sound 'American'. One particular way this was achieved was to extend the range of the voice upwards, in imitation particularly of 'soul' singers, such as Smokey Robinson or Sam Cooke. Among these singers, the high register is achieved with a clear falsetto. Although this technique tends to carry connotations of effeminacy for those familiar with European art singing, particularly the singing of opera (even if castrati have been rare for more than a century), in many African traditions, and arguably within black American traditions, it signifies virility. The clarity of this falsetto is a recent tendency among British rock singers.[9] It is more common to find the high voice associated with a 'straining' quality, carrying the effect of being produced as the result of great effort. I presume that this suggests the unmediated communication of intense emotion. Robert Plant's voice on Led Zeppelin's 'Immigrant Song' is an excellent example of the technique. He sings in high and medium registers and, although both are powerfully projected, they are also falsetto. The tautness of the sound is due to both the stridency of his tone and his freedom from the beat, especially at the ends of phrases. John Lydon provides a very different example of a similar voice. On the Sex Pistols' 'Holidays in the Sun' his register is high, with a very narrow range (arguably only one sung note, close to falsetto). Most interestingly, he wavers not at all from the beat, this perhaps acting as a metaphor for mechanical action.

In recent years, rock singers have (re-)discovered a full-throated vocal style familiar originally from pop singers like Scott Walker. Although it was never a technique adopted by punk singers, it does seem to owe its resurgence to that style. Peter Trudgill (1983) has pointed to a gradual change in the pronunciation and vocabulary adopted by rock singers from the 'mid-Atlantic' of the 1960s to the use of 'features associated with low-prestige south of England accents' by the Clash and Ian Dury. Previous use of such features was associated with 'novelty' records, but in the wake of punk this became a legitimate technique. This suggests to me that punk may have given other singers licence to deviate from the norms of rock singing style, as it gave others licence to deviate in matters of dress, for instance. 'New romantic' fashion was apparently dictated by the desire for peculiarity, and the full-throated, almost 'trained' voice had certainly been little heard in rock before; an example is Spandau Ballet's Tony Hadley.[10] The technique is well exemplified on the Icicle Works' 'Hope Springs Eternal'. Ian McNabb's register seems largely comfortable. There is no sense of falsetto, but a slight straining to reach high notes, which may connote sincere effort, and thus authenticity (again). The voice is resonant and full, the air being pushed from the diaphragm. Precision is the key here: his singing is rhythmically very measured, down to the calculated syncopation and vibrato. Today, the technique is common to rock singing, among vocalists as diverse as Wayne Hussey (of the Mission) and David Bowie. Indeed, in this context Bowie's changes of vocal technique become useful. On an early novelty record like 'The Laughing Gnome' he adopts cockney pronunciation and a near-conversational singing tone, while throughout his early 1970s 'rock' phase he frequently used a 'strained' voice. The later 1970s then saw him develop a rich, full-throated style which has since remained a mainstream of his technique. (Chapter 5 will explore Bowie's changes of style in more detail.)

Throughout this discussion of the voice, I have concentrated on technique rather than on melody. Melody itself has two distinct aspects. The notes that are sung can be considered most concisely in conjunction with the harmonic tendencies of rock, which I address in the remainder of this chapter. The order in which they are sung can be described in terms of the melody's *contour* (essentially the shape traced by rising and falling pitches). In fact, rock traverses a continuum, with contour subordinated to vocal sound at one end (and thus the lyrics possibly more spoken than sung), but contour fore-grounded at the other: the quality of the best ballads of Paul McCartney, for instance, seems to depend on their melody. And, as contour may help to define a repertoire, I shall have subsequent recourse to it in discussions of particular styles (I doubt that a separate typology of melodic contours in rock would be of value). None the less, as Simon Frith never tires of pointing out, it is the *way* rock singers sing, rather than *what* they sing, which probably most attracts listeners, and I think this feature must be paramount in any discussion of rock voices.

Harmonic patterns and formal structures

Next, it is necessary to give an account of the actual notes used in rock, and how these contribute to the form of entire songs. As Chapter 1 has suggested, this is the aspect of music that is most easily systematized, and thus analysis normally accords it most space. That is also the case here. I have placed it at the end of the chapter as a result of my concern with the perceptions music affords in the listener, my concentration on the *esthesic* at the expense of the *poietic*. It may be true that in putting songs together, musicians are primarily concerned with chord sequences and riffs (the positive evidence offered by so many musicians' magazines must be taken together with the more ambivalent evidence offered in Cohen 1991: 136–43, for instance). It does not, however, seem to be true that listeners' own understandings of songs are *explicitly* dependent on differences of chord patterns, although these differences are present. Thus, I am resistant to according it priority over other aspects of heard sound. (This point is extensively argued in Cook 1990.)

There is a fundamental distinction in rock between songs whose harmonic patterns are basic to the song's identity, and those whose patterns are far more incidental. The former group use patterns that repeat through the whole song, or notable portions of it, while the latter tend to have clear period structures. Middleton (1990: 238, and 217) draws a useful distinction between 'the open/closed principle [associated with the period structures] of "bourgeois song" and the open-ended repetitive gestures typical of many pop-dance songs.'

Contrary to critical belief, rock is rich in harmonic formulae (see Moore 1992). In order to investigate the various strategies used, it will be necessary first to call attention to the conventional formal divisions found in rock: verse, refrain (or chorus), bridge, introduction, coda and solo (break). These are categories frequently used by writers and performers, and their ubiquity is sufficient to ensure their analytical value. Through patterns of immediate, deferred and lack of repetition, the stretches of music defined by these categories constitute the formal structures of rock songs. They will normally appear in the region of five seconds (a rather brief introduction) to one minute (a rather extended verse). Verses and refrains will commonly repeat: verses tend to use different lyrics on each occurrence, refrains tend to repeat the same lyric, or a close variation of it. Verses tend to be twice the length of refrains, or sometimes of equal length (especially where an element of narrative is present); only rarely are verses shorter,[11] and here they will tend to be half the length. In contrast, bridges, introductions, codas and solos do not normally repeat, although introductions may recur as codas or breaks.

Songs may use different harmonic/melodic material at the very beginning (introduction) and end (coda), and frequently somewhere between one-half and two-thirds through, often before the final verse. This latter is what I have termed the 'bridge'. A clear example of these three is provided by the Beatles' 'Ticket to Ride'. We have a four-bar introduction (using the guitar riff with which the verse begins), an eight-bar verse and eight-bar refrain, repeated, followed by a nine-bar bridge (actually eight bars plus two, but bars eight and nine are elided), which is marked by the change of pattern in the kit. Two further verses/refrains are separated by a repeat of the bridge, finishing with a two-bar coda (using the guitar riff with which the refrain ends), which repeats to fade. In some (generally later) rock, the bridge is extended into a purely instrumental passage, and hence solo. This is only a tendency, however – in the Who's 'My Generation', the instrumental drum break comes right at the end, merging into a coda.

Rock practice maintains a strong tendency to treat harmonies as indivisible units. Listeners are, therefore, in an either/or situation: at every moment, we are hearing either one or another nameable harmony. Most harmonies are simple triads, although added sixth and seventh chords are not infrequent, while altered triads (such as the suspended fourth) can also be found. In almost all cases, these non-triadic harmonies can be termed 'non-functional'. The distinction between 'functional' and 'non-functional' is neutral, i.e. 'non-functional' does not entail the assumption of a lack of quality. It derives from classical tonality where, in certain styles, a particular chord will lead the competent listener to expect a particular continuation, as explored in example 2.9. In Mozart, the chord of example 2.9(a), a seventh chord on C, will lead the experienced listener to expect a chord of F (example 2.9b) with a high degree of probability. Chords of D♭ or B (example 2.9c and d) would be expected with lower degrees of probability. These chords would thus be acting functionally. In Stravinsky, because the chances of example 2.9(a) preceding *any* other chord are far more equal, that chord would not be acting functionally. The matter of functionality must be treated carefully. Middleton (1990: 105) reminds us that we must beware of expecting triads and other chords

Example 2.9 Dominant seventh on C with potential resolutions

       (a)   (b)   (c)   (d)

to act functionally in rock, a point I have made in Chapter 1. Indeed, non-functional sevenths abound in blues-derived patterns and open-ended structures. Yet there are many occasions when such triads clearly do act functionally, perhaps due to the awareness some musicians have of the classical repertory. Such songs are discussed below.

Although many rock players will find it unnecessary to be aware of a chord as a product of its constituent notes, it will be useful to analyse chords at this level in order properly to explore rock harmony. The most fruitful way to do this is to employ a modal system.[12] I shall first explain how such a system works, and then attempt to indicate its benefits.

According to this system, instead of major and minor scales, we have seven modes, each of which disposes five tones ('T') and two semitones ('S') in a cyclical order, thus: lydian TTTSTTS, ionian (effectively the same as major) TTSTTTS, mixolydian TTSTTST, dorian TSTTTST, aeolian ('natural minor') TSTTSTT, phrygian STTTSTT and locrian STTSTTT. Of these, ionian through to aeolian are the most common, but uses of the other three are not insignificant. Other writers have pointed to the existence of some modal patterns in rock (see Middleton 1990: 198, 200 for discussion of the use of aeolian patterns identified by Bjornberg 1985), but have not suggested the application of a fully fledged modal system. Within each mode, each note can act as root for one triad, yielding seven triads built in the conventional way, i.e. by taking alternate notes of the mode (see example 2.10 for the triads built on the lydian mode.) Only the lydian and ionian modes permit a dominant major triad (i.e. a major triad built on the fifth degree of the mode); and hence permit the strong perfect cadence of common practice tonality. Moreover, the major triad built on the note a *tone* lower than the tonic (the first degree of the mode), which is common throughout rock, occurs only within the mixolydian, dorian and aeolian modes.

Alterations to these modal triads do appear in rock. For instance, again referring to example 2.10, chord III will often appear in its major form, i.e. E–G♯–B (this would be indicated thus: III[#3], to show that the third degree of the chord had been raised by a semitone). But alterations in terms of the *root* of the chord are very rare in practice in rock harmony considered as a modal system. This obviates the consideration of some chords (such as the mixolydian VII) as aberrant. Mixolydian VII is far more common in rock than ionian VII (the relevant data can be found in Moore 1992).

This is the first benefit of adopting a modal system, in that not only does it make sense of tonally 'strange' harmonic sequences,[13] but it does not assume them to be 'abnormal'. The second benefit of this system is one of clarity.

Example 2.10 Lydian mode: scale and triads based on C

Speaking 'tonally', there is always confusion over whether ♭III, in C major, consists of (a) E♭–G–B♭ (on the grounds that the fewest possible alterations have been made to the diatonic chord), or (b) E♭–G♭–B♭ (on the grounds that chord III is necessarily a minor triad within C major). Speaking modally, (a) is best described as aeolian III, while (b) is locrian III. Finally, although I think its descriptive value is most important, this modal system is certainly an intrinsic aspect of the technique at least of guitar and bass players. Therefore, all Roman numeral ascriptions I use are to be understood as referring either to all, or to any particular named mode, rather than to the major scale.

It seems that types of patterns may well acquire specific connotations. Patterns involving a minimal number of elements may connote 'stasis' and 'timelessness' (the guitar solo of the hippy era was frequently executed over a harmonic drone). It also seems to me that sequences which stick rigidly within a single mode (as opposed to using altered triads) may similarly connote certainty, stability, acceptance and even resignation: not for nothing are blues conventionally content to describe the situation. In this context, the music of Madness stands out as exceptional (see Chapter 4).

Open-ended repetitive patterns

The unit of repetition of harmonic sequences in rock is frequently four bars, sometimes eight or two bars, and rarely any other number. The rate of change of harmonies tends to be regular; thus four-chord sequences and two-chord sequences are very common, while three-chord sequences (one chord being doubled in length) are by no means unknown. Why this should be so is a matter of conjecture, although it is probably an expression of the four-beat bar over a longer time-span. Many songs based fundamentally on harmonic sequence restrict themselves to just one, and a discussion of two such songs (Slade's 'Coz I Luv You' and Jimi Hendrix's 'Hey Joe') will prove useful. 'Coz I Luv You' is based squarely on a phrygian IV–I–II–I pattern, stretched over sixteen bars. The pattern repeats six times in all (two verses, solo, two verses, solo), bounded by an introductory I and a closing fade. 'Hey Joe' uses an incomplete cycle of fifths pattern[14] in the aeolian mode and, abnormally, in reverse direction: VI–III–VII–IV$^{\#3}$–I$^{\#3}$. This repeats some seventeen times, divided into three verses (four, four and six repeats of sequence) with a solo after the second verse. To base an entire song on a single harmonic sequence can invite boredom through lack of contrast, and both these songs develop strategies to overcome this. These strategies are subtle, for the incessant sequences reinforce the sense behind the lyrics. Both songs have an intense single-mindedness about them: Noddy Holder's expressions of love are far more those of obsession than a reciprocal process, while Joe clearly feels himself driven to murder and flight. But in 'Coz I Luv You', both the IV–I and II–I moves are executed over a longish time-span, allowing the second to be heard as a variant of the first. Timbral density also grows slowly as the pattern is repeated, and the vocal verses are interspersed with instrumental verses. The verses of 'Hey Joe' are clearly structured as questions and subsequent answers, while the rising scale pattern introduced at the end of the solo is treated motivically, returning at the end – there is hence a difference between repetitions with and without this additional motif.

Other songs use more than one such sequence. Deep Purple's 'Child in Time' is based equally single-mindedly on an aeolian I–VII–I (each chord briefly preceded by its lower stepwise neighbour), which grows to a climax, gives way to a central instrumental section (using I as a drone[15]) and then retrieves the opening section to make a big ending. The effect, however, is no less insistent than those above, owing to the different time-scales involved (nearer nine minutes rather than three) and the obsessive nature of what some drummers call the 'classical' rock rhythm (see Finkelstein 1979):

♩ ♪♪♪ ♩　♪♪♪. The Who's 'Substitute' makes use of a potentially

endless ionian I–V–IV–I for the refrain, but the verse progresses from I through II to V, the first two being decorated by other harmonies. There is thus a distinct difference in a song like this between the harmonic process of the verse and that of the refrain. The verse carries a narrative, marking a change of position between its beginning and end, while the refrain constantly returns to an unchanging position. This takes us into the realms of period structure, with which I shall deal below.

Within any seven-note mode, there are only four ways to continue from one harmony to the next: to remain in place (there being no 'next' harmony), to move in stepwise fashion (up or down), to move by the interval of a third[16] (likewise) and to move by the interval of a fourth (likewise). Remaining in place for any length leads to music based on a drone, which was to become a very common rationale for fully-fledged solos.[17] Stepwise moves are normally highly limited (the mixolydian VII–I is particularly a stock pattern) or conjoined with other moves. Four-stage stepwise patterns are not uncommon (e.g. the aeolian I–VII–VI–V[#3], or 'flamenco' pattern), but longer patterns are rare.[18] Patterns extending a third-based move beyond the second stage are rare when stepping upwards[19] but more common moving downwards:[20] they include the widely used 'Stand by Me' changes (ionian I–VI–IV–V).[21] Third-moves are more notable for being mixed with other types, and for occurring as a single stage, particularly when the requirements of the mode are overriden. Thus David Bowie's 'Suffragette City' and the Doors' 'Light My Fire' are particularly unusual.[22]

In all, patterns using fourth-based moves seem to be most prevalent. Oscillations of I–IV and I–V abound, as do sequences beginning thus and continuing with other moves. However, patterns continuing from I–IV or I–V in cyclic fashion are also numerous. Beyond the second stage, it is rare to find patterns using an entire portion of the cycle of fifths without I as a starting point: V–I–IV–VII, II–V–I–IV and VI–II–V–I are typical examples. These do, however, all appear in rotated form: I–IV–VII–V,[23] I–IV–II–V[24] and I–VI–II–V.[25] The largest number of consecutive cyclic shifts in common rock usage is five, i.e. ionian III–VI–II–V–I,[26] a common sequence in classical tonality, and its very rare alternate version VI–III–VII–IV–I.[27] Sharpwise cyclic sequences (i.e. those whose roots are successively a fifth higher) are normatively ionian, while flatwise cyclic sequences (i.e. those whose roots are successively a fourth higher) are not. Throughout all these sequences, the difference between sharpwise and flatwise moves would seem to be fundamental. Middleton (1990: 200) argues that a flatwise move (e.g. I–IV) traverses less 'distance' than its sharpwise counterpart (e.g. I–V in this particular example), presumably because the tonic pitch is present in both I and IV, but is absent from V. Although this lack of distance rarely seems to be articulated in songs, flatwise moves in general (whatever the mode) do tend to carry connotations of less tension than equivalent sharpwise moves, and modes without a sharpened seventh degree (i.e. those below ionian which do not use a modified chord $V^{\sharp 3}$) can carry similar connotations.

It seems to me likely that all sequences used in rock could be generated from fifth-cyclic sequences by the recursive application of rules of substitution similar to those suggested for jazz by Perlman and Greenblatt (1981) and Steedman (1984), although the rules for rock would prioritize substitution by third-related chords (the importance of fifth-cycles in this were suggested at least as early as Winkler 1978). I have briefly suggested what these rules might look like (see Moore 1992), although much more work remains to be done. Not only may the development of a generative theory of rock harmony enable the explanation of the (musical) competence of performers and writers, it may go some way towards explaining the intra-stylistic competence achieved by listeners.

The open/closed principle

Songs that are based on the repetition of harmonic sequences seem to have quite a degree of freedom in terms of the lengths over which these sequences may be used, and the number of repetitions they may have. In these cases, form is subservient to the operation of the pattern. With other songs, however, form is dominant, and harmonic changes are chosen to fill the required length. Here the terms used in the discussion of local structures by Arnold Schoenberg (1967) are useful. Schoenberg defines a *period* as consisting of two successive musical (i.e. melodic or harmonic) phrases that are in a question/ answer, or open/closed relationship. What is important here is that the music affords perception in terms of the length of the period (verse/refrain), that length being predictable, and in terms of the way each ends. What might be regarded as the normative rock position is the 'open/closed' pairing, whereby the period's first phrase ends on a non-tonic harmony (often V), the second phrase ending on I.[28] In these examples, the period-ending harmonies act *functionally*. The same pairing will sometimes be found in *ballad* structures.[29] These contain four-line verses, with only two different strains of music ('P' and 'Q') appearing in the pattern 'PPQP'. They derive from the Tin Pan

Alley 'sentimental ballad', and should not be confused with the 'ballad' created by folk-song enthusiasts (see Harker 1985: 124ff.).

Closed/closed pairings are less common, presumably because this makes it harder to create a sense of continuity. Both Creedence Clearwater Revival's 'Proud Mary' and Tyrannosaurus Rex's 'Find a Little Wood', which use this pairing, spend a great deal of initial time on I, such that a sense of harmonic progress is not apparent. Among ballad structures, this pairing seems commoner than open/closed, presumably because the ballad structure itself has clear internal divisions.[30] The remaining pairings are found even less frequently. I am unaware of any songs using closed/open pairings. Presumably, having heard a closed initial phrase, an ensuing open phrase will call into question precisely where the period starts. There is no *a priori* reason why such ambiguity should be unwelcome, although the absence of this pairing suggests that it is. Open/open pairings are not unknown, although here phrases are as likely to avoid V as the final chord as they are to use it.[31] The end of the period in these cases is marked only by a hypermetric boundary.

The most important aspect of these period structures is that the harmonies that flesh them out are of secondary importance. Rarely in such periods do we find a repeated harmonic sequence as such (and many such periods would not be harmonically out of place in Mozart). More interestingly, we often find open-ended and period structures existing side by side in the repertoires of many bands, sometimes appearing on the same album, and not infrequently appearing even in the same song. While we must note the qualititative distinctions between period structures (remnants of 'bourgeois song' and private listening practices) and open-ended structures ('collective participation'), rock clearly shows that 'the categories never present themselves in a pure state. They interrelate dialectically' (Middleton 1990: 217). This point is strengthened when we note that the open/open pairings identified above conflict with a strict interpretation of Schoenberg's theory (which insists that the end of a period is marked by harmonic closure): they clearly carry the structure towards open-endedness. So, the differences between the styles of (say) Abba, the Beatles, Bon Jovi, Queen, the Jam and Creedence Clearwater Revival cannot be accounted for purely in terms of harmonic structures.

A second, analogous type of stable structure is that represented by the twelve-bar blues. What is interesting here is not the use of the I–I–I–I–IV–IV–I–I–V–IV–I–I schema (each chord lasting one bar), but the fact that it has taken on the status of a cliché. Very few rock songs that could be described as based on the twelve-bar blues stick rigidly to this harmonic pattern, and therefore the twelve-bar blues can be seen to be a normative structure analogous to the period. Variants can be either subtle or gross.[32] Indeed, for listeners well versed in the blues, simply the sequence I–IV at the beginning of a verse can bring on a twelve-bar blues mind-set. Here, again, harmonies are chosen to fill out the pre-existent structure, which is recognizable even where considerable liberties are taken with chordal durations,[33] a practice at least as old as Robert Johnson.

Example 2.11 Open position guitar chords

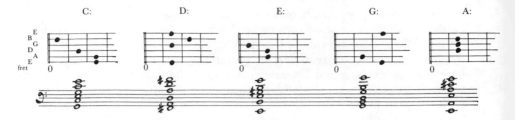

Example 2.12 Capo position chord of E

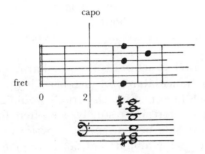

Composing at the instrument

One further distinction, which is always overlooked in any discussion of rock harmonies, concerns whether songs have been written 'at the fretboard' or 'at the keyboard'. Unlike many art music composers, it appears that most rock writers use an instrument in order to develop songs. Here, the mechanistic differences between the guitar and piano/organ/keyboard synthesizer are vital. These are the only common instruments to enable a single individual to have control over harmonic sequences, and also to superimpose on these melodic patterns if required.

The keyboard is comparatively undifferentiated with respect to chord shapes: patterns using white-note roots as tonic are more likely. The fretboard, however, is highly differentiated with respect to chord shapes. The only major chords available in open position are those based on C, D, E, G and A, and the different disposition of pitches within each of these shapes gives each chord a definite spacing characteristic. Example 2.11 displays these chords as they would appear on the guitar fretboard, and also in conventional notation. Thus, a chord of E played in open position is not at all the same as a chord of E played in the D position with a capo on the second fret, as a comparison of the E chords in examples 2.12 and 2.11 shows. If barre chords are not used, the guitar clearly forces a songwriter into a limited repertoire of harmonies.

Equally, the less proficient the writer at the keyboard, the more limited a harmonic repertoire he or she is likely to have, although this may differ from player to player. This yields a clear distinction in harmonic repertoire between many heavy metal bands on the one hand, and some progressive bands on the other. In the beat and rhythm 'n' blues era this helps distinguish the norms of the Rolling Stones from those of the Beatles, and more closely the individual contributions of Lennon and McCartney, since Lennon more usually composed at the guitar, while McCartney frequently composed at the piano. More recently, this begins to account for the different repertoires of, say, U2 and the Eurythmics.

Through the later stages of this chapter, I have intentionally drawn my examples from throughout these past thirty years, in order to demonstrate that the strategies I have outlined probably came into being before the advent of rock (van der Merwe (1989) finds all but the 'open-ended gesture' before the current century), and are probably likely to continue beyond the time that 'rock' remains a useful label. None the less, the way they are used changes through time, and I shall therefore have cause to refer back to these domains – instrumental functions, rhythm, vocal use, harmony and formal patterns – in dealing with the changes of style of rock through subsequent years.

3   *Progressive Styles and Issues*

Progressive rock forms the focus for this study for musical reasons, which will foreground the supposed 'progressive' nature of the music. Indeed, at least until the end of this chapter, it will be best to consider the word always qualified by quotation marks. Its origins are conventionally found in the moment of recognition of a schism between 'rock' and 'pop', a schism founded on pop's commercial nature and rock's innocence of the same charges (an innocence I shall not support) and marked by the release of the Beatles' *Sgt Pepper's Lonely Hearts Club Band* in 1967. (The problematic nature of rock's commercial presence may suggest that the schism resulted less from a recognition than an invention.) As a movement, it was highly heterogeneous, and to identify it wholesale as 'progressive' is a mistake. Some musicians were associated with the ('progressive') aims and ambitions of late-1960s counterculture, always more apparent in the USA than in the UK, but 'association' was normally as far as any relationship went. Hawkwind and the Edgar Broughton Band (for instance) may have tried to put theory into practice by playing free gigs, but few of the musicians were as politically involved either as their audiences believed, or indeed as many in those audiences themselves were (see Denselow 1990: 92–107). The musical techniques Robert Fripp developed in King Crimson are more highly developed than many, as I shall demonstrate below, although he supported no programme for social change (see Tamm 1990, especially 20–23). And, in any case, a high state of development is no indication of progress. Moreover, the recourse to outmoded forms of musical expression (the supposed appropriation of the 'blues') by Eric Clapton, and his later tirade against the practice of immigration to Britain, which led to the founding of Rock Against Racism, sit uneasily anywhere near the epithet 'progressive'. The foundation for many of the cultural practices relevant here was the desire by whites to find blacks 'natural', and I shall critique this in detail below. Because of the contradictions inherent in the notion of a single, 'progressive' programme, I shall treat 'progressive

rock' as a series of related but separate styles, each with their internal consistencies, some of which are not necessarily reactionary, but which deny the
monolith of a single 'progressive' rock.

In their internal consistencies, these styles acquire a relative autonomy, but
it is strictly relative. As with all musical styles, they are grounded in social
practice and historical conditions. I do not intend to offer a discussion of the
cultural practices of the period (many other writers on rock have already
supplied their own),[1] but in order to anchor my subsequent discussion of
styles, one factor in particular cannot be ignored. It seems to me that the most
important feature of mid-1960s Britain in enabling the development of these
styles was the economic situation of the record companies, effective employers
of bands. Not only did they see the world market rapidly expanding, the
consumer boom in the UK yielded them large returns, enabling them not only
to invest in their artists without requiring an immediate financial return (a
return they continued to enjoy until well into the 1970s: See Harker 1980:
226), but also to relinquish a degree of control over the resultant product and
its marketing. This both enabled and encouraged artists to experiment with
music which often was not immediately and widely accessible, and gave them
a sense of control over their musical destinies. Their experimentation was
further enabled by far-reaching technological developments in the studio, and
was also encouraged by an apparent audience demand for involvement with
the radicalism of the protest movement. This allowed 'progressive' musicians
the space to develop an ideology of artistic freedom and self-expression (an
ideology which was also widely constructed by rock critics), within what was
considered a freedom from the constraint of an immediate, dancing, audience:
the term 'progressive', connoted a concern with aesthetic and individual
rather than immediate and communal qualities. The musicians' ideology thus
became integrated into the new youth ideology where 'doing your own thing'
became the operative phrase. In order to help them differentiate this product
from their 'commercial' pop, the major record companies set up their own
'progressive' labels, enabling them to service the fast growing student market.
It is here that the Beatles' release of *Sgt Pepper's* is pivotal, in its indication of
the realignment of rock from its working-class roots to its subsequent place on
the college circuit. The experimentation which, in some respect or other,
characterizes the styles I shall consider in this chapter, is grounded in these
conditions. Into the 1980s, only difficult and proven artists of the stature of
Kate Bush can command a similar degree of record company investment and
tolerance, while other artists who do endeavour to experiment largely do so
away from the ears of the majors and the High Street record buying public.

I shall not endeavour to explain the social grounding of the styles I discuss
here, but in the final chapter I shall discuss the theoretical basis for such
relationships. There I shall conclude that, in Europe and the USA at least,
musical styles cannot be considered entirely socially conditioned.

So, what of the 'progressive' nature of the music that these conditions
enabled? The techniques of urban blues and rock 'n' roll singers and players
had been relatively simple in terms of harmonic structures and metric frame-

works. Prior to 1967, some rock musicians had begun to expand these structures, a process which continued through the following decade with the eclectic addition of techniques taken from styles as diverse as those of Tin Pan Alley, late nineteenth-century European classicism and the recent avant-garde. By the mid-1970s, this process of accretion had reached something of an impasse, at which time the 'progressive' styles were nearing stagnation. Styles which succeeded these have tended to work *within* the limits set by progressive rock, with some exceptions which will come to light in Chapter 4. It thus forms something of a nexus point in the history of rock music styles, at least in the UK. This model is not particularly original. The 'language' of European 'classical' music itself has developed only to reach similar impasses in the late sixteenth century, the early eighteenth century, and the middle of the present century. The model does, however, provide a structure against which 'progressive' styles can be viewed.

The details of these styles themselves raise a number of intrinsically related issues. To deal with these separately from the styles themselves would be to make an artificial distinction that, in turn, would suggest that the styles function with greater autonomy than is the case. Accordingly, my discussion of styles will be interspersed with accounts of the idealization of the blues and of things 'black', the practice of improvisation, and the listening strategies afforded by these styles.

Rock traditions

Rock supports a vast range of labels: progressive rock, stadium rock, classic rock, folk rock, gospel rock, country rock, swamp rock, glam and glitter rock, psychedelic rock, cock rock, rock 'n' roll, rockabilly, ballad rock, melodic rock, synthesizer rock, pomp rock, acid rock, punk rock, art rock, soft, heavy, thrash, hardcore and death metal, hard rock, goth rock, adult-oriented rock, pub rock, authentic rock ... the list is as long as the publicist's thesaurus. Fortunately, many of these descriptions are not of styles themselves, but of institutions (melodies can be found in both stadia and pubs), ideologies (the aestheticism of art rock, or the macho pose of cock rock), critical appraisal (pomp rock is by definition pretentious) and even forms (the ballad, i.e. that derived from Tin Pan Alley: see Chapter 2).[2] None the less, it is necessary to arrive at a position from where the relationship of different styles, bearing at least a superficial resemblance to each other, can be ascertained. There seem to be seven stances that are important in this regard: my guide here has been Raymond Williams's *Culture* (1981a), especially Chapters 3, 6 and 7, although in dealing with a specified cultural activity, the position is necessarily a little more complex than his structure allows.

The initial beat and rhythm 'n' blues (r&b) bands are *formative*. It is in the music of the Shadows, the Beatles, the Kinks, the Who, the Rolling Stones, the Small Faces, the Spencer Davis Group, and many others, that the features set out in Chapter 2 are first encountered with consistency, as a set of stylistic norms. These norms are most clearly conceived in terms of metre and the approach to the beat, vocal tone, the structural role of harmony and, pre-eminently, the setting-up of a musical texture stratified through specific instrumental functions or roles. Formation has gone on elsewhere, of course (the invention of the rules of ska in late-1950s Jamaica, of r&b in late-1940s Chicago or of jazz in late-1910s New Orleans), and these stylistic groupings are themselves interrelated. None the less, the quaintly termed 'British invasion' of the USA in 1964 reinforced the perception of beat/r&b styles as distinct from their American counterparts, a perception that can be validated by comparison of the limits defined by these style groups.[3]

The term 'rock' first came into general use after 1967, to refer to what is now loosely termed 'progressive rock'. The stance that unifies this historical moment is *reconciliatory*. As this chapter will argue, progressive rock takes the stylistic norms of beat/r&b and extends some of them to new boundaries, by incorporating elements of 'folk', 'jazz', 'blues' and other musics. The domains thus explored are normally metre, form (it shows itself above all in formal complexity, expansion and looseness) and to a limited extent harmony, but not texture or instrumental roles. Textural development had to await technological developments, while it seems that instrumental roles have, hitherto, needed to remain static if the music is to be recognized as 'rock'.

'Hard rock' is a useful catch-all term for the 'rock' that arose from one side of the progressive movement, a music primarily based on riffs. Thus, it began as *developmental*, taking as a starting point the early music of the Kinks as one source, Cream as a second and the soul roots of Deep Purple as a third, and developing the linear approach of these bands, while necessarily foregoing musical development in many other areas. What is now called heavy metal (and its offshoots) is but a further stage in this development, a development that has long since moved out of sight of the Kinks' Ray Davies.

The historical links between 'hard rock' and 'punk' are not as distant as they may at first seem (Motorhead used to be frequently cited as exemplars of both). Punk was initially perceived by many to have taken an *oppositional* stance, in terms of general cultural formations (particularly emphasized in dress codes), but also to the music establishment (largely represented by pop, disco and pomp rock). I shall have cause to argue against this perception in subsequent chapters.

The *regressive* tendency works to recapture past glories, from within rock itself. Both Madness and Squeeze were intent on continuing the somewhat quirky, quasi-biographical songs originally produced by the Kinks, the Beatles and the Who, in effect returning to a mode of approach that had run its course. This regression operates both in terms of lyrics and, somewhat, in terms of musical style. Likewise, the 1980s bands who particularly foreground the guitar (Big Country, U2), despite their innovatory approach to texture, tend to be regressive in their attempts to return to a 'pre-progressive' simplicity where authenticity of experience was achievable: Bruce Springsteen is frequently held to be the prime mover here. (Both these movements will receive attention in Chapter 4.)

The development of synthesizer rock in the late 1970s was perhaps the closest we have come to a new formative movement within rock, and perhaps for this reason it is frequently considered distinct from rock. (It was, after all, highly influential in the development of house music, a style which is not accepted by its fans as rock.) The musical development most obviously represented by synthesizer bands was in terms of texture, aided (and almost conditioned) by the meteoric growth in newly available technology. Yet, on closer listening, it can be heard that some of rock's musical conventions remain, particularly rock's instrumental stratification and backbeat. Thus, it is best to see this as exemplifying an *innovatory* stance, within the parameters that rock has itself set up. Innovation tends to be a much vaunted value among various consumers and writers: we applaud those bands or that music *we* like, because it or they are different from the others in some way, but not so different that we are unable to make sense of them. Thus, certain bands and styles become noteworthy because they take the existing features of a tradition and change its direction through introducing features foreign to that tradition.

Each of these stances comes about as a way of introducing new elements into what may be a stultifying style. Even the regressive tendency seems to work this way: the examples I have chosen not only reintroduce spent ideas, but combine these with new attitudes in some other domain (harmony for Madness, texture for U2, etc.). Yet, at least until the mid-1980s, probably the majority of working bands were content to adopt a *consolidatory* approach: much other music is liked because it is similar to what listeners already like, and therefore it finds a ready market.[4] Once the norms of any style have been set, many less well-known musicians work quite happily within them, for example within the pub music scene – small-time, local bands continue to turn out the hits of the 1960s and some of those of the 1970s, and there remains a large market for this live music, primarily because it offers listeners familiarity.

Thus, each of these attitudes to tradition is not monolithic, and a truly detailed stylistic analysis would find bands taking different stances in different areas of their work. Indeed, as the final chapter will show, much of the power of the work of two of rock's style virtuosi, David Bowie and Elvis Costello, comes from their taking up positions cutting across these various stances. What such an analysis suggests most forcefully, of course, is that a stylistic history of rock would not be linear history, but a history full of eddies, backwaters and tidal waves.

The beginnings of progressive rock

Avant-garde fields of 'art' music in the present century have tended to be promulgated by private performance and hand-written scores, largely without respect to commercial considerations. The advent of punk was not too dissimilar: the *constructed* quality of its beginnings was well hidden. Its general un-availability on radio made it seem (even to casual listeners) a 'natural' if unusually provocative movement, knowledge of which was passed on by word of mouth, cheaply produced handbills, fanzines etc. Right from its beginnings, however, progressive rock depended far more on the visual qualities associated with large-scale staging, and on good studio recordings, both of which required heavy investment and therefore high commercial returns. As Frith (1983: 97) notes with respect to both the UK and USA, 'by 1968 the commercial viability of 'progressive' rock was obvious.' This developed through the college circuit and through 'independent' promoters, producers and managers. EMI launched its 'progressive' label (Harvest) in 1968 and the other major record companies followed suit. But at no time was progressive rock a unitary style: it extended from 'art' rock on the one hand through 'hard' rock to styles of 'folk' rock. None the less, there are certain factors held in common by these sub-styles. In retrospect, this music seems to me not to be about destroying the norms of beat/r&b, but to be about extending them through infusion with a variety of foreign influences, and laying out the boundaries (in terms of rhythm, harmony and form at least) within which more recent rock lies. From whatever background they came, these progressive rock musicians were united by a desire to go beyond (rather than deny) the limitations of the seven-inch medium, and hence escape the 'commercial' tag. But, although progressive rock musicians may have felt they were 'expressing themselves' as well as merely delivering commercial products to their labels, even their activity was no less commercially founded than was pop. Aside from matters of musical technique, the only fundamental difference between the two lay in the connotations the style had for its audience: for few students and hippies did the music function primarily as entertainment.

The beginnings of progressive rock are normally traced to the Beatles' *Sgt. Pepper's Lonely Hearts Club Band* (1967), a notable 'concept' album that I shall discuss in detail below. Other influences were borrowed from the American counter-culture that was to produce 'flower power'. These had surfaced in the UK by 1965 and the first appearances of Pink Floyd at underground venues, particularly London's UFO club. Frith and Horne (1987) argue that the art school training of many rock musicians was crucial to their musical development: certainly Pink Floyd are a case in point. Even in 1965, they used what Rick Sanders describes as 'a total environment of light and sound' (Sanders 1976: 9), foreshadowing later attempts at producing a 'total' aesthetic experience, which becomes one of the hallmarks of the entire spectrum of rock. This 'environment' grew directly out of their own experimental studies at Hornsey College of Art (Taylor 1987: 192). The important similarity between these two very different 'beginnings' is that they are both concerned with the production of a unified whole, an entire package ('concept album' on the one hand, 'show' on the other) rather than a succession of separate items.

Accepting that progressive rock takes a reconciliatory stance *vis-à-vis* the pop and beat/r&b traditions, it is necessary to identify the external sources that became somewhat reconciled. Charlie Gillett identifies three main sources for British 'rock' at this time – blues, gospel and folk (Gillett 1983: 376), but this somewhat over-simplifies the situation. There seem to me to be at least six sources to which artists went (or from which backgrounds they came) in order to further the development of rock in the UK. It is my intention to deal initially with one of the clearest of these, the appropriation of the 'blues'. Before this can be done, it will be necessary first to show the relationship between the music of these early British rock musicians and their forebears in the USA, and then to investigate the meaning the 'blues' seemed to have, and still has, for many audiences, musicians and critics in the UK.

'Afro-American' influences

By late 1964, British beat/r&b bands seemed to be asserting a great degree of stylistic independence of their US rock 'n' roll forebears. (Bradley 1992: 62–3 and 71–5 traces the dependence which had existed prior to this.) George Melly reports a conversation with John Lennon which took place in 1964:

> During the course of the party I suggested that despite his [Lennon's] fame and money he was surely prepared to own up that not only did he owe a considerable debt to such Negro blues singers as Muddy Waters, but that objectively they were greater artists. He turned on me with sublime arrogance. He'd admit to no such thing. Not only was he richer but better too. More original and better. We almost came to rather drunken blows.
>
> (Melly 1970: 77)

In an interview given as late as 1982, Lennon stated:

> The only white I ever listened to was Elvis Presley on his early music records and he was doing black music. I don't blame him for wanting to be part of that music. I wanted to be like that. I copied all those people and the other Beatles did, and so did the others until we developed a style of our own. Black music started this whole change of style and attitude that was started by rock 'n' roll, and rock 'n' roll is black. I appreciate that and I'll never stop acknowledging it.
>
> (quoted in Small 1987: 388)

Time clearly focused Lennon's memory. The material taken by the Beatles, the Rolling Stones and their colleagues in the early 1960s came from a variety of (mostly black) US sources (many of whom were Tamla Motown artists): the aim tends to be a near-exact reproduction of the source. To take the Beatles as a first example, 'Please Mr Postman', 'You Really Got a Hold on Me', 'Twist and Shout' and 'Take Good Care of My Baby' come from highly diverse styles, which may be loosely identified within their historical contexts as girl group, soul ballad and dance, and pop ballad. In each case, the Beatles produced a very precise copy of the original, even down to the vocal idiosyncrasies on 'Twist and Shout': the high 'oo' (later to become a characteristic Beatles device in songs such as 'She Loves You'), the pyramid harmony leading into the second half of the song, and the subsequent cracking of the voice on the words 'shake it up baby'. The only notable differences, other than changes of key to suit differing vocal ranges, are changes of instrumentation. Thus, in the Marvelettes' 'Please Mr Postman', the harmonies are filled out by regular quaver chords on the piano. On the Isley Brothers' 'Twist and

Example 3.1 'Take Good Care of My Baby'

Shout', the same role is taken by horns, while on Bobby Vee's 'Take Good Care of My Baby', the whole is based on orchestral strings. In their versions, the Beatles replace respectively piano, horns and strings with rhythm guitar to fill out the harmonies. In every other respect, the differences are minimal (even precise vocal doublings on individual syllables are copied). The subtle changes in vocal lines are often instructive. In 'Take Good Care of My Baby', Lennon and McCartney simplify Bobby Vee's double-tracked original (see example 3.1), which perhaps renders it a little less 'arty'. On 'You Really Got a Hold on Me', although Lennon's falsetto swoop in the second refrain is copied from Smokey Robinson, Lennon alters Robinson's tempered third to a flattened ('bluer') third in singing the title, perhaps over-emphasizing the attempt to 'be part of that music'.

The Rolling Stones adopted a similar approach – Otis Redding's 'That's How Strong My Love Is' is a heavy soul ballad, the Drifters' 'Under the Boardwalk' is more in the pop soul vein, while Buddy Holly's 'Not Fade Away' looks more to white rock 'n' roll. The Stones speed up 'That's How Strong My Love Is', and replace the harmony-defining piano with rhythm guitar, but include a simpler, very soft version of the low horns of Redding's original. 'Under the Boardwalk' is, again, a direct cover, with the guitar

taking on the characteristic ⅜ ♩. ♩. rhythm. On 'Not Fade Away'

they have been more adventurous, pulling it more securely towards r&b, particularly through the incorporation of a blues harp. Whereas Holly employs a call and response pattern between voice and guitar/bass, such that the singing voice is accompanied only by kit, for the Stones the voice alternates with the blues harp, giving a fuller texture throughout. Formally the two versions are identical, and Holly's strummed guitar solo is appropriated by the Stones, although the slower pace allows it to become a little more intricate.

Although further work would be required to ascertain how trustworthy the mass of anecdotal evidence in favour of the precision of 'covers' was, this practice was clearly not restricted to the Beatles and the Rolling Stones. The Yardbirds' cover of 'I Wish You Would' surfaced some nine years after Billy

Boy Arnold's original, and yet it mimics it in every respect, even down to the tempo, the blues harp riff and its ('improvised'!) solo, which is but a slightly ornamented version of Arnold's simple original. The only alterations are the voice's more melodically and rhythmically constrained delivery, and the replacement of piano by guitar.

The unavoidable conclusion to this is that not only was the initial debt of early British beat and r&b to its American (largely black) antecedents enormous, but also that from this seemingly heterogeneous stylistic mix a high degree of stylistic congruence arose, largely through the employment of a single, normative instrumental line-up based on voice, guitar, bass and drums. It was this comparatively unified style that progressive musicians would extend.

Blues as pretext

The ideological identification of 'rock' as a separate music is founded upon the interest shown by substantial, if minority, British audiences in what Gillett (1983: 257) terms 'obsolete forms of Negro music', an interest that first surfaced in the 1920s and that by the late 1950s had spread from audiences to musicians. In this context it is necessary to distinguish very clearly between 'blues' and 'rhythm 'n' blues', recognizing that this was an artificial distinction for the musics' original US audiences (see Oakley 1976: 237–8). For the beat/r&b bands, the music of their immediate American predecessors, i.e. electric r&b, provided much of the early material. Among the artists who helped in the development of progressive rock at a slightly later date, there is a more marked concern for the greater apparent *authenticity* represented by country blues artists, or by urban blues artists touring the UK.

American blues artists were first brought over by Chris Barber in the mid-1950s. On his 1957 tour, Muddy Waters caused a storm by playing through an amplifier, the sort of thing associated with rock 'n' roll rather than 'pure' blues, and hence despised. Although this electrification gradually became accepted, the sense of unease remained. The clearest example of this is Eric Clapton, who despite acknowledging the dominant musical influence of Muddy Waters and Freddie King, spent time tracing back the history of black American musicians until he reached Robert Johnson, a man who acted, for Clapton and for others, as the archetype of the country bluesman – poor, illiterate, full of anguish, naturally talented, and dead.

This search for origins in the blues is the key element in the ideological (as opposed to music-stylistic) identification of 'rock' as a separate music from 'pop', for among musicians, audiences and commentators, there seems to have arisen the sense that if the origin of a style, practice or object can be found, the essence of what it is about can be captured, and magically that essence will transfer itself to the finder. British cultural theorists with an interest in rock have a strong tendency to devalue any style that is not primarily constituted from elements which can be tagged as 'black', and even these 'crossover' styles are often felt to be less worthy than their original black forebears. Although by the 1970s the links with the blues and r&b that had been so evident ten years earlier seemed to be something of a millstone for many rock musicians, even today cultural critics seem to judge rock in terms of the strength of those apparent links. The biggest single point of *condemnation* levelled at much progressive rock was its lack of black influence. Otis Redding and Sly Stone may have been somewhat accepted by progressive fans, but this acceptance failed to affect the music being played by progressive bands. Thus, there tends to be a marked absence of such things as the extended use of vocal melismas, the ubiquity of internal accents and syncopations which change their position within successive repetitions of the same material,[5] subtle vocal anticipations and delays of the beat, the use of 'dirty' timbres and the regular use of the 'soul cadence' (i.e. IV–I over a V–I bass).

We thus encounter this longing for the 'authentic essence' of the blues at a time when the individual artist (typically the guitar hero) was becoming pre-eminent. This should come as no surprise, since both the uncontaminated native and the artist-as-hero are characters in the nineteenth-century romantic search for the rediscovery of a golden age, an age before humanity had become alienated from nature. Charles Keil (1966) discusses this in terms of the 'mouldy fig' attitude towards country blues singers, which is largely a European (and pre-eminently a British) attitude. It entails the assumption that blacks in the southern USA lived in a state of mindless primitivism, in which they expressed themselves through music 'naturally', without the intervening of any musical 'theory'; hence the 'black' sense of rhythm being 'natural' and 'unmediated'. Of course, this attitude can now be seen as blatantly racist, and all the more insidious for remaining unintentional. The function of rhythm in 'black' musics (whether West African drumming or American soul) may be somewhat different to its function in European 'classical' musics, but its function is no more 'natural' in the one than in the other. The blues is also theory-laden, to the extent that it has its own body of rules which are openly demonstrable.

This desire on the part of whites to find blacks 'natural' may be under-standable, in that it represented an attempt to find a measure of 'authenticity' on the part of those who felt their lives were inauthentic, were not their own and were cluttered with commercial pressures. It also represented an attempt to find a music 'pure' and lacking in 'artifice', again since all our music, whether 'pop' or 'classical', was overburdened with these features. The blues were apparently about the 'immediacy of lived experience', perhaps because they were supposedly improvised on the spot: it was not at the time recognized that these improvisations came from the application of melodic, harmonic, articulatory and lyrical formulae from a common stock – no blues singer ever pretended that each thought was 'original'. The 'mouldy fig' attitude is as alive as ever. Small (1987) considers the value of black music to lie in its subversive nature, which accrues to it because it is spontaneous, immediate and 'close to nature'. Frith (1983) talks dangerously of black music being 'felt', perhaps implying that white music tends to be 'thought', and therefore that blacks are incapable of thought. Even more recently, Wicke (1990: 38) has insisted that the blues were 'a pure expression of genuine experience'.

The issue here is the apparent immediacy that can accrue to music employing blues concepts. No musical system of expression is innate – all systems are forms of mediating experience. Yet this erroneous belief clearly affected the music. Many may have been taken with the attraction of declaring solidarity with an oppressed minority of the USA (although by the strange mechanism of lionizing a music that minority had come to despise[6]), but this resulted in the belief among musicians and fans alike that the 'immediacy' of the blues could be transferred to whites simply by playing 'the blues'. The search for essences has now gone further, the essences of the blues being deposited not in America, but in Africa itself, despite the insistence of van der Merwe that:

> nowhere [in Africa] . . . is there anything like the blues mode in its complete form. . . . All the components of the blues mode are to be found somewhere in West Africa, but separately.
>
> (van der Merwe 1989: 131)

Moreover, he traces the characteristic blues harmonic pattern back to early sixteenth-century Italy and France, finding (as we might expect) the roots of other blues harmonic schemes in Europe. To insist that, by employing the blues harmonic frameworks, one is returning to a golden age, a natural state, was a misunderstanding of the saddest kind.

Blues as (con)text

So, what relationship did exist between blues practices and those of progressive rock? I shall argue in this section that the 'inspiration' which some critics suggest the blues supplied (e.g. Gillett 1983: 376) is hard to sustain. It may be that the enrichment of techniques found among the musicians discussed here can be put down to their assumed appropriation of the blues, but in reality, this 'blues ideology' was grafted on to stylistic practices which it only partly fitted. I shall therefore discuss the music of the three bands cited by Gillett (1983) in this context: Cream, Fleetwood Mac and Led Zeppelin.

Cream formed in 1966 from three instrumentalists[7] who were well regarded by fellow musicians. Eric Clapton's roots were in the white appropriation of the blues: having begun with the Yardbirds, he made his name with John Mayall's Bluesbreakers. Both Ginger Baker and Jack Bruce had experience playing in jazz and r&b, notably with Graham Bond. According to Clapton, Cream had been planned as a blues trio 'like Buddy Guy with a rhythm section' (Logan and Wooffinden 1982: 61). In practice, the accent was heavily on improvisation over a basis that sometimes owed something to the blues.

Cream were responsible for many important innovations to the rock vocabulary, particularly those of the riff-based song and extended live improvisations. Although the Kinks' 'All Day and All of the Night' marks the introduction into British rock of the simple repeated riff, this means of construction was taken to new lengths by Cream's 'Sunshine of Your Love'. This innovation was welcomed and has become widely employed. There is still, however, much controversy over the introduction of extended live improvisations: it has become trendy to knock down the man the fans had proclaimed 'God'. Chambers suggests that the counter-cultural *idée fixe* of 'expanding your consciousness' found direct expression in extended improvisations: 'Behind lengthy live improvisations such as Cream's "Spoonful" lay the theme of individual spontaneity, exploration and extension' (Chambers 1985: 111), and it is of course fashionable to decry such a theme now, reeling as we are from the social ills produced by individualist ideology. Frith challenges these improvisations on other grounds:

> By the 1970s there was a general stress in rock on artfulness, on individualized skills; . . . even blues groups were, following Cream, emphasising technical rather than emotional expertise. Black music was, in this context, thought to be *too* direct.
>
> (Frith 1983: 21)

The link with 'black music' is vital, especially in conjunction with the supposed blues base. We see the cultural theorist arguing that 'emotional expertise' is preferable to 'technical expertise', creating the unfortunate apparent division between 'unmediated, black blues' and 'theory-laden white' playing discussed in the previous section. I think Gillett (1983: 384) gets nearer, describing Cream's initial excursions as an 'onslaught of virtuosity and power', in comparison with the 'sexually suggestive' attitude of artists such as Chuck Berry and Bo Diddley.

Clapton's reasons for forming Cream apparently included the need 'to go somewhere else and put my kind of guitar playing in a different context, in a new kind of pop music context' (Ward *et al.* 1987: 396). As can be seen from the diversity of material on the studio sides of *Wheels of Fire*, the context clearly exceeded that of the blues. In terms of style, diversity seems more prized than unity, although instrumentation and timbre do act as unifying forces. Both Howlin' Wolf's 'Sitting on Top of the World' and Booker T. Jones' 'Born under a Bad Sign' are pretty standard blues: the former an eight-bar I–IV–I–V–I, the latter a twelve-bar not moving from I until bar 9. In comparison with early r&b, both are remarkable for their slow speed. 'Born under a Bad Sign' works at about 88 beats to the minute, but 'Sitting on Top of the World' is at a funereal shuffle beat (approx. 42). In both, Bruce's voice and Clapton's guitar fall into a constant call and response pattern. The remaining tracks have varied degrees of relationship with the blues. The Bruce/Brown 'Politician' has a twelve-bar structure, based on a guitar riff overlaid with one and two lead guitar tracks throughout, but both 'White Room' and 'Deserted Cities of the Heart' are fairly standard rock. 'White Room' is formally concise: instrumental, verse (in two parts), repeated, instrumental, verse and instrumental coda, using a modified standard rock beat beneath two standard chord sequences, one for each half of the verse. Over this pattern is laid a sense of continuous growth, whereby Clapton's guitar enters in verse two, in call and

Example 3.2 Cream: 'Deserted Cities of the Heart'

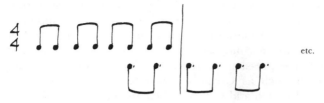

etc.

Example 3.3 Pink Floyd: 'Bike'; Cream: 'Passing the Time'

response with Bruce's voice, building to verse three where the guitar plays throughout. (I shall return to this sense of growth below.) The only strange feature here is the $\frac{5}{4}$ introduction, making use of timpani and violas. 'Deserted Cities of the Heart' is similarly standard, with a solo constructed over a drone, rather than over the chord changes as elsewhere on the album. The only strange turn here is again rhythmic, with the song's straight beat becoming a shuffle rhythm for the instrumental interlude, and the length of the beat increasing by half (see example 3.2). 'Those Were the Days', despite references to Atlantis, is still fairly standard.

The remaining tracks are far from any blues influence, and probably further than 'For Your Love', which had caused Clapton's split from the Yardbirds over precisely this ideological dispute. Both the remaining Baker/Taylor songs, 'Passing the Time' and 'Pressed Rat and Warthog' are strongly reminiscent of the whimsical side of Marc Bolan, Pink Floyd's Syd Barrett and the Incredible String Band. 'Passing the Time' makes use of the same, unusual I–IV^{b7} sequence that lies under Barrett's 'Bike', emphasizing the same vocal pitches (see example 3.3) overlaying a kit-less alternation of $\frac{3}{4}$ and $\frac{4}{4}$, although it uses a rock refrain. 'Pressed Rat and Warthog' is stranger still: Ginger Baker recites an embarrasing piece of whimsy reminiscent of that by John Peel on Tyrannosaurus Rex's *Unicorn*, with a continuous eight-bar sequence in the background. Finally, the Jack Bruce/Peter Brown 'As You Said' is closest to early John Martyn and similar British singer-songwriters. The instrumentation of acoustic guitar and cello is reminiscent of David Bowie's 'Wild-eyed Boy from Freecloud', while Bruce's use of 'modal' guitar tuning[8] recalls that of Joni Mitchell (in the USA) and Martin Carthy (in the UK), first developed at about this time. The use of phasing on the voice was a late-1960s metaphor for psychedelia.

Example 3.4 Cream: 'Spoonful'

In all, then, no style or personality really dominates the studio sides. Clapton's solos are notable but not remarkable and multi-tracking is kept to a minimum, mostly being used to overlay a rhythm guitar track with a lead track. It is on the live sides that the blues influence really comes to the fore, as it was blues material that led to Cream's extended improvisations. 'Spoonful' is memorable in this context: a comparison of the live version on *Wheels of Fire* with the studio version found on *Fresh Cream* illustrates the 'freedom' explored in a live setting. On both albums, the song is clearly little more than a pretext. On the studio version, three sets of riff (6 or 8 bars), verse (16) and refrain (8) are interrupted after the second refrain (the standard place) by a 46-bar solo, while on the live version this solo lasts some 250 bars. In both versions, hypermetre (the sense of a regular grouping of bars into units of 4) exerts no pull once the improvisation has begun. There are three regions in the live solo where Baker's $\frac{4}{4}$ shuffle rhythm pattern (groups of 12 quavers) becomes re-interpreted (after some 45–50 bars, after about 200 bars, and just before the return of the riff). At these points, the triplet quavers seem to become straight quavers, in that every second, not every third, starts to receive an accent (see example 3.4), but at each point a regular mental tracking of the beat breaks down as Baker's accents become slightly sporadic, before he retrieves the shuffle basis and with it the clear beat. This gives a sense of constantly being in the present: the instrumentalists evince no concern for coinciding at the points where the beat is re-established. Most of the interesting details are rhythmic, making use of quasi-tala techniques (explained in the next section). Indeed, whereas in the studio version we never lose the solid $\frac{4}{4}$ shuffle, all three players treat this improvisation as individuals, each moving off on his own flight (this requires no great skill when the whole improvisation is based on a regular quaver and pentatonic E – anything can be made to sound right with literally anything else within these bounds). The elements of structure throughout this improvisation are minimal – at four points Baker eases off, tending to move away from snare and ride cymbal, while Clapton and Bruce slowly take the cue, moving into the middle range and playing more sparsely. Elsewhere, greater activity by one tends to spur the others on to a similar degree, although Clapton's reintroduction of the riff, in mid-bar, seems to surprise his colleagues. The audience's contribution to such a solo can only be minimal, spurring each individual on to greater flights, leading him away from what his fellows are doing.

The most notable difference between the blues as used in progressive rock and the earlier r&b lies in the use of tempo and texture. The textures here are thinner, allowing each player to be clearly heard and encouraging a greater sense of individuality. The tempi are almost always far slower: the sense of the music being drawn out allows virtuoso fills. Thus, early Fleetwood Mac, who were formed out of one incarnation of John Mayall's Bluesbreakers, are far closer to the r&b model. Their second album, *Mr Wonderful*, exemplifies this well. All but two tracks are mid- and up-tempo Chicago-style twelve-bar r&b songs, complete with piano, sax chorus and Jeremy Spencer's reiterative bottleneck guitar. Of the remaining two, 'Love that Burns' is slow, but retains the same texture and instrumentation. 'Trying So Hard to Forget' stands out in this context: not only does it run at about 58 beats per minute, but the instrumentation is slimmed down to voice, guitar and blues harp. Yet the texture is still relatively thick. Partly this is because all three instruments move in the same range, partly it seems to be an attempt to re-create the clichéd, doom-laden atmosphere of the country blues. Although there is no way that this is a black country blues singer, the track does not have the cleanness and resonance of either Cream or Led Zeppelin, particularly because of the guitar's rather muffled tone. On both Cream's 'Sitting on Top of the World' and Led Zeppelin's 'I Can't Quit You Baby', for example, the thinness of texture throws the emphasis on the lead guitarist, whose solos are executed with extreme clarity, and whose riffs define the song.

Led Zeppelin represent a third strand of apparent blues influence. They are often identified as the originators of 'heavy metal' (e.g. in Gambaccini 1982), what Chambers (1985: 123) calls that 'mutant offspring of progressive music', for which a great deal of opprobrium has been levelled at them. Sheer volume was clearly important – fans lauded drummer John Bonham for playing loud enough to be able to dispense with a live bass (bassist John Paul Jones would double on organ), while Gillett (1983: 387) suggests that audiences were '[battered] into blissful submission'. Chambers argues fiercely against the self-indulgent lifestyle their stance promoted and still promotes among heavy metal bands. Led Zeppelin in part seemed to adopt a 'reclusive' attitude which required the fan to be part of the 'initiated', and about which I shall have more to say in subsequent sections. It was manifested in two ways, in (particularly) Page's reclusive lifestyle, and also through their cunning marketing ploy of refusing (virtually) to release singles. Led Zeppelin were to become astute in the commercial arena, being one of the first bands to take control of the release of their material via their own label.

Stokes offers a slightly different analysis of their style:

> Although their overpowering volume and truculent demeanor helped consign them most conveniently to the heavy metal category, Zeppelin actually combined elements of hard rock, art rock and heavy metal.
>
> (Stokes, in Ward *et al.* 1987: 484–5)

This suggests something rather more unified than was actually the case. The first five albums vary greatly in terms of style: it is really only with *Physical Graffiti* that they achieve a clear style, which the rest of their output further explores and refines. The most typical elements of this are present in 'Kashmir', with its chromatic riff and metrical niceties, underpinned by Bonham's mature

Example 3.5 Led Zeppelin: 'Kashmir'

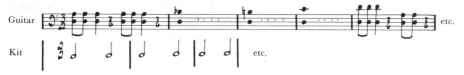

kit style. One of the key features is the crispness of his tone, resulting from his extremely heavy touch and tendency to avoid the ride cymbals. In addition, he frequently leaves the third downbeat of every four empty. In the midst of frequently slow tempi, this contributes a strong sense of continuity, as listeners are constrained to supply this beat internally. Texturally, 'Kashmir' opens in a rather empty fashion (see example 3.5), although kit and synthesized guitar have cross-metres. It also represents a mature approach to the construction of a nine-minute song. On earlier albums, songs of such length were underpinned by a sense of gradual but inexorable growth towards a great climax. 'Stairway to Heaven' is the archetype of this, although 'Since I've Been Loving You' is a no less powerful example. The device is not subtle, but it can be intensely moving, and is normally beyond the capacity of a seven-inch single because it requires time in order to be effective. (Nor is it restricted to Led Zeppelin: Cream's 'White Room' uses the same device, as does Deep Purple's 'Child in Time'.) 'Kashmir', however, makes use of four self-contained stretches of music that are repeated in varying orders. None is really short enough to qualify as 'verse' or 'refrain' in the accepted sense (if necessary they could be labelled verse, link and two alternate bridges), and yet it is almost as if a conventional song has been stretched to its limits.

On the earlier albums, what Stokes terms 'hard rock' tends to predominate. On *Led Zeppelin*, aside from the Willie Dixon numbers, only 'Babe I'm Gonna Leave You' and 'Black Mountain Side' are not based on standard riffs, and both of these use acoustic guitar. Riffs are much in evidence on *Led Zeppelin II*, although 'Thank You' is a sentimental love-song with a standard chord sequence. *Led Zeppelin III* is much more varied, with Page's acoustic guitar highly prominent. Only 'Immigrant Song' and 'Since I've Been Loving You' could have belonged on the previous album: the tone is altogether more gentle. *Four symbols*[9] attempts a more balanced mix of styles, but it is only in 'Stairway to Heaven' that the acoustic ballad actually grows into the riff-based hard rock number, effectively fusing two disparate styles.

Throughout these albums, there is no integrated 'Led Zeppelin style', but only of a number of varied styles that are employed. The most extreme coalesce in 'Stairway to Heaven', although the blues element that is still to the fore on 'When the Levee Breaks' (three-line stanzas and prominent blues harp) is wholly missing from that song. There may be no single unified style, but there are elements that are clearly Led Zeppelin and nobody else. The first is Bonham's kit playing, which I have already mentioned, and in part it is present on the first album: 'Good Times Bad Times' runs at about 88 beats per minute with quavers prominent, as in Bonham's later playing, although hihat and ride cymbals are here very much in evidence. Secondly, although I no longer find Page's guitar style or Jones's bass remarkable, whereas on the first album the bass is comparatively independent and the lead is sometimes multi-tracked over a rhythm guitar (as with Cream), on *Physical Graffiti* and subsequent albums the kit rhythm is dominant. Both bass and guitar riffs now tend to follow exactly the same pattern, independence having been sacrificed to a single-minded unity. Thirdly, Plant's vocal style is so highly distinctive, that all subsequent hard rock vocalists get defined (by critics) in relation to it. The tessitura is very high but the range, rarely reaching down to middle C, is larger than it seems. Tremolos and (less often) vibrato appear on long notes, with a tendency to lose pitch (as an assumed expression of emotional intensity) towards the end of phrases. His tone is far more pinched, however, than that of most comparable figures, from Deep Purple's Ian Gillan through to Rush's Geddy Lee and Iron Maiden's Bruce Dickinson.

Rhythmic interplays and subtleties are often considered the prerogative of soul and dance music styles, where they are used to embellish, but never to obscure the regularity of, the beat. Their absence was frequently cited as a cause of the pomposity of progressive rock. Such interplays and subtleties are actually present in rock, but here they do often break up the even flow of beats. Two songs from Led Zeppelin's *Houses of the Holy* exemplify this well: 'The Crunge', although nominally in $\frac{4}{4}$, adds an extra half-beat to most alternate bars, although in such a way that the voice carries the listener through. 'The Ocean' does exactly the opposite: here, against a $\frac{4}{4}$ basis, the last half-beat of every second bar is elided with the first beat of the next bar, again throwing the sense of regularity. On the later *Presence* we find similar devices: 'For Your Life' threatens to elide the last half-beat exactly as in 'The Ocean', but in this case merely stresses it then carries on as normal. 'Royal Orleans' includes a dramatic time-change, from $\frac{4}{4}$ to a $\frac{5}{4}$ shuffle, where the bars are virtually of equal length. All these devices prevent the pattern becoming too repetitive, although Bonham's mastery of irregularly placed stresses was such that boredom is unlikely on anything but an inattentive hearing.

Although the blues may have acted as a stimulus for all three bands, only Fleetwood Mac were at any time dependent on it. The extensive discussions of Cream and Led Zeppelin show how little their music relates to the blues, despite any ideologically motivated assertions to the contrary. There is an instructive difference in their approaches to the blues material they did use. Whereas Clapton was most insistent on ensuring that the original artist received royalties (at a time when many such artists were still unknown), Led Zeppelin tended to name themselves as authors/composers of tunes that were often only slightly altered (Willie Dixon and Howlin' Wolf are explicitly named on the first two albums). This was an underhand approach, of course, and yet it was perhaps closer to the practice of the country blues singers themselves, for material was clearly public property until the American record companies of the 1930s got in on the act. And Clapton's insistence on black artists' rights makes all the more strange the racism embodied in his outburst on stage in 1976, mid-way through a performance of Bob Marley's 'I Shot the Sheriff', in direct sympathy with Enoch Powell's demands for compulsory repatriation, which provided the impetus for the formation of Rock Against Racism. A clearer demonstration that the romantic, backward-looking attitude of musicians, fans and commentators has no roots in reality could hardly be sought.

The 'unmediated expression' which the blues was felt to embody, and which served to put performers (and critics) 'in touch with themselves' is directly linked to the awe in which the practice of improvisation has been held (although that awe has tended to turn to disdain through the self-centred instrumental displays that many performers indulged). It is, therefore, to the practices of improvisation that I now turn.

Improvisation in rock

Improvisation, that seemingly most ineffable of musical techniques, is surrounded by myths that treat it as somehow magical, in that it purports to bypass the mind's conscious mechanisms, providing a vehicle for performers to express themselves in a fashion unmediated by any other concerns, thus bringing them closer to pre-verbal or pre-conceptual expression. Now it may be true that improvisers do not think through their actions verbally, especially when they are executed at speed, but it cannot and does not follow that these actions escape conscious control. Because what actually happens runs counter to popular intuition, it is vital that the practice of improvisation is subjected to some scrutiny.

All musical improvisations are subject to bodies of rules developed (normally in advance) by the players concerned, specifying both what collections of sounds and/or actions are to be permitted, and what are not. The actions may extend to certain pre-arranged signals, indicating to certain players perhaps to 'drop out', or indicating that a solo passage is about to end. For very many styles, basic rules are shared by the whole community of players. In rock contexts (as in almost all improvising styles worldwide), improvisation consists of the re-playing of formulae, learnt either systematically or in an *ad hoc* fashion, these formulae representing the rules shared by the community. Throughout, what follows is to be understood as descriptive of what has happened, not as prescriptive of what can happen: rules of improvisation are as open to radical change as any other body of rules. I shall focus on the improvising roles of guitarists, keyboard players and drummers in turn.

The 'rules' that a guitarist follows can be broken down into three areas: harmony, rhythm and construction. In terms of harmony, the improviser must respond to, and be restricted by, the harmonic sequences played by the backing instruments. In the body of a rock song, this may simply entail arpeggiated chords, a pre-arranged riff, a set of power chords or some internal line comparable to what the bass may play. In explicit solo passages, the

Example 3.6 Derek and the Dominos: 'I Looked Away'

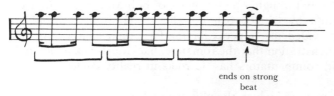

ends on strong
beat

guitarist will have more leeway. On almost all the solos on Cream's *Wheels of Fire*, both bass and rhythm guitar tracks maintain the song's harmonic patterns, restricting the pitches available to the lead guitar at all times. In order for notes in stressed temporal positions not to sound wrong, they must either be consonant to the underlying harmony (which may well be a seventh or ninth chord), or must lead to or from a consonant pitch in a fashion 'logical' to competent ears, normally by step or through the continuation of an established pitch pattern.[10] Even in those not infrequent cases where the harmonic sequence is suspended, effectively being replaced by a single chord or even drone, the lead is still restricted to the notes of the mode underpinned by that drone.

In terms of rhythm, the improviser is restricted to obeying the underlying kit pattern. A guitarist's line will frequently coincide with the crash cymbal on strong beats, particularly to articulate points of climax within a solo. Within this, certain other devices can be brought into play. A key feature of guitar technique is the employment of what, in Indian music theory, is called a *tihai*:

> The essence of the *tihai* is that [its] threefold statement creates the preparation, expression and resolution of tension. Most *tihais* are continued to end on the [first beat of a rhythmic pattern] . . ., though it is possible to end at other points . . . as long as this sounds convincing and not arbitrary or accidental.
>
> (Sorrell and Narayan 1980: 134)

In rock guitar, the pattern is not necessarily repeated only three times, but the device retains the essential feature of consisting of an uneven number of beats, and landing on a strong beat. Example 3.6 transcribes the *tihai* occurring at the beginning of the last solo on Derek and the Dominos' 'I Looked Away'. The device is a standard part of the rock guitarist's technique.

The third restriction is in terms of construction. Most improvised solos are constructed such that they generally move upwards from either low or middle register, this move being executed one or more times and normally ending at the high register. This, again, conforms to the ideal pattern of the first part of an Indian *rag* improvisation, but in rock it appears much more informally. This construction remains common in heavy metal and hard rock styles.

The formulae a guitarist uses tend to be easy to hear. At their simplest, they consist of plucking the individual strings of the underlying chord shapes (e.g. George Harrison's solo on 'Nowhere Man'). More complex solos are either extemporizations on a melody, or are based on specific '*box positions*', used by

Example 3.7 Guitar box positions

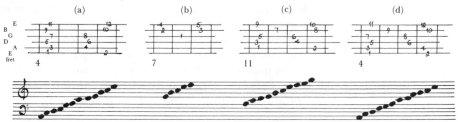

all guitar tutor texts as the basis for improvisations. Example 3.7 shows the three common box positions, labelled (a), (b) and (c), each at the fret on the guitar that will enable the guitarist to play A minor pentatonic (i.e. the minor scale without its second and sixth notes). The notes available at each position also appear in conventional notation. The position chosen thus determines the notes available. The guitarist will play groups of these notes, either ascending or descending, normally in consecutive order (hence my numbering them), moving freely from box to box and, as a change of harmony is needed, moving up or down the fretboard the required number of frets. Variations on these are common: example 3.7(d) shifts example 3.7(a) from pentatonic A minor to pentatonic D minor with a minimal change of finger position. The *box position* thus strictly represents a potential: it indicates the places on the fingerboard at which the notes of the relevant minor pentatonic scale can be found. In this sense, it is similar to the holding of chord shapes, with the exception of the plucking (normally right) hand technique. Chords can be played one string at a time ('arpeggiating' the chord), or the entire chord can be strummed, because each shape specifies only one fret placing per string. Boxes can only be played through one note at a time, since each specifies more than one note on most strings. It is because of the existence of these and similar formulae that the styles of guitarists like Robert Fripp and Richard Thompson stand out, because they tend to construct lines (allowing the fingers to find the notes required) rather than begin from a fretboard position (knowing that what-ever notes result will not sound wrong). Even in noted solos like Ritchie Blackmore's on 'Child in Time', the danger of falling into cliché is constantly present.

The restrictions upon improvisers on other instruments are similar, and with instruments strange to rock it is easier to avoid clichéd playing, as shown by King Crimson sidemen. The solos of violinist David Cross recalled those of Robert Fripp in shape, while those of sax players Mel Collins and Ian McDonald were closer to the cool jazz style often adopted by rock saxo-phonists. For keyboard players, there are established rock approaches to their ensemble use. At one extreme, long held chords can provide an atmospheric background (as in so much latter-day synthesizer rock), while at the other we still find the riff-like, rhythmic chordal playing, derived from jump jazz and r&b by players like Alan Price and Steve Winwood. For solos, keyboard formulae are less easy to specify. The dominant feature seems to be the use of particular figurations or licks (small phrases which can be adapted to almost any circumstance), many of which may come from jazz players, and tend to combine short scalic patterns with standard keyboard chord shapes. These are just ways of filling out a particular harmony and are a direct equivalent to the guitarist's box patterns, which makes imitation between these two instruments very effective (e.g. on Deep Purple's 'Highway Star' from *Made in Japan*). While the licks may have originated with jazz, the harmonic sequences will be those of rock.

The improvising role of the drummer is, of course, rather different. Above the basic beat, any drummer will add fills. The simplest will decorate the upbeat to important downbeats (the 'pick-up'), and move subtly between variations on the basic pattern. There is a great similarity here with the practices of North Indian (Hindustani) drum improvisation. A North Indian *rag* improvisation will employ one of a large number of *tals*, that is, a sequence of a given number of beats (normally from seven to sixteen), with the specification that certain of these will receive stresses of differing degrees. The drummer's role in improvising is to disguise the nature of the *tal* at various points, but without losing track of where it really is – coming out again at a strong beat, such that the audience is amazed at his 'flight'.[11] With rock, the *standard rock beat* can usefully be considered an equivalent of a *tal*, noting that many songs will take as their basic rhythmic pattern a clear variation on this. The early stages of this practice in rock are clearly exemplified by Ringo Starr (see Finkelstein 1979: 37–40) while, as already noted, Led Zeppelin's John Bonham tended to vary the beat by consistently moving between quavers, triplets and semiquavers, often in unexpected combinations.

The more familiar improvisatory role was the drum solo, a now much-maligned rock technique. As with the guitar solo, the essential requirement seems to have been one of balance. Interest needed to be maintained, but the pace needed to be allowed to vary. According to these criteria, Ginger Baker's solo on 'Toad' or Ian Paice's on Deep Purple's 'Concerto' are excellent, with John Bonham's 'Moby Dick' rather lame by comparison. Bonham tended to work with sheer power – over the course of a three minute solo, he reaches climactic points some three times (the first being two minutes in), but these are largely achieved through 'bullets' on the bass drum and tomtoms, immediately succeeded by fills on the other drums. Timbres change, in that the hihat drops out for much of the solo, while the snare does not appear until after the first 'climax', but the return of the cymbals before the final climax seems forced. 'Moby Dick' was, of course, a showcase for the drummer, being sandwiched on disc between very thin slices of guitar-led twelve-bar introduction and coda, and the limits of vinyl space intrude.

Paice, soloing close to the climax to some fifty minutes of near-continuous movement, has had all the preparation done for him. In his four and a half minutes of solo, he keeps the density of movement generally high, playing either twelve (shuffle) or sixteen (straight) notes per (fast) bar, but generates interest by constantly altering the position of what is felt as the strong beat (in fact, playing bars of differing lengths): some dozen times the explicit metre fades, only to be swiftly reinforced (as on Cream's live 'Spoonful'). On at least two occasions this is achieved by lowering the volume, keeping a measured roll on the snare, and introducing initially off-beat bullets on bass and/or tomtoms, gradually increasing their speed. Again, at points he concentrates on particular parts of the kit: snare alone, tomtoms with bass, cowbell (acting as a signal that the solo was about to end). Change is of the essence, then, generally change from climax to new beginning, and motion to the next climax, with ideally only the final climax landing in some sort of catharsis.

The purpose of rock improvisation is not, as it is in many cultures, the exploration of musical material or of an individual consciousness. Most improvised solos serve a dual role. For the listener they extend the moment of experience (the individual song), while for the performer they offer an opportunity for virtuoso display. There is rarely any structural reason why a solo could not be transported to any other song sharing the same key and speed. This is true even in the contemporary work of a figure like Clapton, who is not normally virtuoso-minded. This may also be true of many of those solos that are not improvised. According to Clapton:

> For the most part I can't even remember what I played the night before, so I make it up as I go along. Mark Knopfler is a stickler for detail and he has to play his solos exactly the same every night as signals for the band. But I use the song as a launch pad for going off on a groove . . . I don't dry up . . . I can usually fool an audience. I mean I can play an adequate solo any time.
>
> (Sandall 1990: 84)

It is thus that the role of the improvisation for listener and performer can be separated: solos are not opportunities for players to indulge in concern for audiences by trying to communicate with them. However, as suggested above with respect to the drums, improvisations are not by any means restricted to conventional solos. As we have seen, unlike some other musics, rock songs are not constructed by means of notation. A composer will develop an idea, but will give most performers leeway to interpret that idea, whether it be the precise setting of the standard rock beat, the way the chords are to be arpeggiated, or the way notes are to be phrased. All these elements are aspects of improvisation. If an originator then wishes to exert control over the finished product, this is exerted *after* the other performers have made their contributions, not, as with concert musics, *before* they get to rehearse a piece. Tears for Fears, for example, spent three years working on the album *Seeds of Love*, much of the time being taken up with working on tracks already laid down (Sutcliffe 1989a). This procedure is no longer particularly unusual.

This digression into the practices of improvisation is important, not only because it informs the style of 'blues inspired' bands, but also because it was very much to the fore among those progressive bands who looked to 'jazz' to provide them with working practices.

The jazz influence

The 'jazz' at issue here was not that with immediate roots in the blues, but that which developed ultimately out of the 'bop' movement. In late 1930s USA, as the touring big bands entered a decline, two quite distinct strands of small band jazz playing became apparent. The first developed through Count Basie to the work of 'jump' bands like those of Louis Jordan. It was this style which had an impact on the Bill Haley of 'Rock around the Clock'. The second was intentionally more exclusive, and was typified by the work of Charlie Parker and Dizzy Gillespie. This style, 'bebop' (and later, 'bop'), in its development of new improvisational practices, led directly to the mature work of figures like John Coltrane and what has become known as 'free' jazz, in indication of the comparative impenetrability of that music's improvisational norms. It is this second strand which forms the basis of the playing of Soft Machine (whose name, taken from a novel by William Burroughs, refers to the human being). Their most distinctive, early style has three typical features.

Firstly, tracks tended to be organized according to the bop jazz succession of tune, sequence of improvisations, tune: this structure is always implied, if not explicitly apparent. On some tracks, such as the widely known 'Esther's Nose Job', this may be preceded by a free blown horn intro, while on others (e.g. 'Facelift'), more than one tune may be used. The improvisations are not based on the material of a foregoing tune in an overt way; it is more that the tune forms a frame for the central improvisations. It is only in these composed tunes that any harmonic interest enters the music (as in the succession of dissonant chords opening 'Mousetrap').

Secondly, the instrumental line-up (keyboards, bass, kit) is functionally clear, even with the addition of horns in late 1969. Mike Ratledge's keyboards frequently double both 'rhythm' and 'lead' functions. His syntax derives less from the blues (as does that of progressive guitarists) than from the late modal style of John Coltrane, with his chromatic turns and tiny melodic motifs, his alternating fast runs and long held notes. The horns are most notably used to present the tune in unison, largely in even rhythmic values, over a modal drone pattern supplied by the bass. Even on those occasions where the pattern is not strictly modal (as on the very Coltrane-inspired 'Slightly All the Time', or on 'Drop'), the bass falls into a distinct open-ended sequence, with an equivalent musical effect. Again, the horn syntax seems most indebted to Coltrane.

Thirdly, they had an 'advanced' attitude to time signatures, frequently employing patterns of seven, nine and eleven beats. However, once such a norm had been set up, it would remain in force – constant changes of pattern were not used. Indeed, considering that so much was talked about these 'unusual' time signatures at the time, their effect today seems to be almost minimal. The technique is by no means central to modern jazz.

Although Soft Machine were more consistent than other bands in their use of modern jazz style, their techniques do feature strongly elsewhere. Early tours in support of both Pink Floyd and Jimi Hendrix suggest certain perceived affinities. Soft Machine's improvisational syntax is particularly evident on David Jackson's sax work (with Van der Graaf Generator), while their use of extended time signatures can be found more widely, in work by Yes, Emerson, Lake and Palmer, and even Led Zeppelin. Unison melodies are also found in King Crimson, Gentle Giant and John McLaughlin's Mahavishnu Orchestra. While Crimson and Giant do tend use them as integral sections of songs, Mahavishnu's use parallels Soft Machine's, in that they form riff-like frames for improvised material. For Mahavishnu, the technique permits quite a degree of structural variety. Whereas their 'Open Country Joy' uses a riff simply as a frame, 'Sister Andrea' alternates between two riffs of different characters, while 'Thousand Island Park' makes use of a mock-Renaissance tune (reminiscent of Focus's 'Elspeth of Nottingham'), whose constituent phrases on repetition are interspersed with improvised ramblings.

There is also a marked difference in attitude here to rhythmic coordination beneath framing unison tunes. Whereas King Crimson and Gentle Giant employ a tightness in which the kit tends to double the tune's rhythmic profile, for both jazz-influenced players (Soft Machine) and much modern jazz itself (whether Coltrane's *Love Supreme* or Miles Davis's *Bitches Brew*), the kit tends to supply a regular beat, counterpointed by the irregular melody. For the Mahavishnu Orchestra, this can generate quite a degree of tension, as on 'Birds of Fire', where the violin/bass riff conceives a group of eighteen attacks as $5 + 5 + 5 + 3$, later re-interpreted by the kit as three groups of six. For Soft Machine, only on 'As If' is the kit finally freed from its time-keeping role, approaching a freedom found on Coltrane's *Ascension*. It is this freedom from the $\frac{4}{4}$ bar which seems to characterise the movement beyond beat/r&b norms and so serves to problematize the conception of (some) rock as 'art'.

Art rock

The use of obscure and changing time signatures by various progressive rock bands was, perhaps, the clearest indication that this music was intended to be listened to, for it made dancing difficult. As such, for many commentators and audiences, it appeared necessary to consider it according to the lights of 'classical', or 'art', music. There are actually two aspects to these attitudes found in progressive rock: the first is the art music background of some players, the second is the artistic pretensions of a far wider community of players.

A number of musicians who ultimately found their way into progressive rock had undergone an extensive conventional instrumental training (e.g. Keith Emerson, Rick Wakeman and the members of Gentle Giant). The possible reasons for this apparent change of direction seem two-fold. Firstly, rock was an easier business to get into, was probably more fun and at the time offered a greater opportunity for exploration unhampered by the requirements of the music establishment. Secondly, some musicians were beginning to explore techniques, particularly relating to harmony and form, that were closer to those of a conventional training than to those of pop or soul.

The experience of Gentle Giant seems pertinent. In 1967, the nucleus of what was to become Gentle Giant had a single chart success, 'Kites', as Simon Dupree and the Big Sound. The cabaret circuit, to which they were to be consigned, would have made it difficult to fulfil the musical potential due performers with conservatoire training, a potential which was later to be realized on the burgeoning college circuit and particularly on albums like *Octopus* and *In a Glass House*. For some critics, conservatoire-type training went hand in hand with a perceived lack of 'emotional involvement'. Thus, the concentration on technical craft was discredited, for it filtered 'natural expression', as discussed above. For Gentle Giant, improvisation was little apparent on recordings (although more so on stage), and where it was present it tended to derive from cool jazz rather than from the blues. Additionally, their training perhaps made it easy to think outside blues-based harmonic structures and outside popular song forms and subject matter. 'Knots', from *Octopus*, for example, uses highly chromatic harmonic patterns realized through a dense contrapuntal texture. Although cast as a succession of verses, refrains and interludes, it welds these into a unified drive towards a single climax, effectively realizing the character underlying R.D. Laing's influential *Knots*.

A clear example of the stylistic problems raised by this approach is Emerson, Lake and Palmer's (ELP) *Pictures at an Exhibition*. This is loosely based on Moussorgsky's work for solo piano. As such, the fact that the bass, and frequently the kit (which rarely lays down a standard rock beat anyway), are mostly superfluous hardly matters. It is only loosely based, because ELP take only the first and last two of some eleven pieces in the original, adding material of their own. The 'set' was designed to run continuously, although on the live album solos are applauded in the usual way. The conceptual unity of the album comes not only from the repetitions of 'Promenade' (sections 1 and 3, and also the beginning of side 2), but from the parallelism whereby 'Blues Variation' and 'Nutrocker' (with its twelve-bar blues interpolation) end each side. As we might expect, not all sections (one hesitates to call them 'songs', even where Lake has added lyrics) have the same pacing, and this raises the question of the criteria by which the music should be judged. On side 1, Lake's 'The Sage', with its simple acoustic guitar accompaniment, is an uneasy song that maintains the tension of the side, but its pacing is slow, continuing the contrast set up between the opening 'Promenade' and 'The Gnome'. This tension is relaxed only by 'Blues Variation'. On side 2, 'The Hut of Baba Yaga' fulfils a similar function, resulting in the triumphal grandeur of 'The Great Gates of Kiev'. This works well in Moussorgsky's original, but because ELP have excised much of the material, and thus changed the proportions, the triumphalism seems inadequately prepared. But this criticism results from the application of 'art' standards. Should one look only at individual songs, without relating them? They are clearly related through links in performance. To insist on considering them separately would do violence to the manner of presentation. This album, then, seems to demand the application of criteria derived from art music, to a certain extent, but it seems to set the limit at which these criteria are useful.

Few progressive musicians may have been trained in the techniques of art music, but many were touched by a not unrelated drive towards the self-conscious attempt to validate rock as art, thereby apparently raising the status of the product. This may have been done by disguising the self-containedness of three minute song structures, and employing more advanced harmonies (often imported from jazz and late nineteenth-century European art music), rhythmic patterns (borrowed from twentieth-century Eastern European composers) and electronic sounds (copied from the European avant-garde, especially Stockhausen and Berio).[12] Paul McCartney recalls that:

> We were being influenced by avant-garde composers. For 'Day in the Life', I suggested that what we should do was write all fifteen bars properly so that the orchestra could read it, but where the fifteen bars began we would give the musicians a simple direction: 'Start on your lowest note and eventually, at the end of the fifteen bars, be at your highest note' . . . it all resulted in a crazy crescendo.
>
> (Taylor 1987: 28)

This hardly amounts to influence, but even if it did, was being 'influenced by avant-garde composers' worth striving for? For some artists, the pretensions went even further. A then rather naive Peter Gabriel translates Genesis' 'Supper's Ready' as:

> the ultimate cosmic battle for Armageddon between good and evil in which man is destroyed, but the deaths of countless thousands atone for mankind, reborn no longer as Homo Sapiens.
>
> (Palmer 1977: 263)

The point here is that 'classical' music is popularly perceived as having its own aesthetic, based on its lack of 'survival value' (i.e. unlike heat and water, it is not a commodity necessary to survival), giving it an apparent autonomy, to which rock has always been equivocal. These pretensions clearly suggest that rock musicians were asking for their product to be judged as art. Frith believes this to be a fundamental problem:

> [One of the problems] for rock's claims as art is its continuing function as entertainment. Entertainers neither 'improve' nor 'instruct' their audiences; their music comes easily, while true [*sic*] art makes people work. One solution to this problem was to make the rock audience work too. . . . The trouble with such descriptions of records as the hard work of rock *auteurs* is that they are rarely illuminating, and the image of the individual creator is quickly absorbed into the star-making machinery.
>
> (Frith 1983: 53)

If listeners feel that the function (entertainment) can be imposed by the musicians, this might explain the consistent recourse to fantasy, wherein the illumination is provided by the listener. I shall return to this below. If, however, the listener is free to choose how he or she will use the music, this 'problem' vanishes.

We are now near to the heart of the controversies over progressive rock, which surround two related issues. The first is the notion of the 'concept' album, which, far from vanishing, has grown to the extent that all rock tours have acquired particular identities, existing largely to promote a particular album or set of material as a package. The second concerns the 'fictionality' inherent in the three-minute single. I shall deal with them together since, ultimately, they are indivisible. Both issues indicate the desire to establish a degree of aesthetic unity greater than that of the individual song, and both relate to how the product of progressive rock should be viewed. To over-simplify, the choice is between the functions, as given in Chapter 1, of entertainment (i.e. commercial product) and aesthetic enjoyment (i.e. artistic product).

In 1972 and 1973, Jethro Tull released two albums, *Thick as a Brick* and *Passion Play*. These were particularly well received in the USA, and reached positions 5 and 13 in the British album charts (Gambaccini *et al.* 1988). Live performances of *Passion Play* were poorly received, and both albums (but particularly this one) received such critical panning in the UK that Ian Anderson vowed not to tour again (a promise he kept for a year). Both were considered 'concept' albums in that they played unbroken from beginning to end, with both a musical and lyrical continuity sufficiently strong to lead from one quasi-song into the next (indeed *Thick as a Brick* included reprises and harmonic patterns that would recur in more than one segment), although exactly what the 'concept' was remained rather obscure. According to one report, *Thick as a Brick* was 'one continuous piece of music elaborately con-structed and flawlessly played, yet critically received as obscure and lacking in feel' (Logan and Wooffinden 1982: 120). The charge of obscurity I shall return to, although we should at least note here Paul Willis's description of the 'hippy' attitude, an attitude central to progressive rock:

> Music for the hippies was an immediate apprehension, itself and nothing more: it could not be presented in terms other than itself. It was impossible to decode. It could safely hold contradictory, otherwise unexpressed or profound meanings.
> (Willis 1978: 106)

The remaining critical charges are not particular to Jethro Tull, and can best be discussed with reference to Ian Chambers's loaded comparison of Van Morrison's 'Astral Weeks' (a song widely praised by critics of many persuasions) with Genesis's 'The Knife'. Although *Trespass*, from which the latter comes, is not a 'concept' album, the issues are the same. 'The Knife', according to Chambers:

> develops, through the calculated addition of one distinct musical cell to another, into a type of mini-suite. Preceded by a riff that echoes early twentieth-century Russian classical music, the normal verse–chorus arrangement gives way to a linear sequence of highly structured instrumental variations and solos. The internal musical details are not particularly interesting, but the overall shape of the piece is extremely significant. [It] can be said to offer a musical paradigm for later progressive music after 1970. . . . It is the sequential addition of musical unit

to unit that makes 'The Knife' musically 'complex' (in the accepted 'classical' sense) in a fashion very different from the richness of 'Astral Weeks'

(Chambers 1985: 108–9)

Here, the flawlessness and lack of 'feel' are clearly allied to the purported attempt, discussed in Chapter 1, to achieve legitimation. There are two issues of detail in Chambers's analysis: one is the apparently additive, cellular mode of construction, the second is the derided purported 'mini-suite': on both issues, Chambers is mistaken. His contrast with Morrison's excellent 'Astral Weeks' is based on the erroneous belief, taken from Chester's formative article (1970), that 'classical' music lacks performer-controlled rhythmic subtlety. As I have argued in Chapter 2, this is not the case: the rhythmic norms of 'classical' and 'late r&b' styles differ, as we might expect, but the former is capable of no less subtlety. Chambers's contention that 'The Knife' adds, in a 'calculated' fashion (as if Van Morrison were incapable of calculating the effects of his musical decisions) 'unit to unit' or 'one . . . cell to another' seems, aside from its inaccuracy as a description, to derive from a strange reading of Chester, who suggests that classical 'devices build . . . from basic musical atoms' (Chester 1970: 78). Chambers forgets that, even were this description credible, it would describe the compositional process, not the effect of experiencing the music in real time. As innumerable theorists from Schenker onwards have shown, the complexity of 'classical' music resides below the surface, in the relationships between its constituent layers, a view totally opposed to the superficial reading of the addition of musical unit to musical unit. Moreover, both 'The Knife' and 'Astral Weeks' proceed equally in measured metres, adding rhythmic group (four bars of $\frac{4}{4}$ shuffle for Genesis, two bars of $\frac{6}{4}$ for Morrison) to rhythmic group, leading to cleverly contrived climaxes (the return to the opening material for Genesis, the repeat of the lyric 'could you find me . . . to be born again' for Morrison, with its dramatic shift from oscillations of ionian I–IV to I–VI). Chambers also criticizes the predominantly 'linear' aspect of 'The Knife'; yet what can the 'cross-rhythms set up between . . . double bass, maraccas and acoustic guitar' (Chambers 1985: 107) in 'Astral Weeks' be, if they are not the result of accentually uncoordinated, concurrent linear developments? The large stylistic difference cannot be accounted for by the attribution of the disparaging epithet 'classical'. Neither does 'The Knife' remotely qualify as a 'mini-suite'. It consists of only two alternating segments, whose chief distinction lies in the change of beat from shuffle to straight, leading into a central flute-dominated solo, finally returning to its point of origin. The sub-text of this and similar critical commentary is, of course, the unwarranted assumption that music which seems full of 'feel' represents an unmediated experience, as outlined above.

The notion of the 'concept' album first came to the fore in the Beatles' album *Sgt Pepper's Lonely Hearts Club Band* of 1967, an album that raises a number of interesting points. It represents an explicit attempt by the Beatles to align themselves with an unspecified, 'hippy' position,[13] coinciding with the growing protests over the USA's involvement in Vietnam, the rise of 'flower power' and the concomitant infatuation with Eastern religions. This finds explicit expression in George Harrison's use of the Indian sitar on 'Within you, without you', and in John Lennon's LSD-inspired imagery on 'Lucy in the Sky with Diamonds.' It also results in the tendency to try to find concrete messages within the more obscure lyrics.

From the comments of the artists themselves, made years later, it was not intended as the LSD-inspired *exploration* it has often been taken to be: '4000 holes in Blackburn Lancashire' was apparently a news item propped on Lennon's piano stand as he searched around for an idea for a lyric (Taylor 1987: 29). Yet it is still set apart from its musical predecessors by a number of factors. The most notable of these is its unity in terms of concept. The hype surrounding its launch emphasized this unity. To quote McCartney: 'the idea was to make a complete thing that you could make what you liked of: a little magic presentation – a packet of things inside the record sleeve' (Taylor 1987: 37), with the emphasis on the sleeve.

The 'concept' is underpinned by two further factors that are frequently ignored. The first of these is explicitly musical, representing an early endeavour for rock to build a unity greater than that of the individual, self-contained utterance. This unity is achieved in a number of ways. Firstly, the use of a modulatory bridge between the first and second songs challenges us not to perceive them as separate, while the later reprise of 'Sgt Pepper's . . .' itself provides an apparently unambiguous conclusion. Secondly, there are certain motifs that recur. To cite just the clearest of these: four songs make use of descending functional bass lines at the beginning of verses, three being chromatic and one diatonic (see example 3.8);[14] three songs ('Good Morning', 'It's Getting Better' and 'Fixing a Hole') are based harmonically on I–IV alternations, while 'Lovely Rita' extends this to a cyclic I–IV–VII–III sequence. Thirdly (although it is not the first album to have this), the resources of the band were greatly amplified by the addition of (for instance) sound effects and instruments unfamiliar in rock contexts. *The* fundamental consequence of these changes was that a new set of stylistic values seemed to have been set up – this no longer seemed to fit easily within the mould of simple 'pop' music: it had clearly overstepped the limitations of the seven-inch medium.

The second factor is that the whole album is clearly set within a non-musical context, i.e. an intentionally artificial attempt to create a live club setting, wherein the first song is reprised at the end. It is *intentional*, because no competent listener could be tricked into thinking this was actually a live recording, but also because the most telling event on the album depends on this artifice. The most disturbing song is 'A Day in the Life', which appears last on the album. On its own in isolation, its meaning is hard to determine, full as it is of surreal images and non-specific references. However, the reprise of the title track as the penultimate song creates a closed experiential whole, distanced from the listener, a 'show' that is completed. It is clearly a 'fiction', effectively autonomous, which gives to and requires from the listener nothing more. In this context, 'A Day in the Life' makes the listener step outside the

Example 3.8 The Beatles: falling basses from *Sgt Pepper's* . . .

previous, artificial setting, the fiction, and enter a new reality where the song's 'strangeness' is suddenly made to seem natural, i.e. non-artificial. This does not make its meaning clearer, just more potent.

The boundaries set by the fictionality of the individual song are extremely robust, but have been breached on more than one occasion, particularly in the late 1960s. The rise of 'flower power' was at least in part due to the freedom rock music acquired to deliver an explicit message through its lyrics. In many ways, Janis Joplin was a typical child of the movement: its alternative, counter-cultural attitudes found explicit statement in many of her songs. Yet the popular song is a self-contained entity, with a beginning and end that set it off from reality. It tends to be argued that attempts to deny that fiction automatically entail transfer to the realms of high culture. Yet in 'Ball and Chain', recorded live just a few months before her fatal drug overdose, Joplin succeeds effortlessly in denying that fiction. She makes use of that typical device whereby, mid-way through the song, the band breaks off as she starts speaking to (and almost preaching at) her audience. In other hands this device can be the typical extended live guitar solo (as in Led Zeppelin's 'Heartbreaker'). Vocally, it derives from earlier black revivalist gospel singers: her audience would have expected the band to return to round off the song with another refrain, resolving the tension caused by her words, distancing them from what she had said, in effect saying: 'I don't really mean it, it's just a fiction.' But there was no final refrain. By not packaging the song up, it intruded on her listeners' sense of reality, leaving them to surmize that she meant it, every word of it. The device communicates the strength of her meaning far more incontrovertibly than words alone could ever have managed. The message may be in the words, but their import is assured by a purely musical device. 'Ball and Chain' is the record of a live performance, and I have suggested what the response of competent listeners in her audience would have been. Listeners to the recording cannot speak with the same certainty, for the performance is now packaged and the fictionality has of necessity been restored. We can only say that her use of the device makes it sound as if she meant it. Indeed, for all recordings, 'realistic' effects can only be produced through the manipulation of conventionalized devices.[15] This point will receive further emphasis in the subsequent chapters, where matters of 'authenticity' are further explored.

So, if the single rock song may be thought of as a fiction, even more so is the album with a single concept lying behind it. In many cases, the use of such a structure may well be an attempt to appropriate the autonomy normally held to belong to art music, as I shall show below. A more normal approach, however, is to couch an entire album within a loose narrative. The stylistic breadth of this approach extends from Pete Townshend's *Tommy*, through Roger Waters' *The Wall* to Genesis's *The Lamb Lies down on Broadway*. This last is normative in that it is divided up into separate tracks, which pursue the narrative by expanding on certain moments of it (precisely the approach adopted by innumerable eighteenth-century composers of opera). In Genesis's case, an alternative view of the narrative is provided on the sleeve, but this hardly clarifies its obscurity. Musical returns are made, particularly that of the title song some 80 per cent of the way through, and certain harmonic fingerprints also give a sense of unity, particularly the use of ionian I–IV alternations, aeolian $I^{\#3}$–IV–VI–$I^{\#3}$ patterns (both over static bass lines) and descending bass lines, whether chromatic or diatonic. Further parallels with *Sgt Pepper's* . . . include the way that 'Fly on a Windshield' beckons us into the whole as the heavy entry of the kit seems to change the music's focus (cf. 'With a Little Help from my Friends'), and the use of musical change to illustrate the narrative, as in the remarkable change of tempo on 'In the Cage' as the hero first meets his 'brother'. Despite the fact that very few classical pieces attempt to achieve a sense of unity across spans in excess of half an hour, there remains a widespread assumption that concept albums are intended to do so, playing in an uninterrupted fashion.

David Bowie's *The Rise and Fall of Ziggy Stardust and the Spiders from Mars* is often taken to mark early dissatisfaction with this. Laing tells us this was 'a concept album (a rock notion) executed in three minute songs (a pop form)' (Laing 1985: 24). As such, however, it is not unusual. Even the tracks of Yes's *Close to the Edge* consist of shorter, almost self-contained songs, while Jethro Tull's *Passion Play*, arguably the most extreme example, is in fact ten discrete songs with an introduction, coda and fairy tale. The fact that none of the songs is titled, and that the sleeve lyrics run one into the next, cannot disguise the musical discontinuities between them.

Other bands developed the notion of the concept album more loosely, as a collection of songs on similar themes, or through using common musical devices differentiating these songs from others in their output. Yes's *Close to the Edge* appears to consist of only three songs: 'Close to the Edge' (which runs to some eighteen minutes), 'And You and I' (ten minutes) and 'Siberian Khatru' (nine minutes), but both the former are subdivided into four 'sections'. There is a certain unity of texture throughout the album: composed guitar or organ line(s) in high(ish) registers, underpinned harmonically by intricate keyboard or rhythm guitar figurations and also kit in middle register, themselves underpinned by an active bass guitar, making for a generally dense sound interrupted only occasionally by solo guitar or keyboard passages. Material is also overtly reprised: the subdivisions of the first two songs are perhaps conceits rather than necessities. But there is more than this, for material is also implicitly reprised: for instance, both 'And You and I' and 'Siberian Khatru' develop from I–IV–V harmonic formations. (Covach (1992) suggests there are further musically unifying patterns on this album.)

The development of the 'concept', then, has been decried because the conscious thought involved prevents immediate transmission of feelings, requiring too much work from an audience whom are in reality asking only to be entertained. Clearly, whether or not the music is good, this critical assumption is a basic error.

Listening to progressive rock

Many of the styles of progressive rock differ from both their predecessors and their successors in terms of the most appropriate listening mode to adopt. Jonathan Kramer (1988) argues in a recent study that twentieth-century music, as a broad field, has explored different 'temporalities' from those of everyday reality. Most of these are not relevant to rock, having application to non-strophic forms, but three in particular can help us to understand this particular feature of progressive rock.

Kramer introduces the idea of 'directed linearity', likening it to the experience of rail travel: such travel is experienced as directed motion from an initial point, along a clear path, to a final point. This analogy is used to explore the role of 'functional harmony' in much pre-twentieth-century Western tonal music, although the interaction between listener and music needs also to be taken into account.

Kramer then introduces the idea of 'non-directed linearity'. Here, the sense of motion remains, but the goal is equivocal. This seems to me to describe quite well the time sense of a great deal of conventional rock, wherein a sense of motion is normally ensured by three features: melody, harmony and rhythm. The singing voice approximates to a line rather than a series of discrete sounds, by analogy with spoken phrases. Harmonic successions give a sense of motion from one harmony to the next, although the motion tends only to be very local, arriving back at the original harmony for a repeat of the succession. To be most precise, processive harmonic patterns (such as cyclic sequences) probably induce a greater sense of directed motion than simple alternations of two harmonies, which are closer to a vertical temporality (for which see below). A similar thing happens with the kit, where motion is perceived from beat to beat, arriving back at the original place one bar later.

Kramer also introduces a third temporality that is very useful here, the notion of 'vertical time', where the music is 'temporally undifferentiated'. Pieces of music that explore this temporality

> lack phrases (just as they lack progression, goal direction, movement, and con-
> trasting rates of motion) because phrase endings break the temporal continuum . . .
> phrases are the final remnant of linearity. [Where they are missing] the result is a

single present stretched out into an enormous duration, a potentially infinite 'now' that nonetheless feels like an instant.

(Kramer 1988: 55)

The congruence between this and 'hippy' consciousness is notable. For Paul Willis:

The hippies insisted on the importance of subjective experience and of the 'now'. The past had always had disappointments and the future threatened with 'objectives' and 'plans' which might discredit their belief in something beyond.

(Willis 1978: 90)

This presents the commentator with something of a problem. In attempting to pursue an 'emic' stance (i.e. one from inside the culture), clearly we need a notion of how long 'now' is likely to be. It appears that humans require about $\frac{1}{18}$ of a second in order to be aware of a sense impression – any impulse shorter than this will evade us (Winckel 1967: 53). But a musical 'now' is intuitively longer than this. William James first introduced the notion of the 'specious present', to distinguish between the period of time experienced as 'now' and that which is 'already past'. Ulric Neisser speaks of this in terms of 'echoic memory', a memory that seems to decline over a period lasting between one and ten seconds, depending on the information received (Neisser 1967: 203–5). This accords with the belief held among avant-garde composers who endeavour to incorporate such findings in their music:

The time of memory . . . is the crucial time between eight- and sixteen-second long events. When you go beyond them you lose orientation. You don't recall exactly if it was fourteen or eighteen seconds, whereas you'd never make that mistake below that realm of memory.

(Cott 1974: 31)

So, if we accept the musical 'now' at somewhere in the region of ten seconds, this suggests that hippy consciousness would ignore comparisons made across this boundary. It requires little thought to realize that this approach prevents us talking about the music as experienced at all – at this point, it is necessary to take something of an etic stance (in order, for example, to compare one verse with a subsequent, or to recognize the reprise on *Sgt Pepper's* . . . or in 'Spoonful').[16]

To return to Kramer, with the possible exception of something like the Grateful Dead's 'Dark Star', not even the most radical progressive rock totally eschewed phrases, although it may be argued that this is only a difference of degree. Thus, progressive rock has some recourse to both directed and vertical times, expanding in both directions from the non-directed linearity of much other rock. Probably the most direct, if unorthodox, example is King Crimson's 'Larks' Tongues in Aspic (Part II)'.[17] Example 3.9 is a diagram of the harmonic movement that underpins most of the track. It consists of two types of material which alternate. The first takes off from a g^7 chord, working in cycles of seven beats, although this is overlaid on second appearance with shuffle drum patterns obeying a different scheme. The second makes an

Example 3.9 King Crimson: 'Larks' Tongues in Aspic (Part II)'

unorthodox move from G^{11} to D, via Bb^9, Bb^{11} and Ab^7, with cycles of ten beats. What is remarkable is the voice-leading used to lead from one chord to the next via anticipation in the upper parts (from C to Eb to Gb), arriving on $F\sharp$ over a chord of D with a great sense of inner logic, although the cadence would be unrecognized as such from common-practice tonality. Moreover, the irregular metres (normally seven beats and ten beats) are also finally resolved by the sixteen beat (normative) cycles under the violin solo and the long, unchanging final chord.

What differentiates this directed from a non-directed linearity is either that 'movement away' has been made, or that 'arrival' is a long time in coming – we are working on the order of minutes rather than seconds. At the other extreme, verticality is approached by the long improvisations of, for example, Cream, either over an unchanging drone or where the harmonic pattern has repeated so many times that it is too hard to maintain a count. If a succession is heard only four times and followed by a refrain, a return to this succession will tend to lead competent listeners to expect further movement, back into the refrain or whatever. But, if it has repeated fifty times, even competent listeners will be inured to its continuing, and all sense of motion becomes lost: this, too, is quite simply a matter of the time scale involved. Much of the boredom experienced by aficionados of symphonic and operatic music when presented with rock results, I think, from not listening closely enough to the movement from point to point in what is a non-directed temporality, thereby missing the clues encoding its lack of direction.

An insular path

Vertical temporality is a clear example of an altered (because not ordinarily experienced) reality. As Shapiro (1990) points out, under the influence of LSD the banal was frequently perceived as becoming profound. A similar sense of non-ordinary reality, based on the seemingly banal, underpins much of Ray

Davies's mature work. Is was under his influence that the Kinks became the most notable celebrators of mythical Englishness in the phase preceding progressive rock. This finds its most obvious expression through their lyrics: 'Dedicated Follower of Fashion' was their first hit to break with the riff-based songs of 1965, and was followed by similar songs, such as 'Sunny Afternoon' and 'Dead End Street'. On *Something Else* (1967), the references become a little more concrete. 'Harry Rag' makes use of cockney rhyming slang (it was left to the Small Faces to make the obvious connection between this rosy view of England and psychedelia, particularly in 'Lazy Sunday Afternoon'), 'Tin Soldier Man' is highly reminiscent of the Victorian march, while on 'David Watts' and 'Waterloo Sunset' Davies adopts the stance of the detached observer, which, for George Melly, was their most admirable feature:

> They stood aside watching, with sardonic amusement, the pop world chasing its own tail, and they turned out some of the most quirky intelligent grown-up and totally personal records in the history of British pop. Their ... strength ... was their non-conformism.
>
> (Melly 1970: 99)

Throughout these sketches, Davies's celebration of the past is decidedly ambiguous: he is bleak but also compassionate, and nowhere more so than in *The Kinks Are the Village Green Preservation Society* (1968), whose title track presents a litany of requests for God to save Donald Duck, Vaudeville and Variety, Desperate Dan, the multitude of strawberry jams, the George Cross, Mrs Mopp, Sherlock Holmes, the English-speaking vernacular, china cups, Tudor houses, billiards and more. Even in the English village, the presence of safe American cultural heroes is accepted. Most songs make use of particular timbres and stylistic references to suggest this homely English past. The bleak 'Sitting by the Riverside' sets up a pleasant tune and a touch of vaudeville in the use of the accordion against rising piano string clusters and studio noise (between the verses) to undermine the superficial pleasantries of the idyll. 'Village Green', in which the subject looks back with longing on the village and chums he left behind, evokes the atmosphere through a Handelian, pastoral use of oboe and harpsichord, making use of a fifth-cyclic sequence and descending chromatic refrain, themselves common techniques of Handel. On 'All of My Friends Were There', the references are more concrete – the verse suggests the music hall with its speedily delivered 'comic' vocal and 'oompa' accompanimental pattern, while the refrain settles into an unmistakable waltz. Most strangely, 'The Last of the Steam-powered Trains' (at over four minutes in length the only song to exceed three minutes on the entire album), which uses this image to explore the loneliness of the subject, who seems to have got out of gear with his times, sets this against an unmistakable blues harp and guitar riff. Melly suggests that many of Ray Davies's songs pay 'overt homage' to the music hall, pointing out that, as the nearest we have to an indigenous bourgeois popular music tradition,[18] it is the surest way to break with American influences, Tommy Steele being the best previous example. 'Dead End Street', as a further example, does not conform to conventional standards of verse/refrain (the Tin Pan Alley tradition), nor are its harmonic patterns derived from the blues, although they are comparatively open-ended.

   This overt attempt to use rock to explore musical features seeming to have little in common with those of Afro-American musical traditions becomes, after blues and jazz, a third characteristic of many aspects of progressive rock: British 'progressive rock' in general does have certain musical qualities that serve to distinguish it from its American cousin.[19] In the work of Jethro Tull, this will become explicit. They first hit the headlines at the 1968 national Jazz and Blues Festival, having gained a firm following in underground venues because of frontman Ian Anderson and guitarist Mick Abrahams. After the departure of Abrahams, the eccentric Anderson began to exert his influence on the band, moulding their music into a highly distinctive and original style. By the time of the third album, *Benefit*, Anderson had begun to acquire an unmistakable acoustic guitar style that supplied 'folk' connotations for much of their music. Alongside the reworking of old rural myths, such as Jack-in-the-Green, Anderson went some way towards creating their own – the down-and-out tramp (*Aqualung*), the last rocker (*Too Old to Rock 'n' Roll . . .*), the old sea-dog (*Stormwatch*) – and towards fleshing out others – the wandering minstrel (*Minstrel in the Gallery*), the woodsman (*Songs from the Wood*), the squire (*Heavy Horses*) and so on. Not for the first time in progressive rock, we find the striving for some sort of 'other' understanding, rooted in rather resonant archetypes, and ably abetted by Anderson's eccentric on-stage persona. In Jethro Tull's case, Ian Anderson's concern with subjects placed in a mythical Britain also seems to make itself felt musically. Paradoxically, for a band who have developed largely in isolation from Afro-American techniques, some sixteen or more albums have recorded million sales (despite their generally low profile in terms of the media and the singles market), but largely in the USA. In distinguishing the features which serve to constitute Jethro Tull's style, and which mark it out as distinct from its US contemporaries, I shall discuss in turn construction (large-scale time-spans), rhythm (small-scale time-spans) and, finally, harmonic techniques.

   Their second album, *Stand up*, has been their only UK number 1, but the subsequent *Benefit* (1970) is generally regarded as a first mature offering. Already, two quite distinct approaches begin to show themselves. The influence of guitarist Martin Barre is apparent in the hard rock tone to many tracks, where the chief constructive element is the riff. 'To Cry You a Song' is based on a two-guitar riff of the sort later adopted by Wishbone Ash and, more recently, Def Leppard. At the opposite extreme, the more intimate 'Sossity' is based on an eight-bar acoustic guitar chord succession. These two forms of construction may be conceived as opposites, since the riff lends itself much more to open-ended repetition, while lengthy chord successions invite periodic structures. Much of the time, they are brought into a close relationship one with the other: 'Nothing to Say' opens with a riff that is prominent elsewhere between vocal phrases, but the verse itself follows a five-bar aeolian I–VI–IV–V–V, played three times in total, closing with a sequence III–

$IV^{\sharp 3}-IV-V$. These riffs are not restricted to Barre's guitar – 'Play in Time' focuses on a flute riff, while through later albums Anderson's acoustic guitar style will attract elements of riff. His mature guitar style combines both riff and chord, as demonstrated on 'One White Duck/0^{10}', from *Minstrel in the Gallery*. Here, he plays a line on the lower strings, which acts like an extended riff, while a chordal accompaniment is strummed on the upper strings rhythmically, *between* the notes of the line. A simpler version of this technique is standard fare in folk clubs, and is also used in other contexts, for example by Elvis Costello on 'Little Palaces'. These two techniques remain a permanent feature of Jethro Tull's style, appearing on every album, and the two alternative ways of using them appear throughout, even as far as the recent *Rock Island*. 'Ears of Tin' uses the acoustic, period-based 'folky' style to symbolize the protagonist's longing, backward glance towards his Scottish island, and riff-based rock for his heading for the cities of the mainland. 'Undressed to Kill' mixes the approaches more evenly. Its sixteen-bar verse spends the first four and last four bars on an aeolian I, with a sense of open-endedness, but between these we have the succession $VI-IV-V^{\sharp 3}-V^{\sharp 3}-II^{\sharp 5}-VII-III^{\flat 3}-III^{\flat 3}$, with the final inflection lifting it out of an unambiguous modality, and clearly delimiting the verse.

The title track of *Minstrel in the Gallery* demonstrates a shift away from the riff/period dichotomy by beginning with an extended 'verse', which employs neither a repeated sequence nor a clear period structure. Here, the harmonies only decorate the melodic line, in a fashion hitherto not part of rock. A more stable attempt to develop an alternative to the strophic forms of rock first appeared in 'Black Satin Dancer', from the same album. This was the first of a number of songs to utilize a ternary (i.e. ABA) structure. The song opens slowly and gently, each line taking five (rather than four) bars to sing (a pattern which is again characteristic of all Jethro Tull's work), here over a stepwise descending bass. A central riff section then contrasts, over which a précis of the initial lyrics is sung. After an instrumental section in which flute and guitar trade solos, Barrie Barlow very effectively varying the kit pattern depending on who is soloing, the opening returns. The aim here may well have been to unify what were becoming two greatly disparate approaches (period and riff), but on this occasion the repeated lyrics do not suit the up-tempo central section.

On *Songs from the Wood*, 'Cap in Hand' seems to be the forerunner of the large ternary songs that form the focus of many of the subsequent albums,[20] as a replacement for the looser sequence of 'Baker St Muse'. 'Cap in Hand' is, in fact, doubly ternary, forming a structure which can be symbolised as ABACABA: the set of verses ('B') is surrounded by the band riff and intensely reverberant electric guitar solo ('A'), while the central segment ('C') is a separate whistle dance. In matters of form, Jethro Tull frequently make use of a device consisting of an accumulating texture, from solo acoustic guitar to full band, over the course (generally) of the first third or so of a song. 'My God', from *Aqualung*, demonstrates this most characteristically: the texture thickens and the song comes alive on the entry of the electric guitar immediately *after* the first line of the second verse, rather than before it, as might befit a band less concerned with detail. Having discussed their use of large-scale time-spans, I now proceed to consideration of the small-scale.

Although the standard rock beat is much in evidence throughout their work, the regularity of the beat is frequently transgressed. On *Benefit*, 'Alive and Well and Living in' demonstrates an early version of what becomes a mature technique. The song has two distinct strains. The first consists of five-bar segments (a common grouping for Tull), closing with a two-bar flute phrase (the beginning of example 3.10). A subsequent flute/bass riff and lead guitar line underpin the second strain, ending with the same flute phrase, but here the seventh beat is re-interpreted as a new first beat, in effect extending the length of one bar by half. By *Minstrel in the Gallery*, this technique has become more subtle, as 'Cold Wind to Valhalla' illustrates. Example 3.11 quotes the melodic line from the first part of the first verse, with the acoustic guitar/flute interpolation. Within what is a fast tempo (in excess of 120 beats per minute), the song switches constantly between 4 and 6 beats per bar, while the instrumental interpolation consists of $4\frac{1}{2}$. This has now become a mature technique of extending bars, and sometimes even extending single beats, without interrupting the overall flow. These *additive* rhythms (so-called because they do not derive from taking a temporal unit – bar – and dividing it into equal portions, but from taking a smallest possible unit – here a quaver – and adding together unspecified numbers of these to produce generally uneven-length beats) are common throughout European dance music, also cropping up in English tunes. While the country blues of singers like Robert Johnson can be analysed in terms of additive rhythms, these blues singers are best understood as 'stretching' standard divisive rhythmic patterns (taking a temporal unit and dividing it successively into equal portions) and, since this seems to be the only remote appearance of additive rhythms in rock's heritage, this practice of Jethro Tull's serves to distinguish the music from all branches of American rock.

By the time of *Songs from the Wood*, this and other rhythmic techniques have reached maturity. 'The Whistler' opens in $\frac{6}{4}$, then re-interprets these bars as $\frac{12}{8}$. The effect is subtle, but it means that although the bar's length remains constant, it moves from having six evenly spaced beats to having four evenly spaced beats, each half as long again. The title track is a magnificent example of additive rhythmic technique. All verses follow the same pattern – example 3.12 transcribes the voice of the third verse. Disorientating as this might be were it to appear only occasionally, here it can quickly become a norm. The fact that these rhythms underlie lyrics with unstable line lengths and abnormal numbers of lines per verse is a sure indication that lyrics and music are conceived together. Moreover, whatever sense of syncopation is present is built in to the melody in the form of additive rhythms rather than being superimposed as a feature of performance practice. This could not be notated in standard transcription fashion with the instruction 'syncopate'. Yet the song can still break into a standard $\frac{4}{4}$ rock beat for the refrain, together with standard syncopation.

Example 3.10 Jethro Tull: 'Alive and Well and Living in'

Example 3.11 Jethro Tull: 'Cold Wind to Valhalla'

Example 3.12 Jethro Tull: 'Songs from the Wood'

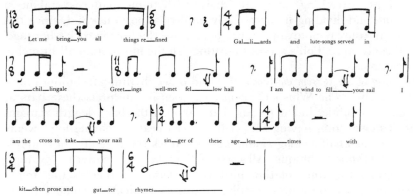

Many songs on this album replace the conventional $\frac{4}{4}$ unit with $\frac{7}{4}$ or $\frac{7}{8}$: both 'Jack-in-the-Green' and 'Ring out Solstice Bells' settle here, while this unit underlies the flute break of the title track: here and elsewhere, the kit approach is exemplary, inventing new rhythmic lines to counterpoint the unusual time signature. This spills over into more regular lengths: the introduction to 'Hunting Girl' could be accompanied by a standard rock beat, but Barrie

Example 3.13 Jethro Tull: 'Aqualung'

Guitar

Barlow's re-thinking of the kit line, with its many unexpected spaces and rolls, gives the song a terrific sense of lift.

In matters of harmony, Jethro Tull are rarely content to remain within any single mode for any length of time. Despite their early music, blues influence is very rarely present. An early example of harmonic exploration is provided by the title track from *Aqualung*. This song's main riff (see example 3.13) emphasizes typical irregularities in both harmony and rhythm. Although the riff falls into four-beat bars, allowing Clive Bunker to stick to a minimal standard rock beat, it extends to seven bars, grouped in highly idiosyncratic fashion as 1 + 4 + 2. Harmonically, although beginning on a chromatic G aeolian, bars 2–6 are best understood as based on G♭ ionian – theoretically far distant. The blues are nowhere in sight, and Jethro Tull seem here to have developed a wholly innovatory style.

As counterpart to these and similar harmonic flights, from *Passion Play* onwards, contrapuntal textures (the practice of proceeding via independent, concurrent melodic lines rather than by block harmonies) become prominent. As I have suggested in Chapter 2, as a matter of rock convention chords are thought of in terms of blocks, rather than as combinations of notes, a pattern of thought that can quickly lead to cliché. On *Songs from the Wood*, the band's tendency to contrapuntal thinking gives the album a great textural richness (which will be considered further in Chapter 4), which extends to a corresponding care over instrumentation: on 'Cap in Hand' flute and guitar are replaced by whistle and mandolin, while the ever-present organ of David Palmer, often playing only single, slow lines in high register, adds textural depth. On 'Velvet Green' the pastiche of renaissance style is largely achieved by the use of contrapuntal lines.

Although these features serve to identify the music of Jethro Tull largely in isolation from Afro-American elements, the style has not remained static. A full treatment would include the way some of these techniques have changed (they are found less on *Stormwatch* than other albums, for instance), the way unusual instruments are incorporated into the ensemble for specific purposes (mandolin and whistle are standard, while pipe organ is not unknown), and the role of synthesizers (particularly on *The Broadsword and the Beast* and *Under Wraps*) and their subsequent abandonment. Such a treatment would take us far from the identification of progressive rock and is, in any case, beyond the scope of this book.

Progressive folk

The presence of 'rural' mythologies, acoustic instruments and additive rhythmic patterns may give limited credence to the belief that Jethro Tull have been influenced by British 'traditional' singing and playing. Charlie Gillett (1983) cites both Pink Floyd and David Bowie in support of his view of the presence of 'folk' influences, but with the benefit of hindsight into how these artists have continued to develop their style, they are not the best examples to use here.

Firstly, it will be necessary to disentangle two customary attributions of 'folk' to rock. The 'neo-folk' movement in the USA, moving through Bob Dylan, Joni Mitchell and artists like the Byrds to Steven Stills, Neil Young *et al.*, became a powerful force in rock, bringing to it a certain lyrical maturity and delight in imagery, and what was perceived as authenticity, due largely to the use of the acoustic guitar. In the hands of a singer-songwriter, this meant that the complete facilities for the invention and performance of songs were in the hands of a single individual: there seemed to be nothing to mediate his or her experience to an audience. Strummed or delicately picked guitars were the norm, as they still are in many English folk clubs today.

This needs to be distinguished from the English folk revival of the 1950s, which continued through the 1960s based around the clubs, where the emphasis was very much on using material from earlier generations,[21] much of it dealing with allegory and disturbing tales of life in all its richness, and on finding new ways to bring this material back into circulation. Indeed, part of the importance of bands like Fairport Convention was the importance of the arrangement – they were not content with simply putting a series of unexceptional harmonies to a melodic line, and their musical emphasis was therefore on line rather than chord. This has always been a stylistic feature of solo guitarists following Martin Carthy, and is now the accepted approach, as demonstrated by bands like Blowzabella and Whippersnapper. This approach is apparent as early as Fairport's influential *Liege and Lief* of 1969, demonstrated on both 'Farewell Farewell' and 'Matty Groves'. It does not feed into the music of the two bands I want to consider here, but does bear more than a passing resemblance to the musical techniques adopted by bands as diverse as King Grimson and Gentle Giant.

Both the Incredible String Band and Tyrannosaurus Rex exemplify the 'folk' strain of progressive rock. Both were initially purely acoustic bands, with ardent followings, and both made use of imagery that emphasized the fey, the 'other'. Deeply rooted in LSD culture, the music of the Incredible String Band (ISB) seemed to concern qualities of gentleness and otherness: as Robin Denselow (1975: 155) put it: 'The songs showed a mystical, pantheist involvement in a very live universe.' Their textures were frequently formed both from exotic acoustic instruments found in other cultures, and from other instruments that do not normally appear in rock. *5000 Spirits or the Layers of the Onion* includes sitar ('Painting Box'), rebec ('Chinese White'), tabla ('Gently Tender'), pipes and bongos over acoustic guitars, while the subsequent *The Hangman's Beautiful Daughter* adds organs, harpsichords, kazoos and others. All these instruments are used to produce connotationally 'gentle' sounds (without strong attacks or piercing upper frequencies), and all are 'other' to rock.

Of greater interest was their attitude to song structure, in which there is a degree of apparent disdain for regularity as great as that of any of the electric progressive bands. For ISB this shows itself in two ways: on songs like 'Little Cloud' and 'Gently Tender', the fey lyrics are compounded by the strange stresses employed – prepositions and conjunctions, rather than the more normal parts of speech, are allowed to fall on strong beats. This extends into highly irregular line lengths. 'Gently Tender' consists of a series of what are recognizably verses according to chord sequence, but the lyrics are stretched and compressed into these, adding to the sense of whimsy. In 'The Mad Hatter's Song', this extends into the form of the song itself, here somewhat sectional. The apotheosis of this approach is the subsequent 'A Very Cellular Song'. Formally, this is no more than a series of pastiches linked by a dour refrain, and all connected only by similar performance style, tempo and perhaps imagery. Indeed, the whole of *The Hangman's Beautiful Daughter* is throughout more calculated in its 'otherness' than the previous album: their subsequent gradual absorption into mainstream rock perhaps testifies to the difficulty in maintaining their original unique attitude.

The Incredible String Band grew out of the folk circuit, and there was at least a tenuous link with folk music *per se*. The output of Tyrannosaurus Rex, on the other hand, was based solidly on Marc Bolan's very private mythologies – their purely acoustic instrumentation was perhaps the only 'folk' connotation their style had, the intimacy this ensured being most strongly a feature of the second folk revival (the first being that of Cecil Sharp and his co-workers). Despite John Peel's early endorsement of them, their range was sadly limited. The style of the initial albums (1968–9) was simplicity itself. Acoustic guitar, almost always with capo, total lack of barred chords and stress on upper strings, giving no sense of bass. High-pitched bongos, frequently played very fast without stress on the backbeat, and high-pitched vocals with excessive tremolo helping to obscure the majority of words. Those that do peek through are rich in possible connotations: princess, Inca, throne, gypsy, Byzantium, galleon etc. Structures are conventional: frequently sixteen-bar verse with eight-bar refrain, where the guitar will break from strumming to double the vocal line momentarily. Despite this seeming uniformity, tracks like 'Wind Quartets' and 'Knight' manage to acquire a certain comfortable intrigue: the former, for example, is perfectly balanced between its tonic minor and relative major, this balance emphasized by the fragility of the accompaniment.

By 1970's *A Beard of Stars*, Bolan had extended the intimate guitar–bongo duo with, most importantly, an overdubbed electric guitar. Both guitar and vocal pitch are also lower, allowing the listener greater access to the words, and on 'First Heart, Mighty Dawn Dart', with its addition of a catchy refrain, all that is missing from the later chart hit 'Ride a White Swan' is the massed strings. Bolan's acquisition of a teenybop audience and sought-after popularity was made with minimal sacrifice of his own imagery, and it may well be that the underground persona of Marc Bolan was the false one. Discussion of the obscure lyrics not only of Bolan, but of so many of the songs I have discussed above, leads me towards a single element which, I think, can be held to underpin British progressive rock. That element is an implicit, but none the less strong, ideology which is *gnostic* in nature. In order to explore this, I shall focus explicitly on the use of fantastic imagery.

Fantasy

The private mythologies of Marc Bolan represent one aspect of the intrusion of the fantastic into progressive rock. Fantasy is the style's only important non-musical source, but in many ways it is the most widely influential. It takes many forms, from the undisguised macho symbolism of Deep Purple's 'Space Truckin'' (where the apparent sci-fi setting is no more *necessary* to the song than it is in so much second-rate sci-fi itself) through to Genesis's 'Supper's Ready', King Crimson's 'In the Court of the Crimson King' and a multitude of others. The sources here are rather less science fiction than the epic fantasy and allegory of writers like Moorcock, Ellison, Donaldson, Tolkien or Peake, or in worse cases the sword-and-sorcery stories of Howard or Carter. Similar imagery can be found in bands as widely differentiated as Emerson, Lake and Palmer ('Brain Salad Surgery'), the Strawbs ('Grave New World'), Led Zeppelin ('Stairway to Heaven', 'Battle of Evermore'), Tyrannosaurus Rex (anything) Cream ('Tales of Brave Ulysses') and innumerable others. Why should there be such a prevalence? Clearly these types of imagery set such bands apart from the 'commercial' end of the market, with their concentration on obscure and occult (in the sense of 'hidden') matters, their lack of obvious personal reference and their clear attempt to provide an alternative way of looking at things, even if this was not clear to the uninitiated. This is a most important point, and I shall take it up below.

The most apparent form of fantasy perhaps surfaced with the early 'space' explorations of Pink Floyd and Hawkwind. Although Syd Barrett left Pink Floyd between *Piper at the Gates of Dawn* and *A Saucerful of Secrets*, the aims of these first two albums are similar. Two types of material predominate, the whimsical nursery-rhyme songs ('Bike', 'The Scarecrow', taken to an extreme in 'Corporal Clegg') and the spaced-out quasi-improvisations. It is from these latter that their early style acquires its conventions. Most important in its absence is the formal division into verses and refrains. 'Intersteller [*sic*]

Overdrive' encloses a largely free improvisation within a semitone-based riff, a 'motif' that underlies many of the ideas on the early albums. The beat tends to remain perfectly constant, with an emphasis on high register bass lines. Twice they drop from the texture, allowing it to 'take off', before returning and gradually re-introducing the beat. The texture is unremarkable: guitar to the left of the mix, organ to the centre, and bass and kit to the right, although the final sequence is thrown between speakers. There seem to be three aspects to the 'space' metaphor as found in Pink Floyd: this phasing effect,[22] the periodic omission of the bass end of the texture and the long, rather uncoordinated guitar lines, which throw up motifs that are developed only briefly before the band move on to the next. On 'Astronomy Domine', the tendency to trebly sounds, and the fact that the voices do not stand out, perhaps adds to this effect, although the rich, low guitar perhaps acts to anchor the texture to earth. 'Saucerful of Secrets' takes this metaphor further: it begins emptily, with no beat, and with each player occupying his own modal space with little, if any, connection between players. When the beat finally arrives, they likewise remain unattached to it. This extreme individuality may perhaps be likened to the almost solipsistic sense of so much science fiction, and also the feel of total self-sufficiency and hence well-being induced under heightened awareness. Ultimately, this tends to turn bleak, as on *Dark Side of the Moon*, *The Wall* and the first side of *Atom Heart Mother*.

The second side of *Atom Heart Mother* consists of a sequence of self-contained songs, far removed from the early spatial essays. It is at this point that a mature musical style begins to assert itself. 'Summer of '68', aside from its neat allusions to the Beatles, the Beach Boys and even the Small Faces, is marked rather by totally regular 4 × 4 metric groupings, by an extremely slow pace and by a sequence that is tonal rather than modal. This sequence is expounded through held chords rather than a riff: indeed, after the early albums, Pink Floyd do not rely on riffs, with their connotations of aggressive energy. In this context, despite the length of 'Atom Heart Mother' itself, the use of vocal and brass choirs, the continual dependence on barely modified sound effects, and the out-of-time layering of elements from earlier in the piece to contribute to the climax, these three aspects (sequence, grouping and speed) remain dominant. The only aspect from the blockbuster *Dark Side of the Moon* absent here is the textural norm of the characteristic organ chords, underlying guitar solos totally lacking in ostentatious virtuosity. This feature was present in their early style, and is recaptured particularly on the title track on *Obscured by Clouds*.

Similar characteristics seem to have underpinned the 'space' metaphors developed by Hawkwind. 'Space is Deep', for instance, originally from 1972, begins with a typical dense texture, using both white noise and filters to provide an 'atmosphere', and combining these with mechanical noises and heavy reverb. As with Pink Floyd, there is a tendency towards longish, open-ended solo sections over simple chord sequences, but with little virtuosity and a tendency for the bass to concentrate on higher pitches. Again, these spaced-out jams represented only one side of Hawkwind's style – that found on

'Motorhead' or 'Silver Machine', for example, is far closer to early heavy metal.

So, although it is possible to identify some musical techniques that may have operated as metaphors for 'space' (both inner and outer), the evidence is not particularly strong. It seems more likely that two non-musical factors are connotationally stronger. The first is the staging (especially light shows) and the overt sensory overload, particularly of Pink Floyd's early shows, while the second may simply be song titles, lyrics and album design. Any other musical sounds that were perceived as slightly weird might well have worked equally successfully.

The importance of the fantastic in rock seems predicated upon gnosis. Classically, gnostic faiths are based on beliefs that salvation is gained by knowledge, rather than by faith or by works or some other means (see Chandler 1988: 44–5). Obscurity is hence to be striven for in their construction, since it intensifies the achievement of the goal. As Chambers (1985: 84–5) notes, 'by 1970, distinct publics, often hermetically sealed off one from the other, were established. . . . Black music was exiled to the far reaches of the white rock world.' This sealing-off is typical of a gnostic attitude: whereas in the summer of 1967 salvation had seemed open to all (even if it wasn't), very soon the language's obscurity encouraged separation. It is here that Peter Wicke's belief in the nature of rock is most pertinent:

> The myth of rock music as a classless youth culture only arose because it was assumed that because teenagers of all social classes were fascinated by the same [beat] songs they must all find the same meaning in them. . . . The most important thing about [early beat] music is no longer the wealth of emotion, the fulfilment of the content and the diversity of associations developed in the artistic structures, but rather the ability of these elements to be open to the symbolic meanings which they receive from their listeners.
>
> (Wicke 1990: 81, 67)

For Wicke, this is true of all rock, although the case is nowhere stronger than in dealing with the imagery of much progressive rock.

Of course, the presence of such imagery is not unrelated to the LSD experience, which set the mark for providing 'an alternative way of looking at things'. That music is necessary to cultural identity is clear, and perhaps nowhere more so than when discussing the hippies. Timothy Leary, arch-propagandist for LSD in 1967 San Francisco, advocated music as a guide to keep you 'on track', while anthropological work into peoples who use hallucinogens to gain spiritual insight suggests that accompanying music is necessary as a 'set of banisters' (to quote anthropological terminology), which can be held on to as a guide while the ego is dissolved (Turner 1988: 71). Clearly Lennon, for one, failed to find it adequate; hence his later vicious attacks on Leary, LSD and the whole cult:

> I got a message on acid that you should destroy your ego, and I did. I was reading that stupid book of Leary's . . . and I destroyed myself. I destroyed my ego and I didn't believe I could do anything.
>
> (Quoted in Turner 1988: 73)

As Turner comments:

> The broken-down ego that was necessary to experience the oneness of the universe
> was an impediment once the real world was returned to because ego assures us of
> our identity and integrity [i.e. wholeness].
>
> (Turner 1988: 73; see also Shapiro 1990: 130)

This obscurity only finally broke down when the falsity of the LSD dream became more generally realized.

In the work of some bands, the unfamiliarity of free jazz and aspects of fantasy were combined to enhance the sense of strangeness. For both King Crimson and Van der Graaf Generator, the recourse to such imagery is tied to a rather 'gothic' sense of impending doom. On Crimson's first album, for example, 'Epitaph' suggests: 'we cross the cracked and broken path; if we make it, we can all sit back and laugh, but I fear tomorrow I'll be crying,' a tone never far away throughout their first incarnations. Four years later, 'Exiles' eloquently mourns the destruction of 'normality', evoking a sense similar to Kay Dick's set of short stories, *They*. Both these settings achieve this rather intoxicating sense of foreboding through similar devices. Both are rather slow in pace; both use the mellotron to hold a chordal background, over which an acoustic guitar clearly arpeggiates the basic harmonies; both are full of textural holes, particularly in the upper registers except at climactic points (which happen to be minor ninth chords in both songs); and on both the drum patterns leave interesting metric gaps. On 'Epitaph', fourth beats tend to be empty, particularly during the funereal bridge section, which uses the baritone sax so effectively (as on the later 'The Letter'), while on 'Exiles' it is the more normal third beats that are empty. Beyond this, each song makes use of other devices to contribute to the effect: 'Epitaph' finishes inconclusively, alternating aeolian VI–V harmonies, while 'Exiles' opens with highly evocative studio-produced wails and groans.

A similar sense is found in some of the uneven Van der Graaf Generator's work, especially on *Pawn Hearts*. 'Lemmings', the opening track, finds equivalent devices to evoke this sense of despair. (What could be more desperate than the closing line, 'what choice is there left but to live'?) Saxophones are dominant, with a rich 'gothic' organ sound equivalent to the mellotron. An acoustic guitar is again pitted against these forces, suggesting perhaps a sense of both purity and vulnerability in the face of these powerful instrumental odds. As with much of King Crimson, augmented triads are in evidence, in the bridge and also in the inconclusive wind-down to an ending. This sense of despair seems heightened by the use of free jazz: 'Lemmings' breaks into a central improvised section clearly identifiable as a free jazz break (more in the style of Cecil Taylor), with the piano resorting to clusters up and down the keyboard, beneath unattached saxophone lines and frenetic drumming. It is these lines, almost unrelated to each other, that are the key; they appear as early as King Crimson's 'Moonchild' (on *In the Court of the Crimson King*).

I have demonstrated in this chapter that progressive rock is marked, above all, by its diversity, a diversity suggestive of a constellatory, rather than a linear, account. As a movement, it has the appearance of having reconciled the basic conventions of beat/r&b with certain conventions from disparate styles ('blues', 'jazz', 'folk', 'art'), but this partial musical reconciliation is accompanied by an equally important disintegration within listening publics, encouraged by the gnostic ideology inherent in the use of fantastic and obscure imagery, itself supported by the apparent 'strangeness' of the stylistic fusions. Thus, many British listeners, at least, did not feel part of this music at all. The practices which identified skinheads, northern soul enthusiasts, teenyboppers, as distinct, distinguished them from the contemporary rock audiences (see, for example, Chambers 1985: 144–48 and 161–67, P. Everett 1986: 104–7 and 120–22) and I suggest they are only irrelevant to this account, rather than unimportant in themselves. The stylistic grounds for the appropriation of reggae by skinheads has never been made explicit. Neither have the important differences in the instrumental timbres used by David Cassidy or the Bay City Rollers, in comparison with rock timbres, ever been seriously described. These await further research by others.

Conclusion: the progress of progressive rock

King Crimson are the best place to end this account of the styles that contributed to progressive rock, for it was they who most thoroughly and comprehensively tested the limits of rock style as they received it.[23] In Chapter 2, I referred to the lack of repetition found in 'Larks' Tongues in Aspic (Part I)'. Although this track has many well-fashioned ideas, none repeats. This suggests a formal looseness, testing to its limits the expected tight structures of rock songs. Some years earlier, on '21st Century Schizoid Man', they had seriously challenged the centrality of the standard rock beat. The archetypal 'heavy rock' song, this has a novel formal approach, using an overall arch structure – verses, composed breaks, free breaks, composed breaks, verses, opening with a powerful heavy rock riff. I have already referred to the free jazz elements (following the guitar solo). The subsequent unison, rather in a free jazz manner, destroys any sense of regular beat, such that the silences that surround its phases are of powerful effect.

The most rigid strictures on invention in rock are those that refer to harmonic patterns and to instrumental functions. Both were under threat from King Crimson. It must be stressed here that all rock uses as its basic harmonic construct the triad, whether major or minor, a construct defined by its intervallic patterning – a space of seven semitones partitioned 4:3 (a perfect fifth, divided major third:minor third). This construct is ubiquitous. 'Fracture', on *Starless and Bible Black*, eschews it. Its harmonic construct has a space of only six semitones (an augmented fourth) partitioned 4:2 (e.g. C, E, F♯, or C, D, F♯). 'Fracture' contains no triads. Moreover, instead of moving from harmony to harmony by step, or by the interval of a fifth, 'Fracture' moves by the interval of a major third. This harmonic language is familiar to listeners to early twentieth-century French music (particularly that of Debussy and

Messiaen), where it connotes a sense of rootlessness. For me, it carries that connotation here too.

The clearest challenge to the normative instrumental functions occurs on 'Providence' (on *Red*), with its unattached, independent lines, which again give the music a sense of being 'unearthed'. Yet despite all these points of challenge, King Crimson were capable of the most beautiful of 'standard' songs, such as 'The Night Watch' on *Starless and Bible Black*, in which the verse/refrain structure is only slightly stretched.

If we are to attempt to pursue the analogy with the Western art music tradition that I raised at the beginning of the chapter, at this moment we have reached a saturation point. All the norms of the music have been challenged – essentially all that remains is for subsequent musicians to 'fill in the gaps'. But here, the analogy breaks down for, in rock, the established domains (form, rhythm, harmony, melody) tell nothing like the whole story. Indeed, over the past fifteen years, all the interesting developments have been in the areas of timbre, production techniques and texture. It is for this reason that I shall outline changes of texture at the beginning of the next chapter. What the case of King Crimson does perhaps indicate is the constraints that surround 'rock' styles. Triads are not obligatory, but harmonic constructs are, and they require a certain aural affinity with conventional triads. The expected pattern of instrumental functions can be overridden, but only against a perceived background of that pattern, accepted as the norm. Finally, since the music is not *primarily* intended for dancing, the standard rock beat can be avoided, as can even the regular repetition of any pattern of beats, but not for long.

As with any artistic movement, both cultural and artistic factors can be cited to account for its existence and ultimate demise. 'Progressive' rock was initially dependent on the existence of an 'underground' culture, spawned by the drug era before its deleterious side-effects were discovered, spurred on by the illusion that individual enlightenment was on the point of being attainable by all, and that global enlightenment could be effected by the youth of all nations if only they could agree on their aims, as exemplified in their reactions to the Vietnam War. It became public because the boom times of the late 1960s gave record companies the confidence to indulge their more experimental artists (an attitude rare today), aligning rock even more with middle-class attitudes. But, as I have suggested throughout this chapter, these circumstances merely enabled progressive rock musicians to respond to earlier styles' presumed lack of artistic control, lack of facility for continuity and developed thought, restriction in terms of subject matter (simple inter-personal relations), lengths (three minutes) and formal patterns (verses and refrains), and restriction to simple harmonic patterns and regular metres and durations. It will be the task of the next chapter to demonstrate some of the ways rock music moved within and beyond the tendencies that constitute the styles cited here. There we shall see that experimentation in the techniques of music remains a key factor.

4   A Profusion of Styles

The previous chapter has led me to conclude that the only positive value to be found in retention of the term 'progressive' is that it encompasses distinctive, contemporaneous styles, which each developed and explored discrete dimensions of rock's stylistic conventions. The diversity of styles which were allowed to live together under the 'progressive' tag precludes any monolithic identification of *rock* in the UK, at least into the mid-1970s: it is only by dismantling the notion of a unified *style* that we can begin to clarify our perspective. In this chapter, I shall argue that the same is true of post-progressive styles, only even more so. Chambers (1985) talks evocatively of 'explosion' and resultant 'fragments' in terms of the period from about 1970–76: the disintegration of stylistic conventions that this implies becomes even more apparent after this date. Indeed, I shall suggest below that one of the beneficial effects of punk was that it revealed, for the illusion it was, the notion that rock styles succeed each other in a linear fashion.

Since my main concern is to identify and demonstrate the internal consistencies of styles, this chapter will again focus on individual examples, but the implication that one leads directly to another, in any sort of parent/offspring relationship, must be resisted. I shall tend to honour their chronologically-ordered origins, but will have occasion to identify other pertinent relationships between them. The discussion is not intended to be exhaustive with respect to post-progressive styles: I doubt that such a programme would be achievable. Returning to my suggestion in the introduction, that rock was structured by a multiply-evolving but coherent set of rules and practices, my choice of styles here is partly guided by the notion of testing the boundaries of that set, boundaries which seem almost to be broached by synthesizer rock, as I shall suggest. In addition, the issue of 'authenticity', which arose in dealing with the 'blues' in the previous chapter, will again prove important. Because I understand 'feeling' and 'expression' always to be mediated, it is necessary to critique the claims of 'authenticity' which are frequently made, since they rest on the notion of unmediated expression. This I shall do in the current chapter, while I shall offer a more thorough defence of this position in the final chapter.

There are two further factors which serve to mediate the responses afforded in listeners by the music, and which do not really begin to have an impact until the mid-1970s. Accordingly, I shall problematize the commonsense understanding of musical timbre immediately following the discussion of synthesizer rock (the style in which the issue is most clearly raised), while the chapter will begin with a discussion of one impact of technology on the practice of listening to rock.

Technology and texture[1]

The mediation of rock through social and cultural formations has received a great deal of attention in recent years – likewise, its historical mediation is frequently addressed. However, there is a further set of mediatory factors that tend to be overlooked, and they are the product of the technology involved in the production of the music itself. Indeed, consideration of these factors is frequently ignored in the discussion of any music, no matter what the style.[2] Musicians (whether performers, composers, producers or anyone else intimately involved in the making of musical sound) are not free to produce exactly what sounds they might conceive, but are constrained by the technology they are working with. That technology may itself set limits on what can be conceived (this argument is frequently made when identifying notation as a form of technology), although in recent years this may have become less the case. Before the late 1940s, this simply meant that the sounds conceived had to be playable on instruments, or at least had to be within the capacity of instrument makers to develop instruments for. In theory this is no less true in recent years, except that the instruments avaliable have been extended by electronic technology. The practical danger here is that it is easy to feel that all the available technology needs to be used. Within popular music in the UK and USA, since the birth of rock 'n' roll at least, innovation has tended to come from two alternating tendencies. The first is that of greater simplification. Heavy metal, for example, was harmonically and rhythmically simple in comparison with most progressive rock, which it followed chronologically. On the other hand, the music of the hit parade has always been simpler than rock in terms of lyrics, while punk began as a technologically simple style. The second tendency is that of greater sophistication. Bob Dylan's early output was sophisticated in terms of lyrics, while much progressive rock took the opportunity to become technologically sophisticated.

The most important aspects of this technological sophistication in practical terms were the use of multi-tracking, with its concomitant control over spatial location, and the development of sound-transforming techniques, resulting in later years in the widespread use of synthesizers. The control over spatial location is strongly related to the use of musical texture as a separate domain, and gives rise to two virtual concepts, of time and of space. Working in the contemporary studio allows musicians such control over the finished product that the lived time of performer and listener are neither co-extensive nor even of equivalent lengths: the recording presents a series of sounds 'as if' they occurred together in precisely this way, but in the studio they have been layered through multi-tracking and manipulated through 'black boxes'.[3]

Texture refers to the presence of and relationships between identifiable strands of sound in a music. The history of Western musical, let alone rock, textures has yet to be written, but it is possible to sketch out some moments in the history of such changes. Middleton points out the *range* of different textures available to studio musicians, arguing that, 'however important the effects and constraints of technologies, these are inseparable from specific *contents* and specific *social functions*' (Middleton 1990: 89). This has a degree of specificity that it is not necessary to provide here, since a textural history is not linear. Moreover, although in many cases there can be a high degree of tension between the musicians' and the producer's control of the product, I am only dealing here with the outcome of those processes.

For rock, the 'strand' of texture is often equivalent to 'instrumental timbre'. It can best be conceived with reference to a 'virtual textural space', envisaged as an empty cube of finite dimensions, changing with respect to real time (almost like an abstract, three-dimensional television screen). This model is not dissimilar to that employed intuitively by producers, but I shall refer to it as the 'sound-box'[4] rather than the 'mix', to indicate that my analysis privileges the listening, rather than the production, process. All rock has strands at different vertical locations, where this represents their register. Most rock also attempts a sense of musical 'depth' (the illusory sense that some sounds originate at a greater distance than others), giving a sense of textural foreground, middleground and background. Much rock also has a sense of horizontal location, provided by the construction of the stereo image. The most important features of the use of this space are the types and degrees of density filling it (whether thin strands or 'blocks'), and the presence of 'holes' in this space, i.e. potential areas left unused. In this respect, earlier styles can seem almost one-dimensional, while more recent styles can make fuller use of the potential, which, of course, has to be set up by and for each individual style.

The Beatles' 'She Loves You' is a good place to start tracing the changes of texture in rock styles: the music's pre-stereo textures can stand for many other recordings of the period. The instrumentation is limited to voices in various relationships, bass and kit, rhythm guitar and occasional lead guitar fills. Its most notable textural feature is its density, so that concentrated listening is required in order to focus on each individual sound source. There are no holes in parts of the texture, which makes the occasional tutti rests very effective. Throughout, the texture is registrally stratified: voices on top, ride cymbal, snare and strummed guitar giving body, and bass giving a firm foundation. There is little sense of textural depth, although the voices and lead guitar fills seem slightly to the fore, and there is no sense that the sound sources issue from different locations. It should be noted that the kit does not reside at the bottom of the texture, alongside the bass. Snare drums and tomtoms fit right in the middle of the horizontal texture, bass a little lower and cymbals, although technically covering very wide frequencies, tend to sit in the top half, rising directly with respect to volume.

Phil Spector's treatment of the Beatles' 'The Long and Winding Road' is, despite his virtual invention of the producer's role, little different. The voice and its almost inaudible accompanying piano fill the middle of the texture, while the strings, chorus and horns (all being sound sources with minimal attack) surround this centre in all directions, but again with little depth. The indulgent nature of the song is not helped by the fact that all the 'backing' instruments fade so gradually that silence is never achieved. The kit and bass are so understated as to be present almost under sufferance, and the opportunity is not taken during the bridge to use them to generate the movement of which the strings seem incapable.

Both these songs tend to define their spaces in terms of blocks of sound rather than lines. Yes's 'Roundabout' concentrates far more on individual lines: even explicit chords function as little more than thickenings of lines. The general texture is dense, resulting from a number of factors. Most lines congregate towards the lower registers: bass, strummed (acoustic) guitar and organ are all lacking in higher harmonics and are also highly active, the bass in particular, although they are sufficiently registrally differentiated to enable ready identification. The central bridge passage uses only parallel voices, kit (central in the texture as always, and spread across the stereo image) and bass riff, but is of thick texture even before the entry of the organ. The reprise of the introduction creates a clear distinction within the sound-box between foreground and background: acoustic guitar harmonics (naturally soft) appear louder and paradoxically lower than rippling organ arpeggios (naturally far louder), which also appear to one side in the sound-box, suggesting a moment's reflection within the surrounding activity. The organ then switches horizontal location to embark on its solo, in which all instruments are 'layered' in the space. This represents a conceptual advance, in that differentiations are made within the overall space, although the only 'holes' present seem to be beneath the acoustic guitar in the absence of the bass.

Jethro Tull's 'Songs from the Wood' represents a further conceptual advance, as sounds can be considered *placed* in this virtual textural space. The opening consists of solo voice backed with parallel voices, but the subtle glockenspiel and flute fills immediately suggest a greater space than that occupied by the voices alone. A variety of conventional timbres are involved: clapping, tambourine, registrally high organ and guitar, gradually filling out the space and thereby expanding the listener's awareness of how much more may be available, until kit and bass finally enter. The texture has gradually spread from a small centre (which was at the time entirely self-contained) to the whole sound-box. The subsequent use of harpsichord, mandolin and electric guitar is quite subtle, but timbres are sufficiently separated to allow them all to be distinguished. Thus, later 'holes' in this texture appear as just that – potential to be retrieved, giving a greater sense of continuity. The central section is particularly notable: interplay between the horizontal centre (bass and kit) and extremes of the sound-box occurs. These extremes are represented by guitars in a middleground with keyboards receding behind them.

Throughout the 1980s, one tendency has been to increase the strength of reverb used, filling out the texture but also putting up a subtle barrier between the listener and the hitherto immediacy of the sound. This is well illustrated by two songs in divergent styles. In Def Leppard's 'Love Bites', the kit has been placed in a focal, central position, with the voice fractionally to one side of the sound-box, balanced by the bass. The guitars fit on either side of these, tending towards the top and encasing the whole texture. The heavy reverb seems to prevent holes forming, even when the guitars are playing just single lines. Yet the backbeat (particularly the fourth beat), struck on the snare and joined in the refrain by crash symbals sounding to either side of the sound-box, is ignored by the rest of the ensemble, as it shoots through the entire texture like a bullet. This emphasizes how potentially empty of all but reverb-created atmosphere the entire space is. It is as if all that happens is 'veiled' except at these moments. (In this song, the bass sustains at the bottom end of the texture, although in more up-tempo numbers the line becomes far more broken.) Technological advance allows the kit to produce a very full sound, with far lower harmonics than earlier kits, and the guitar to produce an equivalent, rounded tone.

U2's 'Where the Streets Have No Name' illustrates a similar filling of space, although with simpler instrumentation. Here, the texture remains the same throughout, but seemingly by design rather than thoughtlessness, creating a texture of great energy. Anything that could disturb this is seemingly re-moved. The guitar is present throughout, covering a small range in a single register, with fast, intricate movement. The static bass (keeping to the root of harmonies rather than constructing an independent line) gives great firmness to the texture, while of the kit, only the ride cymbal is allowed to threaten this equilibrium. The guitar remaining above the voice sets up a perfect platform for the voice to dominate as the only sound source that really moves.

From a decade or so earlier, Wishbone Ash's 'Throw down the Sword' shares Def Leppard's twin guitar instrumentation and sound-box placing – kit central, bass slightly to one side, guitars more extremely to either side – but this is used to different effect, through textural distribution. The minimal use of reverb seems to remove the distancing present in the previous two examples, but with a corresponding lack of textural depth. The crash cymbals set up a haze around the texture here, instead of cutting through, while the twin guitar riff seems isolated within a mass of unused space. It is not until the entry of the lead voice that an illusion of depth is created, owing to the slight added reverb and also to the voice's central position in the sound-box, well above the kit and horizontally distanced from the guitars. The subsequent twin guitar solo, over held organ chords in the same register, helps this illusion of depth, but the overall effect remains one of textural simplicity and comparative emptiness, particularly when measured against more recent styles.

Ultravox's 'Vienna' maintains a constructive emptiness, in large part because of the rethinking of the role of kit and bass in the style of synthesizer rock (see below). In the opening verse the voice appears slightly to one side of the sound-box, with three beats of bass drum slightly to the other. A thunderous fourth beat moves across the sound-box, leaving one side empty, while a solo synthesizer line sits in the centre. These parts are clearly placed within the texture, and no attempt is made to fill this out except at the end of verses, where a full, block chord organ enters at the previously empty side. This greater conceptual separation seems at least partially the result of the more precise control over timbres permitted by synthesizer technology. When the bass and snare arrive, the snare is high in the sound-box, while the bass is foregrounded and low, separating them to a degree unusual in rock.

Finally, Fleetwood Mac's 'Little Lies' illustrates a coming to maturity of the clear construction of a virtual textural space. A vast catalogue of sounds is employed, from synthesized strings and flutes, through a marimba (fulfilling the role of second plucked rhythm guitar), a curious bass 'growl' that appears only on the first beat of a group in the refrain and always at the same pitch, to three types of synthesized samisen- and koto-like sounds,[5] all in addition to conventional kit, bass and voices (solo, solo in parallel and responsorial). But this mass of timbres coexists without any being swamped, because they are all placed carefully within the virtual space, set apart vertically, horizontally (only bass, kit and solo voice appear central) and in terms of depth. Especially notable is the way that, in the refrain, the female voice is placed in front of the ensemble, her parallel lines dropping to 'reveal' the samisen/koto timbres. This suggests a highly impressive control over texture.

Malcolm McLaren's more recent 'Waltz Darling' takes this approach even further in some respects. Its texture is formed from three elements. The rhythm track has three spatially separated aspects (kit, ride cymbal and percussive bass), while the 'song itself' consists largely of voices and synthesized strings. Over these, McLaren places a number of sampled sounds, from speech through to isolated phrases excised from the classical repertoire. Although the whole remains fairly unfocused, the 'placing' of these remnants adds a further layer of play. He even begins to make constructive use of the movement of sounds within the stereo image, a technique barely employed in rock.

The textural density found in 'Little Lies' is of an entirely different order to that of 'She Loves You', although in both the degree of density seems high. In 'She Loves You', it is as if the entire foreground of the sound-box is opaque. In 'Little Lies', it is as if many small areas are covered at different depths. I would suggest that the sound-box enables the conceptualization of varieties of density and, thus, the presence of textural holes. A comparison of a range of texts from the early 1960s through to the late 1980s suggests a clear tendency towards thinking more in terms of a virtual textural space as studio technology develops, involving as this does the beginnings of a re-thinking of the functions of instruments within this texture. Rock remains identifiable in the terms outlined in Chapter 2, yet some of these songs point the way for more subtle textural dispositions within these limits, and for movements beyond it. These dispositions and movements will, to some extent, be charted in what follows.

Glam rock

In his thumbnail sketch of rock history, Simon Frith suggests that 'glam rock' opened up a new perspective for musicians: 'The *image* of the rock star – previously taken to be quite natural (rock was sincere) or entirely false (a cynical sales device) . . . became part of musicians' creative effort' (Frith 1988b: 42). Neither Frith nor any other writer seems to suggest that 'glam rock' may be descriptive of a musical style. Indeed, the stylistic differences between David Bowie and Roxy Music, Lou Reed and the New York Dolls, and even 'glitter rockers' like Slade, Marc Bolan, Gary Glitter and the Sweet, were far more pronounced than the similarities. I would suggest that for most of these figures, the musical style tended to be impervious to the image. We shall see in the next chapter that Bowie's musical style at this time can be adequately discussed without any reference to the notion of glam rock. This contrasts with the style of Roxy Music, which began as a way of exploring a projected image.

I have already noted the vital, but non-specific, influence that fine arts training had on beat musicians (explored in Frith and Horne 1987). For Roxy Music, the influence became specific, for visual concerns were directly translated into image construction, as evidenced in Bryan Ferry's concern with the marketing of the initial albums. Both Ferry and Eno were fine arts graduates, while Eno and Andy Mackay had a lively interest in the radical, improvisatory music of John Cage's followers. Eno, too, clearly found Velvet Underground (themselves influenced by Cage) an important influence, as they offered what he felt to be a merging of the aesthetics of avant-garde and rock musics (Rogan 1982: 13). This merging is not overt in Roxy Music's work, with the exception of Eno's appropriation of the techniques of *musique concrète*, which resulted in his characteristic tape sounds. This virtuosic utilization of extraneous sounds as a form of atmosphere control moved far beyond previous examples, such as Yes's *Close to the Edge*. It was primarily on the first album that Roxy's distinctive style emerged – thereafter it became increasingly difficult to sustain.

Perhaps the most notable musical feature of *Roxy Music* is the total domination of open-ended harmonic patterns, from the almost simplistic dorian $I^{\sharp 3}$–VII–$V^{\sharp 3}$–IV of 'Ladytron' to the chromatic aeolian I–$\sharp VII^{\sharp 3}$–VI–I of 'Chance Meeting'. It seems almost as if Ferry's fingers[6] have found a random triadic sequence on the keyboard, over which he starts to spin a frequently discongruent vocal line. Indeed, the contrast between surface and underlying structure in 'Ladytron' is of more than passing interest. A unit is formed by the immediate repetition of the four-chord sequence. This unit then repeats six times, the first two forming sung verses, the last four underpinning solos highlighting oboe, guitar, sax and piano in turn, before a fade. The introduction, with its slow oboe melody over Eno's disorientating tape effects, giving way to Ferry's minimally accompanied despairing admission that 'you've got me, girl, on the runaround, and it's getting me down', sets up a complex, frenetic surface. Its influence is felt throughout the song, with its rich, honking sax, fast tomtom rhythms and pounding bass. This rich surface, however, hides the most minimal of structures, thus delivering a rich metaphor for glam rock itself. This is reinforced by Ferry's highly distinctive vocal style, in which he almost chokes the words out, with a tremble to the voice, which is apt to shoot out uncontrolled to an unexpected pitch at any moment (towards the end of 'If There Is Something' exemplifies this very well). The actual lyrics are ordinary, but within the strange environment, Ferry's agonized delivery of them suggests less the plaint of the lovestruck than the anguished cry of the possessed.

Texturally, too, this album makes its mark: the traditional instrumental relationships are frequently and subtly overturned. Ferry's piano style is remarkable for its simplicity: frequently just repeated triads or open fifths, allowing Paul Thompson's kit to play a more adventurous role than normal. 'Chance Meeting' dispenses with the kit altogether, the rhythmic layer being provided by a Jerry Lee Lewis piano style executed at an exceedingly slow pace, while the bass spends much of the time at the very top of its range. In the central section of 'Sea Breezes', the voice is underpinned almost solely by a modally obscure bass pattern (in which 'wrong notes' predominate) and a kit appearing right in the foreground of the sound-box, playing a highly varied counterpoint with the bass beat, but eschewing its own normal time-keeping function. Indeed, the album's most interesting instrumental textures seem to hinge on bassist Graham Simpson's idiosyncratic use of chromatic walking lines and high registers. His departure after this album resulted in less interesting textures on subsequent albums. This powerful kit/bass relation is also found towards the end of the second third of 'If There Is Something', as Ferry's protestations of 'love' reach their peak and the song's emptiness, beneath the kit/bass surface, is realized. Texturally, though, it is the environment Eno creates that gives the music its particular aura, from the rather anarchic collections of tape noises that none the less conspire to create the illusion of an unfocused, urban setting, to the effects of tape delay (particularly noticeable on the sax solo on '2 H.B.') and other manipulations. Eno's filling of the textural centre allows the band to dispense with rhythm guitars and keyboards, whose normal role in rock is to prevent those central textural holes.

The sense of image construction is also approached through some interesting attempts at style evocation. As Chambers notes, despite glam rock's student and art school following, its 'primary audience was made up of white, working-class teenagers' (Chambers 1985: 135), thus giving it a place alongside American rock 'n' roll, which had shared a similar audience (Chambers 1985: 33). The punning 'Bitters End', sidestepping the conventional 'big ending' to an album, is a convincing rock 'n' roll doo-wop take-off, even down to the ionian I–VI–IV–V pattern (the 'Stand by Me' changes). The central section of 'Would You Believe?' is similar, being a convincing boogie pastiche (ionian IV–I–V–I), down to the honking sax and backing vocals, while Ferry's overplayed swoops prevent us from taking it seriously.

In comparison, none of the later work of Roxy Music has the ambiguous directness of this first album. Although *For Your Pleasure* matches its atmosphere from time to time, particularly on 'Bogus Man', it also begins to essay a harmonic-structural complexity that is apt to meander. The intense energy of 'Do the Strand' no longer acts as an ironic counterpoint to the austere structure, but is itself necessary because that structure has become cluttered. And, by the time we encounter the weary *Avalon* (1982), swathed as it is in synthesized strings, no amount of open-ended patterns can compensate for its lacklustre rhythmic surface.

So, despite signs to the contrary on the first album, Roxy Music did not develop a musical style with the resilience to underpin the visual effect of glam rock. But, musical practices alone are insufficient to account for the demise of a style epitomizing cultural practices which were, at least for Chambers (1985), far more than a passing fad. The ambiguous sexuality represented by modes of dress, not only worn by performers (particularly clear on the liner photos of *Roxy Music* and most of David Bowie's albums from *The Man Who Sold the World* to *Diamond Dogs*), but by some audiences too (see P. Everett 1986: 126), indicated that sexuality was no longer a merely private concern. It had been forced into the public domain through glam rock's challenge to sexual stereotyping. And, as resistance grew (especially in the tabloid press), this was re-emphasized by the more extreme ambiguity which is now associated with punk (see, particularly, Hebdige 1985). Here, the resultant style of musicians who were themselves indebted, in various ways, to Roxy Music and to David Bowie, was resilient enough to act as a focus, for the general public, of a whole range of cultural practices converging on rejection.

The punk aesthetic

Punk was a short-lived movement whose historical importance may prove to be very limited. None the less, it has attracted such a great deal of attention from cultural critics, largely because its profile was so strong and uncompromising, that it is necessary to ascertain the extent to which their assumptions about its musical conventions are valid. I shall argue throughout these next two sections that misconceptions abound and, indeed, that it was its experimentalism, rather than its anti-elitism, that was its most notable feature. Although we have as yet no detailed explanation of the pre-history of punk, I do not intend to attempt to explore its origins here. Until historians adequately address this question, Laing's account remains satisfactory (see Laing 1985: 1–27). Even a cursory reading of the popular press between 1976 and

1978 would have encouraged the view that punk had a unified musical programme.

'This is a chord. This is another. This is a third. *Now form a band*', instructed Mark Perry (*Sniffing Glue* 7, February 1977). The over-use of this quotation throughout the literature on punk clearly points to the belief that this formed the musical programme of punk, with its stress on mass participation, its re-assumption of unmediated expression (the notion that, having the basic, minimal materials, one can immediately move on to unencumbered self-expression) and its suspicion of ability: as Laing (1985: 62) notes, prior musical experience was of no apparent benefit in the early days of punk. Laing's extensive treatment of punk does indeed suggest that there are sufficient similarities to allow talk of a 'punk' style. However, dealing with the bands with which he spends most time, largely those whose material is still (or again) available more than a decade later, the differences between those content to exist under the punk banner seem almost as notable as their similarities. Accordingly, I shall bring out here both those common elements and those differences within what may be identified as first- and second-generation punk bands, moving in subsequent sections to consideration of the fall-out from punk. Although this may seem a little dismissive of punk itself, it should be recognised that the changes brought about by punk, particularly in the development of 'independent' labels, are still with us and of great importance.

Laing's discussion of the musical attributes of punk is useful: he points to the punk attitude to rhythm as one of the features marking out its sense of difference from other musics. Speaking of the even quaver static bass line (which was already familiar from early heavy metal, e.g. Black Sabbath's 'Paranoid', and to which I shall return below), he suggests:

> 'Holidays in the Sun' by the Sex Pistols begins with the sound of marching feet, a regular, repetitive, definitely unsyncopated sound. This is followed by the drums falling into the same rhythm. This rhythmic monad (1–1–1–1) [is] opposed to rock's conventional dyad (1–2–1–2, where the accent is on the second beat).
>
> (Laing 1985: 61)

I would question whether Laing's 'rhythmic monad'[7] is ever actually perceived as such. In discussing the perception of rhythm, Sloboda (1987: 47) notes that 'If a listener is presented with a set of equally spaced, equally loud notes of equal pitch . . . there is no way in which any rhythm may be said to be present.' This seems to be Laing's position in regard to rhythmic lines that appear without stressed notes. However, Davies (1980) reports research undertaken by Vos (1973) which suggests that, in the absence of other factors, a sequence of undifferentiated tones *will* be grouped by the listener: 'there . . . arose a perceived difference in the stimulus strength . . . where none existed in physical terms' (Davies 1980: 197). In other words, the available evidence suggests that listeners will necessarily impose a grouping.[8]

In the particular case of 'Holidays in the Sun', even undifferentiated marching sounds are likely to be perceived as made by a *pair* of feet. And, of

Example 4.1 Sex Pistols: 'Holidays in the Sun'

etc.

course, such beats (as they become drumbeats) do not occur in isolation, nor are they likely to be perceived as such. The lead guitar enters with a power chord sustained for eight beats and repeated. This is then shortened to four beats, the song's riff filling the next four, with both the first and last notes of this riff anticipating the beat (see example 4.1). At this point, the differentiation between first (bass drum quavers) and second (snare drum crotchet) beats is asserted. Laing's simple distinction between what he calls syncopated (i.e. accented on 2) and unsyncopated (i.e. accented on 1) seems to be the more useful, but even here the even bass quavers hardly *contradict* the standard kit pattern, instead acting *in counterpoint* to it.

The harmonic patterns of 'Holidays in the Sun' are by no means particular to punk, and here perhaps the notion of 'anyone can do it' can be accommodated to what is heard. Yet Johnny Rotten, while almost studied in his refusal to adopt a conventional vocality, none the less creates his own. Laing (1985: 58) has pointed this out with respect to his idiosyncratic pronunciation of 'Antichrist', to rhyme with 'kissed': his general pronunciation owes nothing to rock's hitherto conventionalized American voice (see Trudgill 1983). Moreover, although his pitches owe little to accepted notions of melody, his tracing of a clear pitch contour with his shouted syllables, and his articulatory use of vibrato, clearly defines a distinct vocality.

The Damned's 'New Rose' (1976) was the first widely known punk single, and here we find many elements common to other punk songs. The line-up is restricted to voice, Townshend-style rhythm guitar (i.e. with a touch of distortion, energetically strummed and with only the occasional move into a lead guitar phrase), bass and kit, each playing a minimum number of patterns. A simple alternation of verse and refrain yields to a central bridge with the faint sense of an arpeggiated solo. Each formal unit here consists of a simple boogie formula, all three formulae belonging in the same song solely on account of their proximity, rather than any similarity of contour or pattern. All patterns are grouped in units of four, matching the organization of the lyrics, which are typically declaimed, although less shouted than Johnny Rotten's. By 'Love Song' of 1979, the Damned's guitars have built a wall of sound, over which the vocals are sung rather than declaimed, although this distinction is of minimal import. That year's 'Smash It Up' (part 1) essayed a rather different style, with the staggered instrumental entrances, changes of texture and arpeggiated, undistorted guitar reminiscent of gentler times. The harmonic pattern is again standard, against which the aggression of 'Smash It Up' (part 2), complete with guitar solo, sounds pretty tame.

Their manic edge (with tongue in cheek), which always seems to be slightly

Example 4.2 'Glad All Over'

Dave Clark Five:

I—I will   say   (echo)

Rezillos:

I—I will   say—ay—ay

submerged, comes finally to the surface in 'There Ain't No Sanity Clause' of 1980. Indeed, the rather devil-may-care humour is an often overlooked aspect of punk. The Rezillos' 'Glad All Over', a vicious remake of the Dave Clark Five hit of 1964, taken at great speed, is one of the clearest examples. The original includes the line 'I–I will say (. . .)' (see example 4.2). The syllable 'I' is attacked a second time, and the syllable 'say' is allowed to echo in parallel. The Rezillos re-attack the 'ay', increasing slightly in volume, thereby pointing up the mannered production of the original (who said punk was incapable of subtlety?). The Damned's '. . . Sanity Clause', with its rather hackneyed ionian I–V–II–VI sequence underpinned by a ringing guitar hook, gives an overriding impression of almost breakneck speed. Yet the 'composition' that frequently bubbles up through even the most typical punk songs shows here, in the rather considered guitar solo (which follows the standard registral pattern outlined in Chapter 3) and the underplayed vocal countermelody of the refrain. As Laing insists, the 'incompetence' which was a prized ideological asset is not borne out by the recorded product, which is rather carefully constructed.

An equivalent style is present in the earlier work of Siouxsie and the Banshees. Regular groupings into units of four bars are ubiquitous, underpinned by sequences of four chords. The macabre lyrics are sometimes accompanied by harmonic juxtapositions unusual in rock, perhaps representing an attempt to reinforce their effect. 'The Staircase' uses the highly chromatic lydian $I^{\flat 3}$–$IV^{\sharp 5}$–VI–III, appearing as chords based on tonics of C, F♯, A and E. 'Playground Twist' moves through modes whose tonics share this same, though re-ordered, relationship, i.e. the aeolian modes based successively on A, C, E and F♯, before repeating the cycle. Instrumental textures tend to be standard. The guitar switches between three approaches, all fairly common throughout punk. The first, the high treble chords of 'Hong Kong Garden', and the second, the more conventional arpeggiated chords of 'Spellbound', both add clarity to textures. More dense is the third, the wall of sound created by repeated strumming. (Laing talks of this in terms of a 'buzzsaw drone', and both 'Playground Twist' and 'Spellbound' use it.) This texture, in its impenetrability, connotes at least menace, although its transference to the acoustic guitar on 'Spellbound' seems to modify this connotation. The kit patterns are based on the standard rock pattern, varying from the frenetic 'Love in a Void', with the snare playing on every beat, through to the minimal bass/snare work on 'Hong Kong Garden', where the strummed guitar replaces the even quaver hihat strand. The bass tends to stick to repeated notes, although with some rhythmic variety.

The band's most notable timbral feature was probably Siouxsie's characteristic voice. As with many punk singers, syllables tend to be shot out rather than coaxed out – clear melodies are essayed, even with a smattering of melismatic singing, but individual pitches tend to be separated rather than allowed to flow together. Her range is large, stretching from low alto on the introverted 'Christine' up to the shrill 'Love in a Void', where she is always on the edge of whoops and yelps. ('Playground Twist', with its child-like chanted vocals, acts as a fine summary of her vocal style.) The urgent edge that her voice achieves, particularly clearly on 'Mirage', is created by a very careful pitching of notes slightly flatter than tempered tuning.

In the view of Hatch and Millward (1987), punk, far from being revolutionary, merely crystallized many of the undercurrents already present in the playing of some rock bands. Foremost among these had been: the Velvet Underground, with their eschewal of virtuosity and their explicit coverage of taboo subjects (particularly drugs and sex); David Bowie, who had pioneered the return of the three minute single and explored the power inherent in conscious image construction; and pub rock, which had re-established a place for uncomplicated music in small venues (Hatch and Millward 1987: 160–6). Thus, they suggest that the inherent limitations of the basic punk aesthetic (lack of room for creativity, record company conservatism, limited range of subject matter and minimal chart success) meant that developments of the style were present from an early stage. Such stylistic options were fully apparent at least as early as 1979 (see below), and by the appearance of the Damned's *Phantasmagoria* (1985), their highest placed British chart album, the style had long since become defunct. Although this is no longer punk rock, the bass tempo and the vocal hook of their earlier songs remain on 'Street of Dreams', while the punchy bass tone is still that of the earlier style. This album is richer in its choice of instrumentation, from the use of a 'gothic' pipe organ on 'Sanctum Sanctorum', and big synthesized harpsichord on 'Grimly Fiendish' (a sort of inversion of George Harrison's 'Little Piggies'), to organ, echoed sax and even Spanish-style guitar and castanets on 'Street of Dreams'. This last track also employs textural changes, synthesizer arpeggios learnt from synthesizer rock and the stamp of considered composition in that the basic chord sequence (aeolian V–III–I) becomes transposed up a minor third. Grouping changes are also present, breaking the constant groups of four and allowing the music to breathe.

The Damned seemed to lose touch with their initial following at quite an early stage. Not so the dour Clash, who perhaps exemplify most clearly the sense of identification sought by some punks (as working class) with blacks, of which Hebdige (1985) speaks, through their utilization of a wide range of 'black' music referents (specifically jazz, soul and reggae). These appear particularly on their third and fourth albums (*London Calling* and *Sandinista!*). It is in this respect that they extend the limits of punk, most forcefully in the rhythmic arena. On these albums, they eschew the wall of guitar sound popular among other punk bands, even replacing it with arrangements drawn from styles outside rock. Aside from articulating a standard 1930s period chord sequence through a rock instrumentation (thereby creating a strange, dislocating effect), 'Jimmy Jazz' later brings in jazz-style horns. On *Sandinista!* particularly, Jamaican Mickey Dread's production is very strongly developed, although textures continue once established. James Brown-style horns are used on 'Ivan meets G.I. Joe' while 'Corner Soul', which resembles the Pogues in the raw vocality and use of accordion, is backed by gospel voices. 'Washington Bullets', which in its unfocused anti-USA stance perhaps stands as the album's focal track, makes use of Caribbean-style xylophone and pedal-steel guitar, presumably to evoke the Latin America that the song praises. Not only do black style-referents appear, but explicitly Jamaican techniques too: 'Guns of Brixton' (on *London Calling*) uses a slightly wooden reggae bass beat ('riddim') in conjunction with reggae tomtom drums, in anger at black persecution, while 'One More Time' (again reggae) re-appears as 'One More Dub', a conventional voiceless remix.

The concurrent display of both experiment and convention remains rather strange. Four-square groupings dominate, despite the presence of a twelve-bar blues, 'Brand New Cadillac' (*London Calling*), complete with Eddie Cochran-style guitar. These groupings are frequently totally open-ended alternations of just two chords. 'Magnificent Seven', with its funk bass line, is only the clearest example of this technique. 'Rebel Waltz' essays an eight-bar grouping closer to period structure, and here harmonies are derived not from block chords, but from contrapuntal lines created through multi-tracking and echo. Even here, although the texture is somewhat experimental, it remains un-changing. 'Something about England', perhaps the closest the Clash ever get to nostalgia (complete with synthesized pub piano), seems to strive for a looseness which is never achieved, largely due to the now constricting nature of the standard rock beat. A complete re-think of the same song, 'Mensforth Hill' consists largely of reverse tape segments overlaid with other studio effects. The mixture of external style referents and unorthodox rock pro-duction may not offer a great stylistic unity, but its particular emphasis on the studio does place *Sandinista!* within the larger framework of rock's continuing development.

For many, punk seemed to signify rejection, whether of the excesses of stadium rock bands or of the standards of polite behaviour. This rejection was frequently realized through musical technique in terms of what is usually analysed as *rule-breaking*, although I think it more helpful to think in terms of generating *friction* between a particular song and the conventions of a previously constituted style (I shall return to this in Chatper 5). Some in-stances can be found as early as 1979, while other examples continue to surface later.

The Slits were women musicians (as opposed to vocalists), who made a rare attempt to compete in what is still a male-oriented arena, and their music suggested a great deal of unfulfilled potential. *Cut* (1979) is notable primarily for the multiple influences of reggae. In terms of vocabulary, the word 'Babylon' (signifying 'materialism') is most notably used, on two occasions, to align the band with the Rastafarian antipathy towards consumer culture (this being a punk fixation): 'Shoplifting' is a paean of praise. In terms of rhythm and production values, a reggae aesthetic is utilized most strongly in the sense of the space that is permitted to surround sounds. This is largely because of the production by British reggae producer Dennis Bovell, notable for his work with Linton Kwesi Johnson.

Reggae is also invoked in their approach to volume and vocality. All the instruments tend towards a lightness and subtlety of touch missing from most of punk, even on 'Love und [*sic*] Romance', with its typical punk tempo. The kit is constantly high in the mix (in terms of loudness) and central in the sound-box, frequently superimposing a reggae hihat off-beat upon a standard rock beat. This lightness allows the intricacies of hihat playing not to be swamped, perhaps suggesting an anger clearly under control, and all the more cutting for that. The bass has a typical white reggae feel, i.e. playing on the beat (very few white bassists seem to capture the subtle syncopations of the best Jamaican players), while the strummed guitar tends to act as a rhythmic counterpoint to the kit, leaving a great deal of space. This effect is multiplied on a track like 'Newtown' by the use of a shaken box of matches, a dropped teaspoon, a struck match and odd piano sounds, all of which appear repeatedly and normally on one of the last two semiquavers of a group of four. The achieved effect is of sounds being dropped between the relatively constant rate of attacks of the kit, bass and voice, which is possibly encouraged by sequencer processing.

These songs have greater rhythmic variety than much of punk. A pattern of continuous semiquavers is implied throughout (where it is not actually played), enabling the Slits to play with this sense on both 'Ping Pong Affair'

and 'Adventures Close to Home', moving from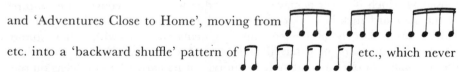

etc. into a 'backward shuffle' pattern of etc., which never

quite takes over. Although grouping patterns are normative, 'Adventures Close to Home' subverts them in a regular fashion. The verse groups 4 + 4, 4 + 4, 5 + 2 (the last coinciding with chord changes), moving into an instrumental section grouped 4 + 4, 4 + 4 + 4, and refrain 4 + 4, 6 + 6 + 2 (where the kit suggests that the voices' 6 + 6 be heard as 4 + 4 + 4).

'Instant Hit' demonstrates an interesting re-thinking of vocal patterns over verses that move from $\frac{5}{4}$ to $\frac{4}{4}$. Two vocal strands (one of which has two-part harmony) imitate each other at one bar's distance, each strand maintaining a two-bar unit, such that the call and (separate) response pattern of the refrain (and of so much rock) is altered here to allow the call and response to overlap to a high degree. This emphasizes a relationship that obtains throughout the album, in which the role of the 'backing' singers is really equivalent to that of the lead voice, a challenge to the apparent hierarchical interpersonal relations of so many rock bands. Much thought has gone into the construction of Arri Up's vocality – not only are some syllables emphasized particularly through tremolo and scream (a technique used throughout those parts of Africa where tonal languages are spoken), but the voice often subverts spoken stress patterns, frequently by declaiming the syllables at regular (e.g. crotchet) intervals, questioning their meaning. In 'Ping Pong Affair', this ably suggests through its distancing effect the subject's disgust with her 'boyfriend'.

With respect to harmony, open-ended patterns predominate, although they tend to be reconciled to conventional verse structures. Single modes tend to operate throughout songs, but frequently the guitar, bass and voice tend to go their independent ways within this mode, such that some unfamiliar coincidences result. However, because each part still makes sense on its own, the effect of such clashes is quite subtle.

The dim echo of reggae is also apparent on the Gang of Four's *Entertainment!* (1979) in their approach to textural space, particularly in the treatment of the guitar. Bass and kit work as normal, with the kit playing a regular pattern and the bass complementing this (all songs on the album are based on open-ended, implicit sequences), while the guitar, employing patterns strummed largely on the treble strings, tends to syncopate against their rhythm. The guitar uses sustain only minimally, thus making for a great deal of emptiness between attacks: the clearest examples of this are probably 'Ether' and 'At Home He's a Tourist'. In 'Contract' and 'Return the Gift', guitarist Andy Gill uses a heavily syncopated series of chords that do not particularly relate modally to the bass pattern, while both the tone and manner of articulation are strongly reminiscent of some of Robert Fripp's more experimental offerings (e.g. his solo in King Crimson's 'Sailor's Tale'). Throughout, the syncopation tends to

come from the use of $1\frac{1}{2}$-beat patterns within $\frac{4}{4}$ (i.e. [♪ ♩ ♪ ♩ ♫♩] or

[♪ ♩ ♪ ♩ ♩]), with a similar effect to the Slits' 'Ping Pong Affair'.

Textures do change somewhat within songs, usually for the equivalent of the break, a reinvention of the Townshend-length guitar solo, although with neither the histrionics nor any need to 'craft' such a solo in terms of registral layout. While the lyrics tend to a greater level of analysis than much of established punk, it may equally be their inventive attitude to texture that earned them the sobriquet 'thinking man's [*sic*] punk' (Clarke 1989: 449).

Public Image Ltd's *Flowers of Romance* extends the minimal aspects of punk, whereby textures tend to remain constant throughout a song. They refuse the listener immediate relief from expected temporal patterns, but construct these without strict reference to the conventions of instrumental function and structure. On this album, each song is underpinned by a different kit pattern, which may vary from the standard rock beat of 'Banging the Door' to the

busy, syncopated pattern (based on ♩. ♩. ♩) of 'Under the House' and the rare $\frac{3}{4}$ pattern of 'Phenagen'. Superimposed on the kit pattern are John Lydon's voice, frequently a bass guitar and a variety of studio sounds. These can range from the disconcerting (the samples on 'Under the House' and the title track, or the running piano clusters on 'Francis Massacre') to the 'conventional' harmonic use of guitar and (synthesized?) accordion and zither. Songs are not structurally adventurous, but they do eschew any notions of narrative or of refrain, the majority perhaps being best understood as consisting of just two freely extended verses. Lydon's voice, although closer to conventional rock singing than his work with the Sex Pistols, emphasizes the desolation of much of the lyrics through its very limited compass (often only three or four steps) and constantly repeating short phrases. The impression tends to be of a minimally coordinated group of individuals, unable to relate, an impression reinforced on 'Track 8' where, although bass, voice, keyboard and guitars all seem to start from the pitch G, they have clearly not agreed on the mode to follow. This comment is not intended as a criticism, for internal evidence suggests that such incoherence may have been the aim. As such, not only has it expressive value, it is exceedingly difficult to capture.

The Fall seem to have acquired the reputation of being one of the hardest post-punk bands to listen to, again presumably because of the unrelenting nature of their textures, which typically appear on *This Nation's Saving Grace* (1985). These are very reminiscent of the Velvet Underground, for example, The Fall's 'What you Need'. Again, the establishment of a basic kit pattern is fundamental, a pattern which then remains constant (and which, as on 'L.A.', is the standard rock beat). The voice is well hidden in the mix, exhibiting a near-spoken, quite offhand vocality, while its lyric details seem to be of little import – 'Gut of the Quantifier' essays a syntax so radical that the lyric seems to have no semantic quality. Although textures tend not to change, in line with the open-ended nature of sequences, most songs make use of two stretches of material, which themselves alternate, a pattern almost archetypal in its simplicity. 'Spoilt Victorian Child' typifies both these points, in its simple oscillation of aeolian $I-V^{\sharp 3}$ and alternation of two textures, each with its own characteristic speed. More subtle divergences from conventional techniques are also incorporated. 'I Am Damo Suzuki' utilizes two rhythmic strands that do not coincide – one for voice and kit, one for guitar and bass. There is perhaps an expectation that these strands will at some point synchronize, but this is not fulfilled. 'Bombast' consists of a simple four-bar unit repeated indefinitely, with kit fills to vary the pattern slightly. Conventionally the kit fills might precede, and thus lead to, the first beat of a unit, but here they appear almost at random.

I have suggested that the punk aesthetic enabled some bands to undertake somewhat radical musical experiments. In their questionable popularity and difficult nature, these have attracted connotations of elitism, which I think need to be resisted: there were many small-time, local post-punk bands who delighted in a similar approach (such as the Diagram Brothers in Preston, or the Very Things in Worcester),[9] and who attracted partisan local followings. Additionally, there were other nationally known bands who, without conforming explicitly to that aesthetic, were strongly influenced by its experimental approach.

The Flying Lizards were one such, achieving national chart success in 1979–80. Again, the establishment of a single kit pattern for each song is of primary importance, and helps initially to distinguish this 'experimentalism' from similar developments in progressive rock. Thereafter, *Flying Lizards* makes use of a great variety of overlaid timbres, from the tinny sounds of 'Money' through to distorted rock guitar ('The Flood'), shortwave and marching sounds ('Russia') and new age synthesizer ('Trouble'). The music's most telling aspect is perhaps the use of the voice, spoken in a matter-of-fact tone, keeping sufficiently close to the underlying rhythmic pattern to convey the illusion of speaking in time, but never succeeding throughout a whole line (such as on 'Summertime Blues', where by setting up a norm of speeding at the end of every line, it conveys a sense of weariness). The overall sense seems to be of a rather reckless humour reminiscent of the Rezillos, but more viciously done. Thus, the guitar solo on 'Money' is a skit on the virtuoso solo, the Brecht and Weill 'Mandelay Song' is taken exceedingly fast, while the trite lyrics of 'The Window' (with its barely threatening reference to the vampire outside) and the thin voice that seems to be unsure of its pitch refer almost to a teenybopper/innocent young girl genre. 'Russia' has less of the humour, its intentional incoherence vaguely conveying a sense of menace, but nothing more precise than that. The flavour of the punk aesthetic is unmistakable.

The music of the Slits, the Gang of Four, the Fall, PIL, the Flying Lizards and other less well known bands, far more radical and challenging now than punk, tends towards a somewhat different understanding of time sense. The largely open-ended sequences are no longer the tightly coordinated instrumental structures of progressive rock, nor the intensional structure of the blues, but are rather blueprints, over which a variety of other layers can be placed. Rather than each moment of music consisting of a series of related layers, conceived together (whether in the mind of the songwriter(s) or during the recording process), there is almost a sense in which the music consists of a separate series of layers, conceived separately and laid over a background of unchanging textures and an incessant kit pattern. It may help to think of this process as one of *design* rather than of *composition*. This sense of design remains unfocused at this point, but as we shall see with the rise of synthesizer rock (largely co-extensive with the later material discussed above), the introduction of the programmable drum machine and, later, the computer into the recording studio, 'design' is brought very much to the forefront. No longer can these post-punk styles be seen as *oppositional* to the mainstream in the same way that punk was when it first arose: all these bands propose, in their different ways, a *development* of some of punk's aesthetic positions.

The punk diaspora

There is perhaps one primary legacy of the punk movement to which subsequent rock styles are indebted. This legacy can best be described in terms of punk's great measure of self-reflectivity, a concern both with the processes of rock and with its own place in rock's stylistic history. The assumption that rock styles succeed each other in a linear fashion could no longer be supported, thus suggesting perhaps the most long-lasting way out of the impasse which existed at the end of progressive rock's dominance. By the late 1970s, a number of earlier (and frequently American) styles were in the midst of revival by young British musicians. Side by side could be found, among others:

> rock 'n' roll (the Straycats, Matchbox, the Polecats), the pop of the 1950s (Darts), 'mod music' (the Chords, Secret Affair...), soul of the mid-1960s (Dexy's Midnight Runners) and ska.
>
> (Chambers 1985: 194)

A related aspect was the recovery of the sort of subject matter originally associated primarily with the Kinks, but also with the Beatles and the Who, namely the apparent reporting of slices of English life, with either an ironic or a bleak interpretation. For the Kinks especially, such reports were delivered from a position of detachment from the songs' protagonists. In the wake of punk, such reports began to acquire overtones of involvement, and this aspect is common in the music that found some chart popularity, as exemplified by Madness, the Jam, Squeeze and Elvis Costello. I shall discuss the work of the first two of these here – Elvis Costello will receive attention in Chapter 5.

As with most engaging styles, Madness's roots were multi-faceted. While the piano gestures towards English pub piano style, and the saxophone is clearly reminiscent of the approach of Roxy Music's Andy Mackay, their most notable early feature was the use of rhythms fundamental to ska. This can be clearly heard on 'Close Escape' (1980), where the remnants of a standard rock beat (snare drum on second and fourth beats) are superimposed upon a ska beat – hihat, bass and piano on the second half of every beat. This is some way from standard Jamaican ska patterns, as found on Prince Buster's 'Al Capone' (Madness's first single was dedicated to Buster). There, only the piano plays the second half of every beat, the hihat playing even quavers, the bass drum playing on the backbeat (i.e. taking over the snare drum's rock role), while the bass plays on the beat as in rock. None the less, the typical ska pattern of the piano is clearly recognizable (it is still a minor part of their style as late as 1984's 'Prospects'). Just as reggae was subsequently to introduce over this pattern a very clear rhythmic sense partly characterized by extreme syncopation and even momentary silences at stressed points, Madness's 'Sunday Morning' of 1982 does similarly, most clearly marked by the bass

pattern .

Perhaps a more central feature of Madness's style is intimated in Dave Hill's comment that their 'basic comic yobbery was tainted by a ripple of unease' (Hill 1986: 39), an unease that can be traced back to specific musical techniques. In part, it seems due to Suggs MacPherson's voice, a voice with

Example 4.3 Madness: 'The March of the Gherkins'

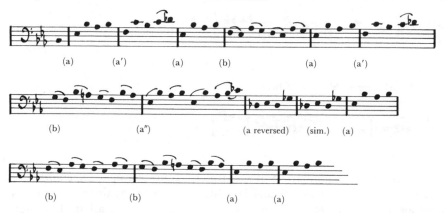

little tone and resonance, half-spoken although precisely at tempered pitch, with syllabic settings that suggest a highly regimented spoken rhythm, although less so than that of rap. However, it seems to be more because of the band's highly unusual harmonic language, which has two primary features.

The pace of harmonic movement tends to be fast – 'Calling Card' is not untypical in its speed of harmonic change, normally two harmonies per bar, although in this song interim harmonic changes parallel the melody very closely, a feature not used too widely elsewhere. On the small scale, harmonic patterns are highly diatonic. The early 'On the Beat Pete', with its dorian I–III–IV–V refrain, is not untypical, but similar patterns can be found throughout.[10] What is abnormal is the way that these patterns are then repeated at unexpected, if diatonic, levels, yielding a chromatic modality superficially secure yet none the less disturbing. The pattern of 'The March of the Gherkins' is schematically represented in example 4.3. Noteheads refer to harmonic roots, moving at the rate of one harmony per bar (two when joined by a brace). Thus, the diagram shows the ubiquitous groupings into a four-bar hypermetre. Two basic patterns are in evidence, marked (a) and (b). Variants of (a) are marked (a′) and (a″). Each of these patterns appears at two levels separated by a tone. However, with the exception of the Db towards the end of line 2 (this begins a third, non-recurring pattern, which is actually a slightly altered reversal of the pattern (a), although, of course, this relationship will not be perceived during the act of listening), all chords are major, and hence the chromatic modality. The words of the refrain, 'Catch me, I'm falling into my past,' with the incipient loss of footing that they suggest, seem to me the best possible summary of Madness's overall style. 'The Blue-skinned Beast', the harmonic roots of which are summarized in example 4.4, is even more highly chromatic (here, all chords are major with the exception of those on F♯ and B♭, which are minor).

The second aspect of their harmonic language carries the medium-scale chromaticism to a more local level, and is nowhere clearer than on 'Shadow of

Example 4.4 Madness: 'The Blue-skinned Beast'

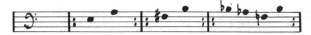

Example 4.5 Madness: 'Shadow of Fear'

Fear'. Example 4.5 summarizes the harmonic roots again – all chords are minor here, except those on D♭ and D, which are major. Again, all harmonies extend for one bar, except those with braces, which last half a bar. This high degree of chromaticism is the direct result of block harmonies, seemingly conceived without reference to a modal centre. Because this procedure is highly unusual in rock, and because it is superimposed on standard textural and structural norms, it gives the music the strong sense of unease identified by Hill (1986).

In other respects, Madness were content to plough a familiar furrow. Thus, the alternation between verse, refrain and bridge (frequently minus lyrics) is normative (as in 'The March of the Gherkins'), and helps to disguise the near-experimental harmonic language. Texturally, as befits their 'local lad' image, the music does not often parade its production values, giving the illusion that it was arranged in a conventional sense rather than multi-tracked. The only occasions where this is less so are the instrumental interludes, where timbres seem to converse from divergent points in the sound-box. The 'unproduced' illusion is partly the result of rhythmic interlocking (thus the voice and the piano's treble register often engage in call and response sequences), and is partly due to the lack of reverb, delay and other studio effects. Even guitar sustain is used only minimally.

The music of the Jam is characterized by explicit, coherent but frequently angry commentary on English life, combined with certain stylistic traits clearly trawled from diverse 1960s popular musics. Initially seen as players of punk rock, they benefited from the coining of the term 'new wave' in that this released them from the negative associations of punk. The link with punk seems in retrospect a little strained. Their music may have shared the highly energized approach of the Clash and the Damned, the belligerent vocal delivery of early songs like 'In the City' and the humourless deriding of 'Mr Clean' may have marked them out, but their overt musicality and debt to both beat and 'commercial' 1960s soul perhaps indicate a truer identity.

This debt to styles from the 'golden age' of pop takes a number of forms. As already suggested, the links with the 'reporting' genre are made explicit in their version of 'David Watts' (by the Kinks's Ray Davies), where the evident envy expressed in the lyrics is more than tinged with disgust, emphasized by

Example 4.6 (a) Cliff Richard: 'In the Country'; (b) Cuff-Links: 'Tracy'; (c) The Jam: 'David Watts'

the crashing snare on every beat, replacing a normal kit pattern. The links, however, go further. The vocal 'pa pa pa pa' introduction to the verse recalls a variety of 1960s styles, particularly those represented in Cliff Richard's 'In the Country' and the Cuff Links's 'Tracy', to which it has great affinity – compare the contour of example 4.6(c) with that of the last two bars of example 4.6(b). All three songs employ analogous vocal passages, and all markedly anticipate the downbeat. The chord sequence underlying the verse of 'Tracy', ionian I–III–IV–V, will also be an important source for the Jam.

Their instrumental line-up (the 'power trio' of guitar, bass and drums) owes less to Cream, Led Zeppelin and ultimately heavy metal than it does to the Who and, to a lesser extent, Jimi Hendrix. Paul Weller retains a liking for some of Hendrix's guitar flourishes and controlled feedback, although he is not prone to Hendrix's occasional self-indulgence. In this, the link to the Who is stronger, perhaps intended as a device to strengthen the 'mod' image and attitude Weller fostered. Examples of this abound.[11]

As Weller's writing experience developed (he contributed more than 90 per cent of the Jam's material), so his stylistic referents changed, and these ultimately produce the contradictions that become such a resonant feature of his work. Although chord sequences common to mid-1960s soul are found in the Jam's early songs,[12] they come more to the fore after about 1980, in conjunction with a growing awareness of the textural possibilities afforded by such a style. In 'Strange Town', for example, the characteristic 'Stand by Me' changes (ionian I–VI–IV–V) sit very uneasily astride the apparent anger of the song's subject, who is lost in London with no one willing to share time with him. 'Going Underground' exemplifies the same thing. Here, the sequence is the ionian I–III–IV–V noted above, to which is set a lyric redolent of punk – the notion of an active 'underground' alternative to the complacency of conventional society.

At around this time, the established instrumental line-up also expands. 'Eton Rifles' employs an electronic organ perhaps reminiscent of Traffic's Stevie Winwood; by 1982, this has mutated into a full soul line-up. This can be heard on 'Absolute Beginners', with its punchy opening trumpet riff, and more particularly on songs on *The Gift*. 'A Town called Malice' again sets lyrics that depict working-class despair against an arrangement and harmonic syntax typical of late 1960s soul. On 'Precious', the transition has become complete, as guitar wah-wah riffs and James Brown-style grunts overlay a full-blown post-Motown instrumental line-up. The distance from here to the Style Council's 'Walls Come Tumbling Down' is but a short step.

There is a deep contradiction between lyrics that speak of despair, anger and action, set against music that connotes, for perhaps the majority of Weller's listeners, the pleasures of dancing and care-lessness. (Even original soul lyrics express less anger than accommodation: see Haralambos 1974.) In addition, the strange rhythmic groupings and comparative freedom from regular verse/refrain structures that appear throughout much of the early material, and that may have been an attempt to symbolize the *disruption* either visited upon or in the hands of the working class, give way to regular groupings and structures with sub-soul attempts at lively syncopation. But the thread of contradiction throughout Weller's writing (for it is strikingly present throughout his work with the Style Council) is so consistent that it cannot be easily dismissed. Either it betokens a lack of technique and a degree of insensitivity to musical effect which is hard to accept, or in turn it must be seen as a sign of something deeper, perhaps a symbol of the bourgeois appropriation and emasculation of working-class means of expression, or even an attempt to signal that such contradictions have no import, that styles have no meaning, and are therefore wholly autonomous.

Punk itself may have been spent as a musical and cultural force by 1980, but its repercussions continue: certain of its stylistic traits have become established rock techniques, aside from the legitimation undergone by the style itself. Indeed, it seems that two extremes are present through much of the following decade, and I shall briefly sketch these here.

The first may be represented by Echo and the Bunnymen. Their reliance on setting up a single, dense texture that reigns throughout each song clearly derives from punk. Two tracks from *Porcupine* illustrate the variety that is still possible within this programme: 'Gods will be Gods' allows subtle changes of instrumentation without varying the overall texture, while 'Higher Hell' introduces instruments successively, finally achieving the full texture at the beginning of the refrain. The perennial four-bar units, frequently based on open-ended alternations of two chords, and the constant kit and bass patterns are also indebted to punk, although the use of heavy reverb, the tendency towards emphasis on bass frequencies and hence the great 'presence' (which can be found across the spectrum from the Smiths to the Mission) perhaps represents a refinement of the punk 'wall of guitar' sound.

The other extreme is perhaps best represented in the work of XTC, with their emphasis on pastiche, overt in their guise as the Dukes of Stratosphear,[13] less so in their Beatles recollections on *Skylarking*. '1000 Umbrellas' strongly recalls various textures, harmonic sequences and melodic contours of the *White Album*, while 'Earn Enough for Us' and 'Big Day' both recall 'Rain'. This leads to a concern with textural contrast, frequently focusing on a great openness of texture (e.g. 'The Meeting Place'), which may mean that the kit is absent, and with textures in which treble frequencies tend to dominate.

Although four-bar units are the norm here too, periodic structures (as in 'Sacrificial Bonfire') are at least as prevalent as open-ended ones.

Throughout this discussion both of punk bands, and of those who developed in the immediate wake of the changes brought about by punk, I have high-lighted the sense of stylistic experimentalism which is widely found. The details of these experiments, however, are very different from the fusions of styles which formed the progressive rock programme: the standard rock beat predominates, while formal and harmonic structures have not been affected by the conventions of jazz, nor those of concert music. There is also very little recourse to fantastic imagery. It may therefore be assumed that the excesses epitomized by Yes, Genesis and similar bands, and which were rejected not only by punk, but also by many of those progressive musicians themselves (in Chapter 5, I shall discuss this in detail by comparing Genesis' *Foxtrot* and *Invisible Touch*) had been firmly removed from the face of rock. This is not actually the case: although self-styled 'prog' bands declined, they have re-mained present in an 'underground' movement (Twelfth Night and Pendragon, both formed in 1978, and Galahad, formed in 1985, are among the most lauded) now covered by heavy metal magazines. Only one of these bands, Marillion, have attracted a wider following, and I shall focus on them in determining the extent to which 'progressive' values, shorn of 'hippie' ideals, remain strong.

Beyond progressive rock

As a journalistic category at least, progressive rock is not dead. Writing in his recent biography of Kate Bush, Kerry Juby suggests that *The Dreaming* was indeed a 'progressive' album, citing fans' apparent belief that 'the songs *need* explanation' (Juby 1988: 107). His implicit suggestion that 'progressive rock' is a generally available *approach* rather than a historically circumscribed *movement* is perhaps too broad to be of great help: a discussion of the music of Marillion and Asia will be instructive. The comparison will also suggest that, although the influence of punk is not restricted to rock *styles* that have arisen in its wake, it does appear to be restricted largely to *musicians* who were not widely active before the late 1970s.

Marillion's name is an intentional corruption of Tolkien's 'Silmarillion', a choice that clearly signalled their desire to appropriate the 'fantastic' attitude outlined at the end of Chapter 3. Right from their formation in 1979, they were regarded as the 'new Genesis', and the apparent influence borders on mimicry. Fish's costumes, make-up and voice recalled those of Peter Gabriel, the artwork on their album sleeves was similarly obscure, although rich with overtones of fantasy, and individual songs had a tendency to lengthiness and the sort of complexity of Genesis's Gabriel-led albums. Thus, after the punk explosion, they were regarded as heralding a return to the progressive era.

In *Script for a Jester's Tear*, they appropriate a number of techniques intrinsic to Genesis's earlier style: the keyboard has a tendency to simple repetition of arpeggios in lieu of constructing lines, particularly on the opening to the title song and on 'Garden Party'. Songs like 'The Web' contain separate musical ideas, in this case two, which alternate throughout the song. On the title track, these ideas appear sequentially, such that the first half falls into a simple aeolian I–VI alternation, while the second part, which is musically entirely separate, uses a mixolydian VI–VII–V–I progression. On the other hand, 'He Knows You Know' uses only a single sequence to underlie some eight minutes. A further technique shared with Genesis is the hiding of the guitar within the texture, highlighting it only rarely, and then with unremarkable solos. There is, however, a notable difference in style: once a pattern and texture have been set up, Marillion are content to continue them without variation, fitting the words to the music rather than giving the illusion of their having been invented together. Thus, the music is full of precise, rather than varied, repetition. It seems to me that they have learnt from punk, where this technique is almost ubiquitous, and have to a degree *reconciled* fundamental elements of that style with some aspects of progressive rock, particularly in their penchant for extended songs and obscure lyrics.

Although lacking these two elements, the techniques employed by Asia seem to have greater congruence with those of progressive rock. Formed from members of progressive bands (Geoff Downes and Steve Howe from later incarnations of Yes, John Wetton from King Crimson and others, Carl Palmer from Emerson, Lake and Palmer), Asia were clearly uninterested in pursuing the lengthy song structures that had been the practices of their previous bands, but these practices inform their collective work.

Their first album contains nine songs: two of them were reasonably successful singles. None of the songs is much over five minutes, and not only in this area have they altered earlier practices. The standard rock beat predominates, although Palmer is constantly introducing variations that complement Steve Howe's guitar work far more evenly than they ever did Keith Emerson's displays. Standard verse/refrain structures also predominate, with regular metric groupings, hook refrains and interesting, but standard, harmonic sequences. The real difference between Asia's and Marillion's approaches lies in the fact that for Asia, within this standard outline, nothing stays the same for long.

'Sole Survivor' stands out in this respect. Formally, it consists of an introduction, two verses/refrains, bridge, verse and final refrain to fade-out. The introduction remains metrically uncertain, due to the syncopation, as $\frac{4}{4}$ bars are extended by one or three beats (example 4.7 gives an outline of the kit pattern here). Each verse consists of a four-bar aeolian VI–VII–I$^{\#3}$ sequence repeated three times, closing with IV–V–VI, leading into the refrain, which constantly alternates I–IV. Each line of the verse is, however, articulated differently: over a constant bass/kit pattern, the guitar invents a secondary melody under the second line, while the keyboard does likewise for the third, this linking into the verse's cadential line. Again, the guitar adds a solo melody under the refrain, rather than filling it out with a riff or simple chords. The bridge then slims down the texture considerably (it has hitherto been a

Example 4.7 Asia: 'Sole Survivor'

thoroughly conventional mix for bass, kit, organ, guitar, lead and harmony voices), building from a point of relaxation with layered keyboard strands to a return of the introductory riff and so with full force into the final verse. Thus, what is on the surface a very ordinary song is enlivened by attention to detail, a degree of detail learnt from time with bands like Yes, Genesis and King Crimson.

The remnants of progressive rock found in the music of Asia are normally hidden from critical gaze: they were considered an AOR band, perhaps as Britain's answer to the countless 'faceless' bands of American rock (Kansas, Toto and REO Speedwagon, for instance). According to Barnes (1990), adult-oriented rock (as an American radio programming format) grew out of American 'progressive rock', and tends to consist of 'white', 'safe' rock, with something of an emphasis on playing music from the 'golden age' (about 1967–75). Thus, music that seems to continue in a similar style will attract the term as a style label. One problem is, however, that 'progressive rock' is itself constituted from a variety of styles (as explored in Chapter 3). A second problem arises from importing an American formatting term to a British context, where formats do not operate in the same way. Music considered 'AOR' will be found amidst other album- and live-oriented rock styles on (national) Radio 1 (Tommy Vance and Alan Freeman in particular have stayed with this music), while the 'classic' stations (the other format particularly relevant to rock), such as Capital Radio's 'Capital Gold', rely almost exclusively on singles material. As a result, it seems to me unhelpful to use 'AOR' as a style label in its own right, particularly for British rock, where it has in any case been sparingly applied.

Hard rock and heavy metal

Stylistic echoes of both progressive and punk styles come together in what Chambers has identified as 'the true centre or "mainstream" of recent rock culture' (Chambers 1985: 124). If this is so (and it partly depends on whether one places this centre in the stadium or the club, in the USA or the UK), then it is clearly valuable to attempt more than a crude definition of what the style entails. Chambers uses the single, all-inclusive term 'heavy metal', but I would suggest that this over-minimizes the differences of style that can be found. I think it worthwhile to attempt to distinguish between heavy metal (and its offshoots) and what, twenty years ago, was called 'hard rock'. For Ken Tucker, each new generation of headbangers is accompanied by a new generation of bands. Thus, Deep Purple are replaced by Black Sabbath, replaced in turn by Ozzy Osbourne and then Metallica, while even Led Zeppelin are charged with having codified heavy metal's basic formula, which consists of blues chords, high register vocals and lyrics combining mysticism, sexism and hostility (Ward *et al.* 1987: 485). This represents an uncritical and not particularly accurate view of a style few non-partisan writers seem to take seriously.

What follows results from the detailed analysis of a variety of British bands and artists commonly grouped in this way: Black Sabbath, Deep Purple, Def Leppard, Magnum, Gary Moore, Motorhead, Nazareth, Saxon, UFO, Uriah Heep and Whitesnake, together with less detailed work on bands and artists as different as Anthrax, Exodus, Robert Plant, Judas Priest and Iron Maiden, and various bands from the USA (Metallica, Boston, Heart, Bon Jovi and others). I would propose initially that the labels 'hard rock' and 'heavy metal' be thought of as points on a style continuum. Some bands cannot be exclusively categorized, but there are many features that clearly differentiate bands along this continuum from those outside it.

Taking all the bands commonly lumped together under the heavy metal/ hard rock label, whether original (early 1970s), new wave (early 1980s) or more recent still, the first factor that serves to identify them is structure. Contrary to the view of Tucker and others, blues chords and the twelve-bar structure are increasingly rarely encountered.[14] UFO's *Phenomenon* (1974) may utilize a standard twelve-bar structure on 'Built for Comfort', but such a structure would be entirely out of place on Saxon's *The Power and the Glory* (1983) or Magnum's *Wings of Heaven* (1988), to choose two bands at either end of the continuum. (One exception to this comment is provided by Whitesnake, who consistently have recourse to blues structures and explicit lyrical reference to the 'blues', even when this is accompanied by other structures.)

The second factor concerns speed. Songs tend to use one of three distinct speeds: about 80, 120 and 160 beats per minute, with a leeway of about 15 per cent on these figures (the speeds might be labelled 'laid back', 'up-tempo' and 'frenetic').[15] The former tends to be used primarily for sentimental love songs (what have become known as 'ballads'), which are rare at the heavy metal end of the continuum. Frenetic speeds may seem to have developed from punk (where this speed is common), especially in thrash metal from Motorhead on, where an aesthetic of rejection of established social standards is frequently explicit. Yet it should be noted that Nazareth's 'Razzamanazz', a 'hard rock' song in other respects, used this speed as early as 1973.

Associated with these differences of speed are two broad manners of guitar articulation. The first is the generally delicate arpeggiation of harmonies, without effects pedals, which is used at 'laid back' tempi; the second is the use of power chords, normally combined with distortion (from a fuzz box pedal), which underpins faster tempi. In heavy metal, this frequently takes a characteristic form of alternation between power chord and repeatedly plucked bass

Example 4.8 Metallica: 'Harvester of Sorrow'

Guitar

string. Example 4.8 illustrates one such riff from Metallica's 'Harvester of Sorrow'.[16] These two manners of articulation will frequently appear in the same song, where the delicate opening may function as preparation for the attack of the song proper, as in Gary Moore's 'Victims of the Future'.

The third factor is that of instrumentation and associated texture: here a clearer difference between heavy metal and hard rock can be observed. Heavy metal tends to be firmly based on the power trio of guitar, bass and drums, frequently with the addition of a second guitar. Hard rock tends to add to this an organ or synthesizer, allowing not only timbral variety in the interplay between the two (such as that indulged in by Deep Purple's Jon Lord and Ritchie Blackmore), but also the creation of atmospheric 'settings' with long, held, frequently high register keyboard chords. Both hard rock and heavy metal tend towards a density of texture, generated by the hard rock keyboards and by heavy metal's tendency towards greater use of guitar distortion.

A fourth factor concerns the voice and subject matter. There seems to be a general distinction between the madness/violence/occult leanings of heavy metal and the less extreme macho posing/love songs that hard rock has inherited from popular song in general. Hard rock is further distinguished by its high male[17] voice, highly resonant and with ubiquitous vibrato on long notes. Refrains tend to be marked by the addition of high backing voices in parallel harmony. Heavy metal seems to be less concerned with vocal theatrics, polished tone and harmony voices, although the variety existing between the singing of Saxon's Biff Byford and the near-punk vocality of Metallica's James Hetfield prevents any more concrete generalization.

Finally, formal predictability at both ends of the continuum is high. Verses frequently consist of two strains, the first of which may be based on a drone (this likelihood is higher with heavy metal), while the second is more likely to use a definable chord sequence, acting as a transition to the refrain.[18] The first of these strains will frequently consist of a four-bar metrical group repeated once. Hard rock refrains will tend to use a common four-chord sequence, and are more likely to act as a 'hook' than are verses. Period structures seem to be foreign to these styles.[19] Guitar solos are found in most songs: hard rock solos tend to be based on conventional box positions and will often be highly virtuosic in their execution; heavy metal solos may be less concerned with speed and more with distortion. In hard rock, these solos tend to grow out of the material the guitar is already playing (as throughout Gary Moore's *Victims of the Future*), while the heavy metal solo is more likely to arrive as if from nowhere. With the recent rise of new (largely American) 'guitar heroes', such as Yngwie Malmsteen, Steve Vai and Joe Satriani, we seem to move into yet another category. Notwithstanding Vai's highly inventive recent work with Whitesnake, critical opinion tends to suggest that the programme of such guitarists clearly distinguishes them from Clapton and Hendrix. This programme is frequently dismissed as empty virtuosity, and it is perhaps no coincidence that Yngwie Malmsteen's technical figurations (judging by his *Rising Force*) seem so reminiscent of those of the nineteenth-century violin virtuoso Paganini, whose work was similarly dismissed.

Taking all these factors into account, although there are points of similarity between hard rock and heavy metal, my impression is that heavy metal is perhaps the most formulaic of rock styles (and hence, the rock style that permits the subtlest play of significances[20]). A brief comparison of Black Sabbath's *Paranoid* of 1971 with Motorhead's *Overkill* of 1979 will suggest how these factors come together in practice. Both these albums are identified as heavy metal, and many of their features are foreign to hard rock. On *Paranoid*, the bass is comparatively immobile in terms of pitch throughout, frequently playing on every quaver. The kit relies heavily on the use of ride cymbal, the guitar chords have heavy sustain, while the voice tends to stick to a single melodic phrase that is repeated four (or more) times for each verse. Riffs are the norm, either melodic riffs over a drone or short 'power chord' riffs almost always lasting for two bars. Structures remain close to the 'introduction, two verses, break, verse, play out' formula common to pop since the beat era. The standard rock beat is evident throughout, while phrase endings often

syncopate ｜ ♩ ♩ ♩ ♩ ｜ as ｜ ♩. ♩. ♩ ｜. The voice is pitched

high, without resonance, but with a strong preference for tempered pitch. Structures are truly 'open-ended' – there are no examples of period structures. Some eight years later, Motorhead's *Overkill*, although heralded as the first of a new breed of 'thrash metal' really differs only in its speed. Here, 'Limb from Limb' can be analysed as a twelve-bar blues, but it does not use the standard 'blues chords' as Ward *et al.* (1987) suggest. The structural pattern, which is clearest on the verse of 'Stay Clean' (eight bars of riff based on I, four bars based on V, four bars based on I), can be regarded as normative. All the other comments made in respect of *Paranoid* apply equally here.

Hard rock, being less formulaic, cannot be summarised in quite this way. A comparison of Deep Purple's *In Rock* with, say, Robert Plant's *Now and Zen* reveals that their similarities of style need to be discussed separately in terms of the factors enumerated above.

Thus, although the normative uses (headbanging?) and forums (stadia) for the styles of hard rock and heavy metal may overlap almost entirely, it seems to me valuable to acknowledge the differences between them. On the one hand, this enables the clarification of styles of 'thrash metal', which clearly derive from heavy metal rather than hard rock. The constant semiquaver plucking (see example 4.8) that became a basic feature of thrash guitar in the wake of Iron Maiden's *Killers* of 1980, is not found among hard rock guitarists. Likewise, the lengthy structures of Metallica, which consist of a series of (melodically unrelated) riffs, are far distant from the chord sequences of hard rock refrains.[21] On the other hand, this clarifies the influence of hard rock on bands as varied as James and Jesus Jones, whose styles seems to have nothing in common with heavy metal. Jesus Jones appear to combine standard verse/ refrain structures and kit patterns that are derived (ultimately) from James Brown's 'Funky drummer'[22] with hard rock guitar. Guitar solos, although infrequent, tend to use the speed and tone reminiscent of players like Gary Moore, while some songs are underpinned by power chord riffs.[23] James employ similar structures and kit patterns, while verses and refrains often use the same chord sequence. 'Government Walls' uses both the delicate plucked introduction leading to power chord 'song proper', and also the guitar solo growing from its riff that I have identified above for hard rock. The voice, however, has a studied ordinariness lacking in range and resonance, and would sound very empty in a hard rock context. Indeed, these bands exhibit no more than the influence of that style.

Even this cursory survey would suggest that the single label 'heavy metal' is inadequate with respect to style. If Chambers's placing of this music in the mainstream of rock culture is correct, there are both room and cause for a great deal of research. Two particular questions would seem worthy of further exploration. Firstly, to what extent do the subtle differences between different brands of 'metal' (about which fanatics make great play) equate to differences of musical style; and secondly, to what extent are such differences accompanied by similar differences in the use to which the music is put, and hence its significance for the styles' respective audiences?

Synthesizer rock

By the early 1980s, the 'mainstream' of rock culture had seemed to be flowing not with guitars, but with synthesizers. Indeed, the late 1970s saw two seemingly opposed developments in rock which have proved to have long-lasting consequences, and against which the continuity apparent within hard rock and heavy metal styles stands out. The first of these developments was the apparent renegotiation of the relationship between artists, their material and their producers undertaken by punk musicians, a renegotiation that emphasized a return to simplicity in many spheres. The second was the wholesale adoption of new technology, represented initially by the synthesizer, which apparently opened the doors to a whole new range of complexity. The synthesizer was not merely another electronic instrument with its own specific characteristics, like the Hammond organ or Fender guitar (although it began by being used as if it were), but held the promise of a hitherto unheard of control over timbral resources.

Viewed against a historical perspective, the synthesizer is not a particularly new instrument. As long ago as 1897, the American Thaddeus Cahill patented the first electronic instrument, which he called the *sounding staves*, while 1923 saw the first appearance of Theremin's *theremin*, on which sound was produced and changed by the proximity of the hand to an aerial, rather than through a keyboard. One of the most interesting features of synthesizers in general is their potential freedom from the restrictions of tempered pitch, a potential largely unrealized in rock, with its slavish adherence to the familiar tempered scale. The first oscillator-based synthesizer was constructed in France by Givelet and Couplex in 1929, although it was not until 1964 that Robert Moog's technical advances enabled the synthesizer to become usable for performance in real time (see Mackay 1981). Until the early 1970s, all synthesizers were monophonic, thereby dictating their use as soloing instruments, encouraging players such as Keith Emerson and Rick Wakeman to employ them as exotic additions to the conventional keyboard arsenal.

By the late 1970s, polyphonic keyboard synthesizers had become available, making the instrument almost as versatile as other keyboard instruments. Of the factors that contributed to synthesizers' success, the desires to appear 'hi-tech', to build on a new base in the aftermath of punk and to retreat from that style's aggressive confrontation seem most noteworthy. Not only was the synthesizer a static instrument as opposed to the guitar, which could literally be wielded, but the sounds used lacked the force of attack of the plectrum on the guitar string. Although the synthesizer itself did not demand a change of dominant style, it became associated with one, thereby bringing with it a fundamental problem.

Gary Numan was one of the pioneers of what constituted 'synthesizer rock': both 'Are Friends Electric?' (with Tubeway Army) and his own 'Cars' exemplify the style clearly (and it represents a style, rather than just the addition of a particularly notable instrument). Both exude bleakness, an impression matched by Numan's pale demeanour and static pose. The bleakness is largely achieved through the intense minimalism of the music: 'Are Friends Electric?' interchanges three short ideas, effectively riff-equivalents but not used as the basis for any extension. Bass, kit and fuzz guitar are clearly present, and the voice has a very dead-pan delivery. The synthesizer timbre is very clean and totally lacking in distortion, a characteristic common to much of the style. Most importantly, however, the pitch material does not have a pentatonic basis, setting it clearly apart from styles of rock that consciously owe their origins to rhythm 'n' blues. 'Cars' has dispensed with the guitar, and represents a further textural simplification as the upper synthesizer line is in rhythmic unison with the kit. This 'minimalist' technique, the result of bare, uncomplicated textures and brief, repeated ideas, results in a degree of innovation within rock: the term is not one of approbation.

Synthesizers also form the basis of the work of Orchestral Manoeuvres in the Dark (OMD): in their case, the Emulator, an instrument that enables the precise synthesis of sounds normally produced by conventional instruments and ensembles of instruments. (Contrary to received opinion, until the recent generation of digital machines and samplers, synthesizers were notoriously poor at mimicking most musical instruments, whose sound-shapes were far too complex for them. The piano proved most difficult of all.) The development of the Emulator and equivalent instruments has been a matter of great concern to many established players of conventional instruments, since it is perceived as depriving them of something of their livelihood. Such concerns go back at least as far as the Moody Blues' conversion to the mellotron (not a synthesizer, but essentially a keyboard attached to banks of pre-recorded tapes) as an alternative to taking an orchestra on tour. OMD, however, tend less to mimic established timbres than to create new, smooth ones (i.e. timbres with uncomplicated wave-forms), which they combined with a minimal approach similar to that adopted by Gay Numan. 'Electricity' employs a four-chord pattern, repeated throughout without variation, and brought about through three distinct synthesizer lines. 'Enola Gay' has the same structural features, with just one synthesizer 'tune'. The same can be said of later singles: both 'Souvenir' and 'Maid of Orleans' employ equally simple melodies (in the latter song, setting up a strong sense of irony against the anguish of the lyrics), over a drum machine and a synthesized bass totally lacking in attack qualities (the percussive edge of the original 'unsynthesized' instruments).

On the Human League's *Dare* (1981), every sound other than that of the voices was synthesized. It marked the marriage of synthesizer rock with the contemporary phase of disco, but it carries the style's minimalism even further. The rate of harmonic movement remains constant throughout the album, over what is still just the standard rock beat. The bass part no longer develops its own melodic line, playing only the root note of each chord, an approach perhaps inherited from punk. These chords are normally simple close-position synthesizer triads: they thus cover a far smaller pitch-range than would be the case were they on guitar, and the sound is thinner and the register higher than guitar chords would be. Thus, there is a clear textural hole beneath them, which is well exploited on 'The Things that Dreams Are Made of', where it reinforces the clinical regularity of the drum machine and general flatness of the mix, to which little reverb has been added. Forms are simple, too, often just consisting of verse and refrain, each built of harmonic sequences of two or four chords, with an introduction bringing in timbres one at a time, 'layering' these and perhaps producing a sense of expectation of the song proper. Although this is an established technique, it is used exhaustively here. On occasion, chordal structures are even more minimal: the basic pattern of 'Seconds', for example, combines triads (three-note chords) with dyads (two-note chords); see example 4.9.

Overall, most examples of this style use the following elements: a standard rock beat in the region of 120 beats per minute; textures consisting of syn-

Example 4.9 Human League: 'Seconds'

thesizer melody line, plus chords, plus voice, plus kit and bass, with clean timbres; harmonic patterns of four chords; vocal melodies of precisely repeated phrases, often further back in the mix than with other styles, and with a studied, deadpan delivery. An exception to this norm is provided by the Eurythmics, who introduce a great deal of variety into almost every one of these domains. In so doing, they exemplify a problem, explicitly concerned with the use of the synthesizer, which in spite of being frequently only implicit, is fairly prominent. In order to pursue this, I shall need to consider timbre as a separate musical domain.

Timbre and its gestural qualities

In discussions of European concert music, the timbre of a sound is represented by the instrument that plays it; in discussions of avant-garde electronic music,[24] it is represented (if at all) by its wave-form. In much music it is taken for granted, as a 'given', despite the fact that most players are concerned to acquire a particular distinctive tone, which will frequently be described in terms of its position on a continuum running from 'pure' at one extreme to 'dirty' at the other. John Shepherd (1987b: 158, 163) flies in the face of contemporary musicology by suggesting that timbre is almost the primary domain. Although I cannot agree – one of the greatest problems besetting contemporary musicology (and contemporary music) is the belief that any particular domain has priority, a problem I have endeavoured to circumvent in Chapter 2 and all my subsequent discussions of styles – Shepherd's emphasis is welcome, for particularly in music where the construction of timbres becomes subject to precise, conscious control, via synthesizers, timbral qualities can no longer be taken for granted.

Put simply, the problem encountered in consideration of the effect of any 'electronic' music is that of alienation, which is dramatized by a consideration of the differences between the characteristics shared by 'acoustic' instruments (which here can be stretched to include electrically driven analogues of the fretted and keyboard instruments, e.g. the electric guitar and organ) and purely electronic sound sources (particularly wave-form oscillators). Positions of listeners with respect to the gestural constituents of music are pretty complex, and rarely the subject of theory.[25] What follows must therefore be regarded as somewhat provisional.

All so-called 'acoustic'[26] instruments produce sound when a human body sets something in motion, whether a string (e.g. on a guitar), a column of air (e.g. on a saxophone) or a membrane (e.g. on a drum). Listeners will almost certainly have encountered this process, at some stage, on a visual level, and many will have experienced it at a physical level too. Listeners can therefore imagine what it must be like to be in physical control of the production of the sound. 'Air' guitarists (those who mime to guitar solos and riffs) rehearse this control as an almost irresistible physical response, but these gestures need not be those of control, they can be those of response: music produced by acoustic instruments may seem to call out human gestures. Thus, the 'rise and fall' of a sung melody is produced by a tensing and subsequent relaxing of the vocal cords, while a gradually rising guitar line requires an increasing constriction of the body, as the left elbow reaches the left side, and the left hand approaches the right. Some would follow Susanne Langer (1942) here in suggesting that these 'gestural' qualities can be felt in some way analogous to events in listeners' private mental and physical worlds. For these reasons in particular, listeners can relate to the music of 'acoustic' instruments on more than abstract levels.

The potential problem with music produced from electronic sound sources is that all these things are missing. Fundamentally, all that needs to be done is to press a button. And – this is the vital point – the button that elicits a sound from an electronic sound source does not bear the same order of relationship with the resulting sound as the 'button' (e.g. the key on a keyboard) on an acoustic instrument, where the relationship is virtually unitary (the same key always produces the same sound, within quite precisely defined limits). Edward Lippmann notes, in discussing electronic avant-garde music, that:

> the absence of a true acoustic source gives rise to a curious effect in the evocation of attention, for noise and abrupt sounds are automatically responded to as signs of activity and significant environmental events rather than for their inherent formal properties or sensuous attractiveness. Thus when we can find no source that gives this kind of meaning to such sounds, and when we cannot even imagine the nature of a possible acoustic source, we are subject to a strange frustration. We are forced back upon immanent objects and intrinsic properties, but at the same time we attend to our response itself and are unable to suppress the spontaneous suggestion of environmental objects and occurrences and the in-sistent demand that we identify and locate them. This problematic situation colors the whole character of music based upon electronically reproduced noise.
>
> (Lippmann 1977: 71)

Thus it is hard, if not impossible, for a listener to get inside the action required to produce the sound, and there is a danger that music based on such electronic sounds could alienate listeners. As the popularity of synthesizer rock shows, this is not the case.

Let me propose two paradigmatic categories, which I have adapted from Emmerson (1986). The first category refers to the origins of music's consituent . timbres. These can be defined as *natural* (i.e. they were produced, or seem to have been produced, by a voice or an 'acoustic' instrument) or as *synthesized* (i.e. they have been built at a synthesizer or a computer). The second category is the class of gestures the music suggests. These can be *human* (as discussed in the preceding paragraph) or *mechanical*. Although rock's sounds emanate from speakers or headphones, they create the illusion that they are emanating from a human body, through the medium of the reproductive and/or amplification system. With most rock, and all pre-synthesizer rock, the categories *natural* and *human* will link up in opposition to the categories *synthesized* and *mechanical*, which are not found. In synthesizer rock, this pattern begins to blur, as synthesized sounds and non-human gestures come into play. In these cases, we return to the possibility that such sounds could be irrelevant to listeners. But, since they are not, what factors in the music serve to prevent the sounds alienating listeners? A possible solution can be demonstrated through the Eurythmics' rich 'No Fear, No Hate, No Pain', which embodies a timbral complexity absent from the bands discussed earlier. Immediately, it must be said that the presence of a recognizable pattern of beats affords the listener a comfortable initial range of responses, but the song consists of much more than just this pattern.

'No Fear, No Hate, No Pain' sets up a very clear opposition between 'natural' and 'synthesized' sound sources. Inverted commas are necessary here, because I (and, in my experience, other listeners) can no longer be sure just by listening that a sampler has not been used: thus, the actual source is less important than the apparent source. This opposition is not left un-mediated, and it is these mediations that I shall focus on.

Firstly, the timbral constituents of the song are highly varied. Listeners are presented with two human voices, a synthesized bass and drum machine, a 'tinny' synthesizer timbre, real or sampled orchestral strings and oboe, a few identifiable sound effects, and a whole mass of unfamiliar, 'unearthly' syn-thesized sounds (similar sounds have long been used to accompany images of barren planet-scapes and abandoned, floating spaceships in science-fiction films). The two voices come, of course, from the same singer, and this is recognizably the case. However, they are separated both in the stereo image and by differences of intonation and lack of linear continuity – there is no way that this precise relationship between them could be produced in a single take, even if the stereo image were to be ignored. Thus, immediately, the vocal sound (that produced by the one instrument all listeners have access to) suggests a strange reality. Within this, the unusual (percussive) playing of orchestral strings provides a link between the *natural* timbre of the voice and the *synthesized* sounds. The almost mechanical precision of the strings suggests that they may be synthesized, but their sound is natural. The two sets of synthesizer chords, the latter especially 'tinny', played as they are with an inhumanly regular vibrato, are mechanical in terms of gesture. The 'unearthly' chordal sounds of the centre of the song, unaccompanied by a drum layer, are explicitly linked to the voice at the end via the sound of the very recog-nizable oboe. Annie Lennox's only response is wordlessness, which suggests a momentary transcendence of the emotions of song. The sound effects (especially the machine-gun rattle) suggest artifice (in the sense that the tinny sound produced by a toy prevents it being confused with the 'real object' of which it is in imitation) and I would suggest that, given the quality of equipment used in the recording, this result is intentional.

Overall then, natural and synthesized sounds are not set apart, but are mediated by sounds that resist unequivocal placing within either category. Moreover, both are made to sound artificial in some manner: the meaning of the song's lyrics is not transparent, while the 'splitting' of the voice and the tinny synthesizer chords and sound effects give a heavy sense of irony. This irony is itself congruent to the apparent meaning of the lyrics, and thus the song makes the point much more powerfully than if the lyrics had just been spoken. They appear to concern the despair of drug addiction, although in a confused manner that seems to redouble their meaning. Thus, the unfamiliar, alienating synthesized sounds are brought into the fictionality of the song because it so easily affords the interpretation of the natural sounds as themselves alienating.

Authenticity re-constituted: guitar bands

If the synthesizer affords alienation of the listener from the immediate production of the sound, the guitar represents the opposite, as no mediatory forces *appear to* intervene between the finger and the string. Thus, far from dissipating in the wake of Bob Dylan's acquisition of an electric guitar, the issue of the 'authenticity' of rock remains open:

> In the context of the synthesiser bands prevalent in popular music in the early 1980s, the work of committed *guitar*-based performers, like Big Country, U2 and Bruce Springsteen, was actively taken to signify commitment to the 'classic' values of rock tradition.
>
> (Middleton 1990: 90)

This is not, of course, quite the same issue. The stylistic similarities between electric Dylan and early Springsteen suggest that attributions of 'community', 'creativity' or 'honesty' are read into the musics from outside (Middleton 1990: 139–40) – the way 'authenticity' is constituted changes with respect to time.[27]

I have already raised this issue in Chapter 3 with respect to the situation in the 1960s. Twenty years later it remains problematic, and Middleton offers an analysis that may be found useful. For him, any 'culturalist' approach to music will foreground 'authenticity'. Since all such approaches suggest that music and culture are structurally related (see Chapter 5), 'This ... encourages a stress on the notion of "authenticity", since ... honesty (truth to cultural experience) becomes the validating criterion of musical value' (Middleton 1990: 127). The supposed 'authenticity' that 'folk' music (whence the idea originates) has for many is, he argues, mythical (rooted, for example, in the Romantic critique of industrial society) but within it hide real processes, such as 'continuity' and 'active use' (which combine as 'tradition'), which suggest the notion of 'appropriation': the recognition that all music originates outside ourselves, prompting the question 'shall I make it mine?' Middleton argues that we have, in fact, a number of avenues open to us, ranging from 'appropriation' and the milder 'acceptance', through 'toleration' and 'apathy' to downright 'rejection'. The suggestion is that what we (ideologically) declare 'authentic' is the music we find easy to 'appropriate'. As Frith points out, the authenticity associated with guitar-based performers is not a close-kept secret:

> What's new about the rock/ad agency tie-in is not the exploitation of stars' selling-power as such ... but the use of anti-commercial icons to guarantee the 'authenticity' of the product they're being used to sell.
>
> (Frith 1990: 90)

In clarification, he argues that throughout 1985–6 Springsteen was 'the most valuable rock sales figure'. What none of this answers, however, is why such music invites wide appropriation. That it is more than the simple use of guitars is evident: Echo and the Bunnymen, Whitesnake and Black Sabbath (see previous sections) are not cited in such contexts. While a discussion of the styles of Big Country and U2 will not in itself provide complete answers, it will suggest avenues of further research.

The 'sound' of Big Country, and the sense of open space their music seems to create, is commonly noted:

> The feel of open space, of things rousing and stirring, of sounds clear, high and clannish. . . . [*The Crossing* is] bigger than life, the perfect soundtrack for one awe-inspiring stare into the Grand Canyon at daybreak. . . . Grand Canyon and a good part of Texas between the two enormous roaring guitars. . . . The rolling thunder of Big Country's guitars can still fill the Grand Canyon. . . . Overall beauty and power.
>
> (Reviews quoted by May 1985)

While this journalese smacks of promotional material, it is worth pursuing. How music may accurately portray such a sense is difficult to discover, although it clearly relates to matters of texture, and listeners might expect a relaxation of a rigid time sense.

The opening of '1000 Stars' constitutes a texture Big Country return to time and again: the kit opens with a standard rock beat, but with much additional work on tomtoms – Mark Brzezicki's drum style tends to underplay the cymbals in comparison with most hard rock drummers. A high guitar enters, with a full sound but a predominance of treble frequencies. It uses a fast, slightly irregularly picking pattern, without individual notes being particularly distinct, before adding a voice midway between these two in the texture. The absence of the bass at this point is important, so that right at the beginning a textural hole is present in the lower registers. This placing of the voice(s) *between* the kit and, frequently, both guitars, becomes a standard technique: the bass tends to one side of the sound-box, balanced by the solo guitar on the opposite side. Elsewhere in the texture, holes tend to be minimized – on 'Lost Patrol', for example, the high degree of guitar sustain fills holes in higher registers, while the kit works very hard to do the same a little lower down. Despite this, the guitars tend to be mixed quite low, avoiding a top-heavy texture, and if anything it is the kit tomtoms, right in the centre of the texture in both dimensions, that seem to be mixed highest.

Equally consistent in Big Country's work is a certain idiosyncratic attitude to harmony and its use in musical structures. Their approach can perhaps best be summarized as an almost puritan diatonicism. Not only do harmonic structures eschew chromaticisms of any sort, but individual vocal and instrumental lines do too. Yet the band's harmonic structures are anything but bland – they are truly modal in the sense put forward in Chapter 2, and more so in the musicological sense, since any identification of tonic is frequently ambiguous. The refrain of 'Where the Rose Is Sown' illustrates this rather

Example 4.10 Big Country: 'Where the Rose Is Sown'

well. The pattern can be characterized as an ionian VI–I–V–III, although these chords are only weakly realized owing to the radical mobility of the bass (see example 4.10). Its effect is somewhat parallel to the 'pan-diatonicism' employed by Stravinsky, who frequently used this technique to evoke a ritual grandeur,[28] a point to which I shall return.

This radical diatonicism is linked to grouping structures. Four-bar structures predominate to such an extent that, where they are replaced by three-bar, or alternating three- and four-bar structures (as in 'Heart and Soul' or 'Flame of the West'), the disruption affords a powerful effect. These four-bar groupings are achieved, in the main, by open-ended structures where V–I patterns are normally avoided, especially at either end of groups. Third-related moves are far more common (e.g. the aeolian I–III–IV–I pattern of the refrain to 'Flame of the West'). This slight harmonic unorthodoxy mitigates the unremitting regularity of groupings, although the constructional device is so intrinsic that the 'open-endedness' of the harmonic structures is never allowed to flower. 'I Walk the Hill' makes use simply of periodic ionian IV–I–V–I (verse) and I–V–IV–V (refrain) progressions, both taking four bars, normally doubled to yield verses and refrains both of eight bars' length. The instrumental introduction is likewise a 4 + 4 pattern. The entire song can be characterized thus: introduction (4 + 4 bars repeated); refrain (4 + 4); verse (4); refrain (4 + 4); verse (4 + 4); break (4 + 4; 4 + 4); introduction (4); refrain (4 + 4); verse (4 + 4); break (4 + 4; 4); refrain/break (4 + 4; 4 to fade). This alternation of 'verse', 'refrain', central instrumental break and opening instrumental material acts normatively, even on those few occasions where the harmonic structure is not open-ended but periodic, as here, and on 'One Great Thing'. This latter song's opening period, ionian IV–I–V–VI, IV–I–VI–V, is answered, following the centuries-old pattern, by IV–I–V–VI; IV–I–V–I. Although there is thus a clear distinction in types of structure, it is not accompanied by any marked difference in either sentiment or sound.

Example 4.11 Big Country: 'Steeltown'

Example 4.12 Big Country: 'Flame of the West'

Big Country's approach to the use of the guitar is also rather distinctive. They use nothing that approaches the conventional riff, nor do they use power chords or harmonies explored through simple strumming and picking patterns. The most obvious aspect shared by all these approaches is the use of syncopation – Big Country's restriction of occasional syncopation to the voice adds to the sense of regularity and inevitability (congruent to their grouping and open-ended structures), which remains a powerful aspect of their style.

Example 4.11 reproduces the guitar introduction to 'Steeltown', which thereafter continues as the equivalent of the riff underlying the verse. Example 4.12 gives the solo guitar line to 'Flame of the West', which appears as an introduction to the vocal verse and bridge. Both these lines are characterized by a number of factors. They tend to be quite fast, cover little more than an octave (the range of the Highland bagpipe) and are sometimes a little indistinct owing to the heavy reverb used in the mix. However, they are never displays of virtuosity and are not improvised – the repetition of guitar melodies acts to identify individual songs, and serves to fill the space between stanzas: such lines could not be transported from one song to another, unlike the improvised guitar solo of a heavy rock song. Frequently these solo lines tend towards a high degree of pentatonicism, but with an emphasis on the major third above the tonic that is missing from 'blues' derived pentatonic guitar solos (i.e. the scale is of the form C, D, E, G, A rather than A, C, D, E, G).

The voices used do not seem particularly notable – they are full-throated, in a high tenor register and with a limited range, but pitches are always attacked precisely with a tasteful minimum of glissandi and no roughness (except for the frequent ejaculated 'ha'). The only type of syncopation is as shown in example 4.10, where every successive half-beat tends to be anticipated. Their vocal techniques are thus congruent to their guitar techniques.

In terms of rhythm, these guitar lines are very measured (notes tending to appear on the beat), with a preponderance of ornamental semiquavers, such that a particular pattern of ornamentation will be normative for a particular song. Examples 4.11 and 4.12 illustrate two such: the first beat of each bar for example 4.11, and the third (and eventually the second) beat for example 4.12. This 'consistency of ornament' technique is fundamental to the Highland *piobaireachd*[29] (see, for example, MacNeill and Richardson 1987: 38–47). Many listeners have commented on the frequent allusions to the sound of the Highland bagpipes in Big Country's 'swirling' guitar breaks, and this technique may be a factor in this evocation. A further factor might be the consistent use of drum rolls to fill the spaces between beats (particularly noticeable on 'Come Back to Me'), for such a drum technique is a mainstay of Scottish massed pipe and drum bands.

U2 present an equivalent 'authenticity', and it seems more than coincidental that they are also described as creating a great sense of 'space' in their music (the fact that both Big Country and U2 are frequently portrayed in the open, against backdrops either of open sky and bare, unpopulated hillsides, or of deserted heavy industrial sites, may not be irrelevant). Like Big Country, U2 frequently make use of registral emptiness between guitar and bass, which the voice is free to fill, and which may contribute to the spaciousness, but there the overt similarities seem to end. As early as *Boy*, four clear characteristic aspects of U2's style can be found, which remain in force up to the album *Rattle and Hum*.

The first of these is the open-endedness of their harmonic sequences, which frequently consist of no more than two chords that alternate, often without any clear structural sense of verse, refrain or break. In a few cases (so few because the bass largely remains static), this approaches the diatonic style of Big Country (as on 'Exit'). Partly as a result of this, songs seem almost totally to eschew repetitive 'hooks': the clearest exceptions are on 'With or without You' with its ionian I–V–VI–IV, 'Red Hill Mining Town' and 'Unforgettable Fire', each of which has a mixolydian I–V$^{\#3}$–VII–IV refrain, and 'Where the Streets Have No Name' with its clear sixteen-bar verse (two bars per harmony) on this mixolydian pattern: I–I–I–IV–VI–V$^{\#3}$–VII–VII. It is not until *Rattle and Hum* that they make use of periodic structures, as in 'Van Diemen's Land' and the conventional twelve-bar 'Angel of Harlem'.

The second aspect is the bass playing, a driving style that develops from punk, sticking to the root of successive harmonies without creating a clear sense of line. Although playing on even quavers is the rule ('Red Hill Mining Town' stands out precisely because this pattern is broken), the speed is much slower than normally found in punk bands.

The guitar also seems to derive from punk on the early albums, but it later slows and coalesces into two approaches (most songs include at least double-tracked guitar, relating to 'rhythm' and 'lead' tendencies), these representing their style's third characteristic aspect. Many songs open with a high guitar arpeggio repeated over a unit of either one or four bars, dividing this unit in the ratio 3:3:2, and put through a treble roll-off filter and digital delay unit, giving a very controlled echo. Riffs are entirely absent, songs often being underpinned either by this way of playing, or by semiquaver-repeated strumming patterns reminiscent of punk 'thrash' (but more gently executed), which often sink into pure rhythmic semiquaver 'hacking' (strumming the strings but stopping all the strings from vibrating with the left hand, leaving only the attack of the plectrum to reach the pick-up).[30] Although the guitar textures become more refined on the later studio albums, their defining characteristics have not changed.

The final main aspect of their style is Bono's voice, which, from the earliest albums, also seems to have had affinities with punk singing. 'Twilight' from *Boy* exemplifies this clearly: there is little sense of precise tempered pitch, while on the word 'twilight' itself, the first (high) pitch is overshot, falling back to a second pitch a fifth away. Throughout some six albums, the tessitura of Bono's voice has gradually dropped, such that by *The Joshua Tree* he has settled on a conventional 'tenor' range. A further aspect of this approach is that melodic 'hooks', i.e. melodic ideas with a particularly strong pitch and rhythmic profile, are absent. Recitative is the predominant vocal technique, apparent in both 'Promenade', with its total lack of repetition of melodic material, and 'A Sort of Homecoming', with its constant repetition of a single melodic shape. This latter procedure is almost normative (appearing as early as 'A Day without Me'), with Bono leaping to a relatively high pitch and then falling back. Long ago, the ethnomusicologist Curt Sachs called attention to this archetypal shape (which he called the 'tumbling strain'):

> The most fascinating of the oldest melody patterns may be described as a 'tumbling strain'. . . . In their most emotional and least 'melodious' form, such strains recall nearly inhuman, savage shouts of joy or wails of rage and may derive from such unbridled outbursts.
>
> (Sachs 1962: 51)

Although such speculation is unverifiable, it may contribute here to the sense of authenticity, particularly since it is often combined with a near-destruction of any clear syllabic pattern in the lyrics, suggesting their only sense is as articulated cries, as on 'New Year's Day'.

Further typical vocal techniques are difficult to verbalize. Bono makes use of two that are reminiscent of Siouxsie Sue: his voice often *catches* when moving from note to note on a single syllable, combining this with sudden downward swooping acciaccature (e.g. 'Shadows and tall trees'), and *yowls* – circling a main note with glissandi before arriving on it. He is also rhythmically inventive – although tending to conform to strong beats, he rarely pays attention to intermediate subdivisions, relating his singing much more to speech, and thereby constructing a more immediate relationship with his audience.

So, what is it about this music that affords connotations of a sense of space? Most likely, these will result from the overall texture. Aside from the wide registral gaps at the openings to many songs (thereafter the guitar will frequently fall to the vocal register), the great use of digital delay on the guitar (giving very immediate echoes) and the high degree of apparent reverb (the 'atmospheric' background, wherein any textural holes are felt to be only temporary) both seem to contribute greatly to this effect, as if the sound were bouncing around in a great amphitheatre.[31] This, combined with the use of long sustained organ chords/notes and sometimes high sustained guitar pitches, becomes most apparent on *The Unforgettable Fire*. A possible additional factor is the fact that, especially from *The Unforgettable Fire* onwards, textures often progress from an initial guitar (possibly combined with voice) through the gradual addition of bass and kit, and frequently a second guitar layer. 'With or without You' is a more sophisticated example of this where, after the texture has filled out to its greatest extent, it returns to its lowest point and begins to build again, forming a coda. One further device, which is shared with Big Country, is Larry Mullen's general avoidance of cymbals, in particular hihat. Comparison of U2's *War* with *The Unforgettable Fire* makes this plain – the sense of space is much more apparent on the later album.

A characteristic experience of wide open spaces is the difference in perceived motion between events in the near and the far distance, the *difference between these* giving the sense of space.[32] Both Big Country and U2 (and other bands for whom images of openness seem important, such as the Alarm and Simple Minds) symbolize this with much intricate surface movement (drum and guitar picking/strumming patterns) overlaying minimal underlying (i.e. harmonic) movement, which in the case of Big Country, as discussed, is slower than even a conventional harmonic analysis would suggest. This polarization of speeds, combined with the musics' registral layout, connotes a sense of open space and grandeur.

In the way they have re-thought rock texture, Big Country and U2 in particular have provided a clear stylistic alternative to the guitar-based hard rock and heavy metal styles discussed earlier. Since, as Middleton (1990: 90) suggests, the music of these bands signified a commitment to hallowed rock values, at least some part of that commitment is likely to be found in the different way the style is constituted. I have already pointed to isolated features of the music of Big Country and U2 that seem to embody these: the use of guitar, the incorporation of 'pipe and drum' effects in the music of Big Country, and Bono's vocal techniques. I also feel there is a link to be made between this 'authenticity' and the imagery of open spaces.

In Chapter 3, I suggested that technical features associated with the blues have been used in rock to imply the authenticity of experience undergone by various players. Here, I need to take the argument further, and point out that it was the rural blues, rather than its urban counterpart, that was primarily felt to carry this sense, the rural blues being closer to the music's magical origins. Players like Big Bill Broonzy, who would play electric guitar in the USA, had to switch to acoustic guitar when playing in the UK. It is the rural associations here that are important. It may be that we have to take on trust certain stages in the development of the blues from the field holler, but the origin of the blues in the open spaces of Texas, Louisiana and Mississippi is at least an article of faith (see Oliver 1969: 17–20). Thus, it is in its association with such spaces that the blues acquires one important strand of its authenticity. Therefore, I would suggest that the creation of a sense of open space in a style only loosely related may also carry connotations of removal from built-up, industrial areas, and hence a nostalgic return to the romanticized notion of pre-industrial existence. For Big Country, the connotation is strengthened by the explicit recall of pipes and drums, and their link to matters of Celtic myth. Although this argument is far from conclusive, it does help to account for the noted difference in signification.

Authenticity re-constituted: roots rock

Over the past fifteen years, there has arisen a new set of styles that are, at least tangentially, associated with rock, styles that are frequently subsumed under the headings 'roots' music or 'world' music. The problems associated with these labels are legion. 'World' music assumes we can be aware of music from anywhere else; it also implies that other styles (e.g. those of Wagner, Frank Sinatra and Bessie Smith) did not originate in the 'world'. 'Roots' music, although perhaps a better term, still carries essentialist assumptions. We are, however, stuck with the labels, at least while the musics continue to be marginalized. Two distinct sources for the constituent styles can be isolated, both of which retain 'authenticity' as an ideological issue. The first comes about as an aspect of musicians' continual desire to develop their own distinctive approaches, while the second relates more specifically to the musics from which these influences come.

In Chapter 3, I referred briefly to the music of Fairport Convention in discussing the English folk revival of the 1950s and 1960s. Their fusion of the instrumentation of revivalist players (especially fiddle and acoustic guitar) with a rock rhythm section (largely electric bass and drum kit), decried by some on the same grounds as Bob Dylan's collaborations with The Band (e.g. on *Planet Waves*), led to the coining of the style label 'folk rock'. The formula was sufficiently popular to sustain them and others (e.g. Steeleye Span) for many years, although it did not mean that the strict revivalist instrumentation and practices fell out of favour: the two approaches co-existed quite successfully, and players like Martin Carthy moved easily between the two. By the later 1970s, however, the British folk club was once again becoming the setting for an elitist, melancholy pastime, with the 'finger in the ear' and 'Arran sweater' clichés largely true. It was neither energetic nor (therefore?) of any appeal to a younger mass audience. Two broad attempts were made to change this state of affairs.

The first was that of the long-established dance bands (e.g. the Oyster Band, Blowzabella and Tiger Moth), who began to 'modernize' the style, at least in part through the use of drum kit and electronic amplification, thus re-establishing a link with practices of the previous decade. The second was the development of what was almost 'punk folk', which first became widely known through the Pogues, formed in 1983. Their (then) leader Shane McGowan had been involved in a minor way in the original punk movement, and it is perhaps unsurprising that their music was performed with a well-rehearsed carelessness, as on *Rum, Sodomy and the Lash*. Speeds vary on this album, but the up-tempo numbers (e.g. 'The Sick Bed of Cuchulainn', 'Wild Cats of Kilkenny', 'Billy's Bones') are in the region of 150 beats to the minute, which is very fast indeed. Their instrumentation connotes informal dance – banjo, concertina, penny whistle, strummed guitar, autoharp, piano accordion, supplemented by electric bass and kit. Although the listener may be primarily aware of a complex, energetic interplay of instruments, this energy overlays simple structures, both in form ('The Old Main Drag' is rather a conventional ballad) and particularly in harmony: most songs are based throughout on primary (I, IV and V) triads. Thus, on Eric Bogle's renowned 'The Band Played Waltzing Matilda', the starkness of the sentiment is well matched by the band's refusal to add the passing-notes and inverted harmonies of many of the other available versions.[33] The seeming carelessness derived from punk is most apparent in the vocal approach: the words tend to be spat out, the voice having no resonance, no vibrato and no sense of shaping of phrases. This is true not only of McGowan, but also of Cait O'Riordan's voice on 'I'm a Man You Don't Meet Every Day'. Although within the revivalist traditions, female performances of 'men's' songs were an established practice, here it perhaps comes more from a belated punk desire to invert the norm: thus, 'Billy's Bones', usually a fine lament, is tossed off at breakneck speed.

The Pogues are not alone in this approach. The Men They Couldn't Hang may pitch their voices more precisely, but they adopt a similar delivery and speed. On Bogle's 'Green Fields of France' (widely known as 'Willie McBride'), the uncluttered arrangement and halting pacing (four beats of band alone after every three beats of accompanied singing) serve the song well. The stylistic distance from here to more explicitly post-punk thrash bands like the Wedding Present is thus quite small. The latter's 'My Favourite Dress', for example, is at the slow end of their generally fast repertoire. The instrumental delivery is similar to that of the Men They Couldn't Hang, while the melody is similarly intoned rather than composed: the only marked stylistic difference is the use of electric, rather than acoustic, guitar.

This nod in the direction of 'traditional' material is not restricted to British 'folk' styles. For example, overt Africanisms have been part of the stylistic mix since the days of progressive rock.[34] A history of the influence of such styles on rock would include mention of at least four notable events.

First is the output of the expatriate Nigerian/Caribbean Osibisa, who charted in the early 1970s and continued touring for well over a decade. Second is the 1967 field recording of Burundi drummers, which appeared initially on a single (by Burundi Steiphenson Black) in 1971, backed Joni Mitchell's 'The Jungle Line' in 1975, and re-appeared as a backing track behind Bow Wow Wow and Adam and the Ants in the early 1980s. Third is the signing of Nigerian Sunny Ade to Island Records in 1983, to which the general awareness in this country of the 'Afro-pop' explosion can be dated. Fourth is Paul Simon's incorporation of Southern African musicians on *Graceland*. Despite the unease felt in some quarters over the album, it has caused a meteoric rise in British public interest in African musics.[35] For the second and fourth events cited above, the impetus behind such usages seems rather superficial, either for the sake of fashion or to utilize exotic sounds not ordinarily available to us (and in Simon's case at least, it served well to revive a flagging career).

The main problem with this revitalized interest in other musics is the connotations that are attached to them: broadly speaking, we are in the midst of a re-run of the 1960s idealization of the blues, but for blues now read the musics of Asia, South America and Africa, but especially Africa. In this respect things are even more insidious, for Africa is still, simplistically, seen as the source of the blues itself, that totem-like entity of which we are all expected to be in awe. Ian A. Anderson, one spokesperson for the progressive branch of the folk/roots movement, puts this most succinctly in a recent editorial in the magazine *Folk Roots*:

> Apart from the musical and visual excellence [of the programme on Mali in the BBC2 series *Under African Skies*], the programme was the best illustration I've yet seen – in particular the quotes from the participants – of why we keep pointing to Africa as an *inspiration* to people who want to make modern music from their own roots.
>
> (*Folk Roots* 77)

The longest interview broadcast was with that doyen of African pop, Salif Keita, who has become a jali. The jalis have been, for some centuries, the hereditary musicians of Mali, Guinea, Senegal, Gambia and the Ivory Coast. All came from the Mandinka, a people who trace their history back as far as the powerful Mali empire of the thirteenth century. Their original role was four-fold: to praise the king and nobility; to recount family histories and genealogies (these being an oral people); to encourage acts of bravery in battle; and to commemorate the dead. These roles remain even today, but now the jalis are patronized by religious leaders, politicians and wealthy businessmen. They are much in demand at weddings, ceremonies for child-naming and circumcision, and the like. New music has grown alongside the old since the nineteenth century and is still doing so, while techniques have more recently changed to include amplification (even at weddings in enclosed rural compounds), the use of instruments like the electric guitar, and well-rehearsed arrangements with set introductions and choruses, replacing traditional improvisational techniques.

Against this background comes Keita. According to the interview, he was born a member of a noble family who were not allowed to demean themselves by becoming singers. And, being albino, he was subject to discrimination. On deciding to become a singer, he was largely ostracized, but became a highly accomplished jali, this involving the acquisition of their styles, material and functions. Through the 1970s he did an apprenticeship in West African dance bands (with their mixture of Cuban and Congolese styles) before getting breaks to record in the USA in 1980 and in Paris from 1984. Although initially aimed at a Mali audience, his music now became more widely popular. His 'Mandjou', for instance, praises a previous president of Guinea and that president's ancestors all the way back to the early Guinean hero 'Mandjou'. It was held in high critical regard, although its sound is remarkably similar to the London r&b sound of 1964–5.

Against all odds, then, Keita entered and succeeded in this (lowly) profession hitherto closed to those not from musician families. I will paraphrase the translation of the interview he gave. Paris had better recording facilities, so he left Mali in order to 'blossom' as a musician, to open himself out, to 'discover himself' and to 'discover show business', in the process discovering other styles and places before ultimately returning to Mali. He wants to make music for the whole world, and he also wants to be in show business, which means leaving Mali, because to be in show business you have to sell to a wide market. All this, of course, is against the traditional jali belief that a musician's wealth should come directly from the gifts of patrons (Keita himself has apparently gained much wealth in this way, including two Mercedes from one patron). The parallel should by now be obvious: Keita is talking in very much the same terms used by other commercial musicians throughout the past thirty years, whose popularity has convinced them of their own apparent importance.

Keita's music is clearly part of the complex processes of change in which many African states find themselves, processes which have profound effects on traditional attitudes and practices. The transition from feudal to quasi-industrial societies has gathered pace in recent decades, and has been combined with a renewed interest in indigenous musics on the part of the major record companies, exerting their influence so as to have a share in any style which gains popularity outside its own region. A full analysis of their role is out of place here, but Wallis and Malm (1984, particularly 74–119) is a valuable study of their impact. Radio 1 disc jockey Andy Kershaw commented on these changing practices in a short article for the *Radio Times*, bemoaning the lack of air play for such music on Radio 1:

> I blame African-music experts for deterring people with an appetite for hearing new sounds – that snobbish idea that one has to be an expert before the music can be properly enjoyed. And largely I think, because the musicians are black and from the developing world, TV producers and critics have tended to be over-reverential and uncritical of African music. It should be treated for what it is – pop music: exciting and great fun.
>
> ('Voice over', *Radio Times* 23–29 September 1989: 79)

Although I equally deplore the damaging, uncritical stance that surely exists, his quote contains a sub-text that is highly invidious: it is that we should exploit this music, because it is just 'fun, pop music'. It seems to me that the onus is on listeners and musicians from the 'developed world' to learn that this is not 'quaint', but neither is it just 'pop'. It is a classic case of double-bind. Keita's music has become sufficiently Westernized for it to be acceptable pop music, for most 'underdeveloped' nations have been convinced that the acquisition of Western technology, and hence Western social practices, provide the answer to all their ills, and of course Western cultural commodification cannot be separated from Western industrial technology.

This may seem a particularly depressing picture, but there do seem to be approaches to the incorporation in rock of non-Western musical techniques that escape this idealization, and here the lack of distinction between 'rock' and 'roots' that I have been assuming thus far will come into focus.

In 1982, while working on his fourth solo album, Peter Gabriel finally managed to stage the first WOMAD (World Of Music And Dance) festival, which put musicians from Burundi, Egypt, China, Indonesia and elsewhere alongside leading British rock acts. Gabriel's interest in issues in the developing world had surfaced before: his anthem to South African black rights leader Steve Biko appears on his third album. WOMAD has since gained influence as an organization promoting awareness of other cultures' musics, but its influence on Gabriel was most notable, in that it has coloured his music, particularly on that fourth album. Most listeners to West African drumming are overawed by its surface complexity. This is normally spoken of in terms of 'polyrhythm', whereby different patterns of beats are played simultaneously by different drummers. Alongside this surface complexity there runs a relatively simple 'time-line', i.e. a rhythmic stratum that repeats indefinitely as a performance guide, and that improvising drummers re-interpret in different

ways. Throughout West Africa, the 'time-line' ♩ ♪♩ ♩ ♪♩ ♩ is

ubiquitous. Gabriel is said to prefer the 'simpler' rhythms that can be heard alongside the complexity of the surface of West African drumming, and it is to this that he refers: it is particularly clear on 'Rhythm of the Heat'.

Within the rock mainstream, Gabriel's concern and interests are shared by Kate Bush, with whom he has worked. Her earlier albums are notable for their use of, for example, Irish instruments (as on 'Night of the Swallow'), but a wider awareness first surfaces clearly on 'The Dreaming', title track of her critically disliked fourth album. Regarding this, she comments:

> The Aboriginals are not alone in being pushed out of their land by modern man, by their diseases, or for their own strange reasons. It is very sad to think they might all die. 'The Dreaming' is the time for Aboriginals when humans took the form of animals, when spirits were free to roam and in this song as the civilized begin to dominate, the 'original ones' dream of the dreamtime.
>
> (Juby 1988: 103)

The parallels between this track and Gabriel's 'Rhythm of the Heat' are striking. Both are built around rhythm tracks rather than harmonic patterns: both are based on $\frac{12}{8}$ for the richness of rhythmic interpretation it permits (this metre equally underpins the West African 'time-line'). Both the tracks are built up through the use of Fairlight computers, permitting highly sophisticated control over sound synthesis and sequencing. Each musician thus has total control over the final sound, rather than leaving anything to the vagaries of the interaction of performers (although Bush has said she prefers the 'magic' of people performing together). The harsh, metal percussion of the conventional kit is missing on both tracks, replaced by heavy drums (Bush emphasizing second and fourth beats, Gabriel only fourth). In addition, Bush employs an Aboriginal *dijeridu* for programmatic purposes, Gabriel employing a similar-sounding percussion track. Both songs are based on drones, although Bush's does have a minimal harmonic content. In both, the voice sings in a near-monotone, the effect of the lyrics related to chant, while small units are repeated constantly: aside from basic rhythm and melody, this is particularly true of Gabriel's string and pipe tracks. Both songs are redolent with low frequencies, helping to suggest the air of unease and menace. 'Rhythm of the Heat' then follows its African antecedents by breaking into a tempo faster by a ratio of 3:2. This technique is common among West African drum ensembles, and the way it is manifested is very similar to Gabriel's song. In their use of rhythmic layers as compositional starting points rather than harmonic patterns or melodies, both Bush and Gabriel are less reliant on keyboard or guitar than had been normal hitherto in rock, and this new approach is largely responsible for the music's stylistic originality.[36] Both are also ultimately dependent on computer-generated rhythm and free-generated sounds, but the fact that these sounds can be 'named' in terms of conventional instruments, and that the sounds have complex overtone structures (unlike the bland timbres preferred by many synthesizer rock bands), reinforces the argument above, where I suggested that, to avoid alienation between the listener and the synthesized sound, it was necessary to provide a timbral 'bridge' to the world of established instrumental colours.

Bush, in particular, has continued the process of bringing together these unfamiliar instrumental sounds with the fundamental elements of rock. This can be done subtly, as on 'Running up That Hill', where the kit is devoid of cymbals (thus suggesting connections with African drum ensembles rather than the rock kit), or by a more thorough incorporation of such sounds, as on *The Sensual World*. 'Never Be Mine' is almost a compendium of the album's stylistic developments. Bush makes use of both the nasal tones of the uillean pipes (Irish bagpipes, also known as 'union' pipes) and of the full-throated voices of the Trio Bulgarka, a trio of female Bulgarian singers who were first brought to the UK in the mid-1980s. Both the pipes and the trio create the same sounds they would in their more usual contexts (the arrangements for the trio were made in Bulgaria with the intimate involvement of Bush), and they overlay open-ended sequences with minimal harmonic change and no distinction between conventional formal units. The stunning 'Rocket's Tail' moves from a subdued opening in which Bush in accompanied only by the Trio's voices, through to a hard rock shuffle pattern incorporating a blistering guitar solo.[37]

A comparison between Kate Bush and Richard Thompson is instructive here. Bush began in the world of rock, only gradually incorporating 'roots' elements. Thompson began as an integral part of Fairport Convention, and is thus still seen as a primarily 'roots' musician (see the record reviews and readers' poll pages of *Folk Roots*). Although his sympathies are reputed always to have been more with 'rock' than with 'folk', he has certainly made use of techniques with a long heritage, such as the 'riddle' genre employed on 'We Sing Hallelujah' (1974).[38] By the mid-1980s, however, despite the power of his lyrics, his musical style has shed all remnants of 'folk' styling, 'Did She Jump or Was She Pushed', from *Shoot Out the Lights*, being indistinguishable from rock. That such distinctions are still insisted upon in some circles points to the continuing *ideological* nature of the debate over authenticity.

Although the influences of rock on non-Western musics (particularly those of Africa) are well attested, my discussion of the recent work of Kate Bush and Peter Gabriel suggests that the direction of influence is by no means one-way. This does not necessarily mean that we are ultimately heading for a homogenized popular culture. The ethnomusicologist Bruno Nettl draws a distinction between what he terms 'Westernization' and 'modernization'. He points out that non-Western popular musics share certain traits: mass media dependence; European triads; textures consisting of voice, plus instrumental ensemble, plus percussion; use of both Western and traditional instruments; lengths of between three and five minutes; and simple metres based on groups of three, four or six beats. Many non-Western musics influence each other: in Brazil both Amerindian and African influences are strongly present, East African music mixes aspects of Caribbean, European and Arabic styles, while Iran makes use of Arabic, Indian, Western, Caucasian and Turkish styles (Nettl 1985: 84–5).

None the less, for many cultures the incorporation of 'rock' and related techniques is all part of the process of the modernization of industry, the urbanization of society and the secularization of musical culture, and does not represent a pale attempt to reproduce Western popular music *for a Western market* (except that represented by the tourist, perhaps). Indeed, in their survey of the music industry in twelve varied nations, Wallis and Malm insist that: 'The common development that has involved more local music-making than anything else in the . . . sample, has been the emergence of national styles of pop and rock music during the Seventies' (Wallis and Malm 1984: 302). Rather than suggesting, therefore, that all new popular styles must relate to such styles in Western Europe and the USA, this suggests that new fusions can be developed,[39] perhaps providing that musicians keep their eye on their own home market. The best guarantee against homogenization would be for such musics to remain somewhat marginalized. But this would require the musicians to be in a position to resist the power of the transnational, major record labels to take up and exploit unfamiliar styles. To return again to the analysis offered by Wallis and Malm, these major companies retain an interest in many small countries, precisely because it cannot be forecast from where the next fashionable style will come. This presence may be effected through local, 'independent' companies, or by the direct presence of the majors themselves (see also Collins 1985: 117). As we have seen in the case of Salif Keita, resistance to this presence may be neither possible nor desired.

I suggested earlier that innovation in rock has tended to come from two opposed impulses. The first demands greater simplicity with respect to one or more elements which have become obscure through excessive complexity; the second demands greater sophistication with respect to one or more elements which have become simplistic. The development of rock from the punk era onwards continues this interplay, only here many of the techniques seem to have origins in the punk and progressive movements respectively, and may well continue to do so while such musicians remain active. This can give seemingly paradoxical results: the new 'progressive' rock of Marillion, despite its lengthy structures, uses punk techniques of continuation, while the more concise work of Asia still uses progressive techniques. The structural simplicity of synthesizer rock is a direct continuation of the straightforward structures of early punk, but in its attitude to timbre and texture, it begins to develop the musical domains left untouched even by King Crimson. The sophisticated textural developments of a band like U2 combines with a bass technique which remains as simple and solid as that of the first punk bassists. The style fusions attempted by Peter Gabriel and Kate Bush recall the general progressive programme that I have previously outlined, but with none of the harmonic complexity associated with most progressive bands. And so on. What my analysis does not attempt to do is try to explain how degrees of sophistication and simplification co-exist within the same cultural practices or if, as I suspect, they do not, then to what extent the publics for these various styles remain 'sealed off' one from another. The answer to this question must await further research.

5   *Meanings*

In Chapters 2, 3 and 4, I have been particularly concerned to trace the internal dynamics of rock styles, what I called in Chapter 1 the music's 'syntactical' meanings, without much explicit reference to the music's delineations, or 'analogue' meanings. The primary reason for this approach was, of course, that such stylistic conventions are frequently the result only of conjecture, which has rarely and unsystematically been subject to verification and refutation. The many forward references throughout the last two chapters will have suggested that these two types of 'meaning' are hard to separate in practice. Since the issues surrounding meaning are not intrinsic to separate styles of rock, they will form the focus of this chapter. Perhaps a key issue here is the level at which analogue meanings are determinable. Is it reasonable to try to isolate the meaning of individual rock songs, or does meaning reside in styles and the practices they involve? More pressing still is the issue of just what counts as meaning at this point. For instance, can the meaning of a rock song be reduced to the meaning of its words, in which case why bother to sing it? If it cannot, then what purposes are the music serving?

The organization of the chapter is related to the dichotomy expressed above. In the first two sections I shall assume that all individual rock songs have discernible meanings, which can be communicated, as performers express themselves, to listeners. The problems associated with the notions of 'communication' and 'expression' will become apparent. I shall then switch my attention to the meanings involved in repertoires of songs, explicitly those repertoires formed through applying the concept 'style'. In previous chapters I have assumed an understanding of style as relatively passive, whereby styles become historically constituted through the practices of particular bands, which practices thereby set up discernible stylistic conventions. I shall close with discussions of music wherein style is used as an active ingredient in a seemingly self-conscious endeavour to construct a new layer of meanings.

Communication

> If you want to come up with a singular, most important trend in this new music, I think it has to be something like: it is original, composed by the people who perform it, created by them – even if they have to fight the record companies to do it – so that is really a creative action and not a commercial pile of shit thrown together by business people who think they know what John Doe and Mr Jones really want.
>
> (Willis 1978: 154)

In speaking of progressive rock in this way, Frank Zappa was encapsulating the ideological terms in which rock is differentiated from pop. The distinction lies, here, not in a refusal by musicians to enter the commercial sphere, but in a conception that that sphere is sufficiently wide for a freedom of self-expression to be fought for. Similar arguments have been raised regarding glam rock, punk, the early beat groups and even the more recent 'guitar bands'. The relationship with the industry is never actually as clear-cut as Zappa pretends. Although he would prefer to see musicians occupying a role in direct opposition to that of the rest of the industry, they cannot be so easily separated, as I shall argue in the next section. However, the conspicuous importance of the ideal of self-expression is thus signalled.

In day-to-day social interaction, we communicate to one another by expressing ourselves, primarily through language and bodily gesture, and additionally through such less ephemeral modes as dress. All such expression tends to have a minimum of originality. In rock, originality seems to be prized as a mark of self-expression, supposedly unencumbered by mediative forces, as exemplified by the virtuoso guitar solo. This common-sense understanding cannot, however, be supported; if self-expression is to be expressive of any-thing, if it is to mean something to the recipient of the expression, that something must be encoded as a system of signs, and encoded in a form that a listener can interpret meaningfully. 'Meaningfully', in this context, presum-ably asserts the necessity of some sort of congruence (some sort of agreement on the *rules* of the exchange, or the *sign system*) between the listener's inter-pretation and the performer's intention. Whether the latter can ever be dis-covered in any other way (in order to check the success of the communication) is open to intense doubt, but that is an issue I decline to pursue here. In rock, as in any art form enjoying only partial autonomy, communication cannot take place 'unencumbered', but is mediated on two principal levels: that of the *internal code*; and that of the *contingent factors* which determine what music will reach which ears, by what means, in what context, etc. etc. The remainder of this section is devoted to a discussion of the former, while the latter is the subject of the next section.

To discover the degree of communication possible through music, it is necessary to return briefly to the topic of musical meaning raised in Chapter 1. There, it was suggested that music can be said to have both *syntactical* and *analogue* meanings, both of which are said to be 'communicated' in a rather unspecific sense. Many writers, however, have felt compelled to attempt some specificity, and to define the codes that might make it possible to translate analogue meanings into words, an enterprise which is considered to lie within the field of semiology.[1] In describing this enterprise, Laing (1985: ix) states that 'a sign consists of a signifier – the sound or sight of the word "punk" – and a corresponding signified – the mental image or idea evoked by the signifier.' Laing's work is highly persuasive for most aspects of punk, although it disappoints in the limited space he devotes to the sounds. Summarizing his discussion of tempo and rhythm, he suggests:

> The fast tempo combined with the anti-syncopation tendency of many punk songs supported the connotation of urgency of utterance which declamatory vocals and their lyrics evoked. For if the pace of a song no longer functions as an impetus to dance it then becomes a sign that the singer needs to get across the message as quickly as possible.
>
> (Laing 1985: 63)

On the contrary, it does not necessarily become such a sign: the fast tempo and declamatory style could equally be read as a desire simply to eject the 'message',[2] or even to prevent its being 'got across', by virtue of its very pace. There is no single set of significations supported by its body of signs.

Tagg's important article (1982), cited in Chapter 1, makes use of a more thoroughgoing musical semiology reminiscent of Cooke (1959), whose intentions are typical even if his content is not. Cooke's repertoire is European art music, and his approach primarily melodic, relegating harmony, rhythm, volume and texture to secondary roles as 'characterizing agents'. Two quotes will exemplify his tone: the first is a general comment, the second more particular.

> That the major third should be found to express pleasure should surprise no one, since it is present . . . early on in the harmonic series: it is nature's own basic harmony, and by using it we feel ourselves to be at one with nature.

> If to fall in pitch expresses incoming emotion, to descend from the outlying dominant to the point of repose, the tonic, through the major third, will naturally convey a sense of experiencing joy passively, i.e. accepting or welcoming blessings, relief, consolation, reassurance, or fulfilment, together with a feeling of 'having come home' . . . [combined with] the sweeping confidence that takes for granted that all difficulties are over.
>
> (Cooke 1959: 51, 130, 167)

Two main problems surface here. The first is his appeal to 'nature' as final justification, which implies the superiority of the European art tradition. The second was disinterred by the aesthetician Monroe Beardsley (Beardsley 1981). In a carefully argued discussion, Beardsley points out that Cooke, having discovered that certain melodic motions possess a particular quality that can be metaphorically described by an emotion-word, jumps to the conclusion that the composer must therefore have been expressing that emotion (Beardsley 1981: 61–2).[3] This problem has not, I think, been overcome by subsequent writers.

A more recent, and more directly relevant, example of a similar approach has appeared in a recent article by Sheila Whiteley (1990). She applies it to the music of Jimi Hendrix and, unlike Laing, does so with extended, close reference to musical detail. Much of her argument consists of attempting to show that Hendrix's 'Purple Haze' and 'The Wind Cries Mary' encode the experience of acid and marijuana trips, respectively. For 'Purple Haze', she notes the 'sheer volume of noise [that] works towards the drowning of personal consciousness,' the mesmeric effect of the melody, based as it is on a recurrent motif, which suggests a mood of obsessiveness and absorption, and the overall effect of 'drifting':

> The sensation of drifting is . . . fed by phrasing and articulation. In the lead break the guitar meanders in an almost raga-like noodling around the notes, again suggestive of a state of tripping where a fixed idea/concept/point takes on a new reality. In conjunction with the feedback and distortion there is a feeling of incoherence.
>
> (Whiteley 1990: 46)

Of course, this analysis is firmly grounded in the lyrics, which would not seem to admit of an alternative interpretation, but volume of noise, repetition and meandering, on which her argument hinges, do not in themselves ensure that what is being encoded is an acid trip. (Neither can I accept that Hendrix even begins to encode incoherence: the song's coherence is assured by its extremely limited harmonic and rhythmic vocabulary.) Likewise, for Whiteley, 'The Wind Cries Mary' 'encodes the effect of marijuana through the gentleness and inner-directedness of its style.' In the absence of the lyrics, surely no such assertion could remotely be contemplated, and thus it would be possible to point to any musical effects to support the apparent message of the lyrics.

These three illustrations exemplify together what are for me the three chief difficulties attending semiotic interpretations of individual songs. The most immediately relevant is the notion that meanings are locked into the sounds by musicians, the listeners' task being to unlock those meanings, i.e. that musicians communicate unequivocal meanings through expressing themselves. I shall return to this below, in investigating the concept of the *persona*. Immediately, however, I shall focus on the two remaining difficulties uncovered by these illustrations. The first of these is the translation of syntactical meanings into words, while the second concerns the type of meaning which is being encoded, and I shall consider them together.

In her discussion of 'inherent' and 'delineated' types of musical meaning, Lucy Green (1988) insists that the former cannot be described in words; as soon as words are employed, the discussion automatically begins to concern the types of delineation that music has. The words that critics use to describe the music's syntactic domain are no more than rough approximations, which frequently appear as biased readings because they are not adequately grounded in the sounds. This difficulty is, I think, overcome in Philip Tagg's exhaustive study of the Abba 'mega-hit' 'Fernando' (Tagg 1991). Tagg's method is deceptively simple. The entire song is first broken down into musemes, which are the smallest stable elements ('minimal units of musical meaning'), so called by analogy with the word 'phoneme'. Correspondences are then sought between these musemes and their appearance in other examples of both similar and only tangentially-related styles. Not only is this stage necessary, but it is so time-consuming that I have never seen it properly undertaken in equivalent studies. The musemes are then both analysed in terms of their syntactical functions, and also related to their 'paramusical context', by which Tagg means 'words, pictures, actions, social habitat etc.' (Tagg 1991: 12). This lengthy process of analysis provides Tagg with a number of conclusions, one of the most valuable being

> that there is really only one main process in *Fernando*: FROM problems and emotional involvement in an exotic and exciting environment TO happy reminiscences at home about that environment and those events. This interpretation means that the verbal longing from 'home' to the liberation struggle in the Andes . . . may even be false, a sort of musical-emotional 'lie', a bit like irately yelling 'I'm not angry!'
>
> (Tagg 1991: 102)

It is not the actual conclusion that is reached that concerns me here, but the type of conclusion that it is. Tagg is suggesting that the syntactical meanings of the music allow us to come to an understanding of the *attitude* held by the musicians towards the ostensible meaning of the lyrics. In other words, the music is not signifying ideas themselves, but is implying attitudes towards the ideas proposed by the lyrics (and Tagg does not argue that this attitude was either consciously held or consciously portrayed by Abba). It seems to me that it is conclusions of this type, conclusions which focus on the signifying of attitudes rather than ideas (see, for example, my previous discussions of Slade's 'Coz I Luv You', Jimi Hendrix's 'Hey Joe', Janis Joplin's 'Ball and Chain' and the Eurythmics' 'No Fear, No Hate, No Pain'), which are the least likely to reduce to cases of loaded readings, and are thus most worthy of note.

In order to discern the attitudinal relationship between music and lyrics, it is necessary to focus on the lyrics themselves. It is perhaps because of music's persistent ineffability and resistance to enquiries that attempt to refer it to 'the outside world' that many commentators write as if it is merely a pleasant backdrop to the lyrics, and concentrate either on interpretation of the lyrics themselves or on the persona embodied in the human voice. After all, this voice is the primary link between the artist and the listener, being the instrument shared by both. A rationale is provided by Frith's suggestion that 'It is through the voice that star personalities are constructed . . . The tone of the voice is more important in this context than the actual articulation of particular lyrics' (Frith 1987: 143). This is one of the few areas where detailed audience research has been carried out, and there seems to be much support for his contention. In one such recent report, Priasky and Rosenbaum (1987) conclude that, for American youths, listening to any particular song because of the content of its lyrics was the least well-supported reason for listening to it at all. Yet because the lyrics are there, it is easy to apply to the song techniques of narrative analysis derived from literary and film theory. While this can be a valuable exercise, it can too easily be allowed to stand for an understanding of the song itself (i.e. the combination of sonic qualities and lyrics), an issue Frith (1989) raises.

To give a detailed example, in a generally useful survey of Elvis Costello's lyrics, David Gouldstone asserts that

> it is chiefly on his lyrics that Costello's reputation is founded. Naturally it's his music that initially attracts people to his songs, but by and large it's the words that make them stay. It's quite common to hear him described as rock's best lyricist after Bob Dylan.
>
> (Gouldstone 1989: xii)

This view is unsubstantiated (as such views usually are). My main concern, however, is that despite his stated insistence that the meaning of the lyrics is affected by songs' sounds, he discusses those lyrics in virtual isolation. Regarding the vindictiveness of 'Hand in Hand', for example: 'the pill is not even sugared by the unremarkable tune' is all he has to say on the music, bemoaning the song's lack of distancing and irony and its 'apparently uncritical portrayal of gloating malignity' (Gouldstone 1989: 33), which makes it for him a revolting song. Yet the irony that he desires is clearly there in the music, most notably in the one-dimensional, almost mock-triumphal repetition of I–V–I harmonies (particularly the final martial anticipation of I) and the long subdominant (chord IV) pedal, ensuring that the final coda is over-prepared. Similarly, by failing to take into account the attitude set up by the music, so many other analyses of song lyrics are not only incomplete, but lead to erroneous conclusions.

Aside from their role in signifying ideas, lyrics also play an important role in enabling listeners to construct an image of the persona embodied by the singer. Durant argues that one of the most important differences between the sung speech of rock and the spoken speech of conversation is the anomaly in communication resulting from 'shifters':

> What is most extraordinary about first- and second-person pronouns in rock songs is the possibility of identification they evidently establish: the possibility to superimpose the person of a listener on the 'I' of the singer, an identification which creates the effect of the rock singer speaking out on an audience's behalf; or alternatively, the possibility of the listener occupying the position of second-person addressee addressed by that 'I' of the singer.
>
> (Durant 1984: 203)

Thus, the meaning even of the lyrics cannot be fixedly encoded in them by the singer, but they represent a ground for negotiation, the listener ultimately construing them relatively freely. This means that listeners are involved in actually constructing that persona, for themselves, on the basis of the sounds heard and their competence in the style employed.

A further, related, site of negotiated meaning is in the non-verbal sounds uttered in the course of singing. Here, the code is based not on the *precision* of the emotion felt, but upon its *depth*:

> Pop songs celebrate not the articulate but the inarticulate, and the evaluation of pop singers depends not on words but on sounds – on the noises around the words. In daily life, the most directly intense statements of feeling involve just such noises: people gasp, moan, laugh, cry . . . people distrust the silver-tongued, the seducers, politicians, salesmen, who've got the gift of the gab.
>
> (Frith 1983: 35)

These articulatory noises are largely inaudible to conventional musicological enquiry in its concentration on the piece of music as an abstract entity rather than a performance. The *persona* projected by the singer through the song is thus not dissociable from the means of representation, the song itself (see Cone 1974: 29–33).

So, the identification listeners may make with the singer, in whatever way, can only ever be partial, mediated by the ephemerality of the music itself, the questionable role of the lyrics and the very fact of having to construct the persona of the individual to whom we are listening. Because of this necessary incompleteness, even here, it cannot be asserted that communication takes place between performer and listener.

The mediation of self-expression

Even if we are resistant to denying that rock singers express themselves in communicating with their audiences, this 'self-expression' is further mediated by a variety of factors that induce a tension between what musicians may want to do to or for listeners, and what circumstances enable them to do. These mediative factors can be summarized as those involved with the actual business of making sounds (whether in the studio or in concert), the role of the recording companies (most importantly their management and promotional activities) and the process of getting these sounds to the ears of listeners (largely via the media industries). The first of these has already surfaced throughout this book, while many writers have ably discussed aspects of the music industry from their own points of view – I am only concerned here with the ways that they mediate between the musician and the listener.[4]

The very process of putting a record together and selling it is frequently likened to that of constructing a market and designing a product to fill that market – in other words, the audience is identified, and then it is the musicians' task to service that audience. David Bowie exemplifies this most explicitly: as Frith and Horne say of him, 'the biggest and most influential stars . . . are precisely the ones who design their own *fans*' (Frith and Horne 1987: 15).[5] In creating this market, artists presumably created room for self-expression, but there is a fundamental paradox regarding this freedom, in that it is only available as long as the musician finds an audience: here most clearly, self-expression implies communication. Frith (1983: 63) argues that this freedom is further limited, and that determinations of the meaning of individual expressive acts must be contextualized (largely within the debate over the apparent values of authenticity and commerciality).

Frith (1990) identifies what he calls the 'rock' model, which portrays the accepted relationship between the musician and the rest of the industry. My explanation of it looks something like this. When a band first attract the attention of the industry's 'artist and repertoire' (A&R) staff sufficiently to win a recording contract, they will probably have a devoted local following. This in itself is unlikely to ensure wider success: the A&R team discovers 'potential', which, in order to be worth investing in, will have to be geared to a larger market – Frith (1983: 102ff.) points out that all A&R decisions are made according to financial criteria. Hence, before the band can reach this market, their original expressions of self, as perceived by their home audience, will be further compromised. The musicians will not necessarily be unwilling to acquiesce in this: after all, it is the A&R department that 'knows the market', while the royalty system means that the musicians have a vested interest not only in producing what they would wish, but also in producing what will sell. As Laing (1985) points out, this sharing of the marketing risks means that the equation of 'good' with 'commercial' (what has quality will sell in quantity) comes ever closer. What goes on to tape in the first place, who produces it, how long is to be set aside in the studio, how it is to be marketed and distributed, all this may receive input from the musicians, but unless they have already proved their worth they will have no veto.[6] Much of the decision-making at this point is in the hands of the producer, a record company employee, whose task begins with administrative decisions regarding the studio session, and then continues with what is conventionally understood as 'moulding' the original ideas of the band. Frith argues thus: 'Record producers . . . act as the link, the mediator, between musicians as artists and their music as commercial product' (Frith 1983: 110–11).

This view of the producer's role seems to me a little skewed. The producer *may* have a minimal effect on certain domains of the music (the pitches and rhythms, the lyrics and the basic instrumentation), but on other domains his (rarely her) role is of supreme significance, particularly in terms of texture and timbre as these are shaped at the console, and sometimes in terms of form (the pattern of verses, refrains and solos). Thus, to argue that these domains are *mediative* is to argue that the music is constituted according to the same criteria that conventional musicology proposes, in opposition to the arguments I have previously put forward. On the contrary, the producer's role must be seen as equating to that of the performing musicians: he is at least as much *auteur* as the song's originator(s). Struthers argues that the control exercised by the musicians over the finished product has become progressively reduced:

> A clear indicator of where effective control lies in the studio is seen in the design of the recording console: one noticeable feature of recording has been the gradual consolidation of its control over recording sessions.
>
> (Struthers 1987: 254)

It is for this reason that I have, throughout, referred to the products of rock *bands* (including the producer) rather than attempting to unravel the contribution of various *individuals*, which it is not possible to determine from the recording alone.[7] Thus, although the producer's role may be minimal in respect of the music receiving a live performance (it will not be minimal if the music has already been recorded), it is fundamental in the studio.

Once a band has achieved sufficient success to enable their record company to begin to recoup its investment, both partners will have a vested interest in maintaining their market share (as a measure of audience interest) and, hence, quite possibly a partial stylistic stasis. At this stage, musicians may reach a peak in artistic control, since the formula of which they are part clearly works, although they will only maintain this control while they remain popular. Wicke (1990) argues that the musicians' position is somewhat complex. Although musicians will probably have a shared viewpoint with their local following in their early days, success will necessarily be accompanied by a growing independence from an audience identifiable in detailed terms, yielding a degree of felt autonomy on the part of the musicians.[8] To be sure, there are rock bands who have taken an audience along with them in pursuing new directions but, in the absence of methods of measuring the extent to which this is the case, it would appear that outstanding examples are few. At this point, then, the majority move into a phase where their individual voice is no longer valued. They may be re-packaged, or they may drift into obscurity still avidly communicating, but with a contracting audience.[9]

Pursuing the model whereby mediatory forces are interposed between the musician and the listener, we come to the forces apparent in the media. Their strength is asserted by Barnard:

> In mass-mediated culture, listeners and consumers can never constitute their own tastes; the choices are limited in the first place, all manner of pressures bear down to limit not only the diversity but the availability of cultural products.
>
> (Barnard 1989: 187)

His text covers well the relationship between musicians, recording companies and radio broadcasting, and I shall not broach these matters here, except to note that the relationship is largely symbiotic, and somewhat stationary.

The 'cosy' relationship may be under attack from the growth of videos, and their regular use of live performance footage. This growth is coincident with the altering relationship between the live performance and the recording. Whereas the record was originally seen as a form of promotion itself, promotion for the live performance, it is more the situation now that the live performance (or, more correctly, the tour) acts as promotion for the album. Thus, a tour is normally packaged to contain a mixture of items from the current album and a set of clear audience favourites. Indeed, as Frith (1988a: 205–25) suggests, the video has, at least in part, come to act as a surrogate live show, itself acting as promotion for the recording, a process which may complete itself when the video supplants the recording entirely.

This relationship is not the only one that has changed. In the recent article in which Frith discusses the 'rock' model at some length, he suggests that it has now been superseded by what he calls the 'pool' model:

> The dynamic here comes from [the international entertainment media]. There are no longer gatekeepers regulating the flow of stardom, but multi-nationals 'fishing'

for material, pulling ideas, sounds, styles, performers from the talent pool and dressing them up for worldwide consumption. The process is, from both the musicians' and the audience's point of view essentially *irrational*. Who gets selected for success seems a matter of chance and quirk, a lottery, and success itself is fragmented, unearned, impermanent. The 'creative' role in this pop scheme is assigned to the *packagers*, to record producers, clothes designers, magazine editors, etc.; they are the 'authors' of success.

(Frith 1990: 113)

Although I have argued that producers have always had something of this role, this clearly represents a changing situation for rock musicians, not least because it distinguishes between rock and other styles purely on the grounds of what else the *package* is to consist of, rather than on the musical constituents of the style. This means that the control musicians have over their expression is even further diminished. This does not, however, necessarily entail video and television replacing radio as rock's primary promotional medium. Barnard (1989) has suggested that radio has the ability to sustain interest in a song that the visual medium cannot match, because while the impact of repeated television clips dissipates over a period of days, repeated radio plays of a song maintain listener interest.

The points that I have raised here seem only to strengthen the general conclusion of the previous section, that a simple model which proposes that musicians express themselves in unmediated communication with an audience does not stand up to scrutiny. The sense that audiences make of music does not result from the decoding of any previously encoded message, but from the making of sense, by listeners, within a range afforded by the music they receive. This extends to the persona 'projected' by musicians, which will vary from song to song and from listener to listener and is thus in large part created by those listeners. And, finally, it extends to the channels of access leading from musicians to their audience, over which those musicians have very little control. These mediations are crucial.

Style and identity

I have argued above that both the practices of rock, and its objects, cannot be conceived as embodying unequivocal messages which are communicated, in part due to the necessary flexibility of any resultant interpretation. In the remainder of this chapter I move from consideration of individual songs and their mediation to the consideration of styles and their mediation, and in this section I shall focus on the notion that the meaning of styles, in relation to other pertinent cultural practices, *can* be considered fixed rather than flexible.

Throughout previous chapters I have implied that styles are subject to historical change. Here, I wish to focus on this explicitly. As a concrete example, the music of Elvis Costello could not have preceded that of Smokey Robinson: Costello rose as part of the 'authentic' pub rock/punk rock movement, itself partially a revolt against disco, which was rooted in the Philadelphia sound of the Trammps and the O'Jays, which in turn was partially dependent on the sound of Tamla Motown. Not only has Costello employed some of the attributes of that style in the arrangements on *Punch the Clock* and the syntax of *Get Happy*, but his vocal and lyrical tone would not have been found before the advent of the punk aesthetic (this stylistic consciousness is discussed in detail below).

A reading of historical accounts of 'teenage' culture would tend to suggest that styles of music, like those of fashion and behaviour, simply replace each other. Thus, an outline of stylistic change would emphasize the replacement of the Mersey beat and London rhythm 'n' blues of the early 1960s, via the music of the mods and rockers of the mid-1960s, by the psychedelia of the 'swinging' pop culture and hippies in the later 1960s. This in turn would be seen as leading in some way towards the styles of art rock, heavy metal and skinhead stomp at the turn of the decade, the resurrection of teenybop and the rise of disco in the early 1970s, the creation of punk in the mid-1970s, and the growth of both politically aware musics and the synthesizer-dominated bands of the late 1970s etc.[10] Although some of these styles occur in opposition (indeed, Hebdige (1985: 130) has suggested that such oppositional cultural practices are normative), on this model styles die out and are replaced by others. Although the timescale is far shorter, the model is similar to that posited for the European art music tradition, wherein successive styles and their associated sets of values achieve dominance in turn (Modernist succeeds Romantic succeeds Classical, etc.).[11]

Now, as long as 'rock' is considered a teenage music, this view is inevitable, for the teenage years are few, and the gradual acquisition of maturity is accompanied by marked changes. Rock, however, cannot be defined simply as a teenage music, and not all people change their listening habits as they age. Although the issue is not simple, it must be recognized that bands who came to the forefront as part of teenage culture in the late 1960s and 1970s are either still current or, more interestingly, reforming. Examples abound: Charles Shaar Murray (1989b) reports on the revival of Pete Townshend's *Tommy*; Phil Sutcliffe (1989b) discusses the reformation of Anderson, Bruford, Wakeman and Howe (who have since been re-absorbed into Yes); Mark Cooper (1989) discusses that of Ten Years After and others; Adrian Deevoy (1989) examines the continuing success of the Rolling Stones. What is important is not that these bands may have stayed together, but that their stylistic changes have been kept to a minimum. While nostalgia may be an important element (whether catered to or created by compact disc exploitation of back catalogues), some of these bands continue to appeal to a now-teenage audience. In contrast, earlier bands on the cusp of the rock/pop divide, such as the Easybeats, the Tremeloes and the Swinging Blue Jeans, have long since transferred to the cabaret circuit. For the rock bands, this means that their styles are still found useful by listeners.

Therefore, although within rock there will be a time before which a style cannot appear, there is not necessarily a time after which it can no longer have a place (see also Wicke 1990: 73ff.). The extension through historical time so prized by art music aficionados is thus also an attribute of rock. The corollary to this is that either the cultural attitudes that enabled the formation of the music must still be prevalent, or the music is being used to serve a new function, that of the re-creation of those attitudes in the spirit of nostalgia. Of course, this may not be deemed a particularly healthy situation. Charles Shaar Murray notes that

> sixties culture . . . rules the roost. Removed from the hubbub of the times, the old songs and film clips continue to resonate; not for what they signify or even for what they once signified, but simply because of . . . the magical aura they possess because they once signified something.
>
> (Shaar Murray 1989a: 33)

Some writers would argue for a causal relationship between a musical style and its parent culture, on the lines of the 'homological' model. Clear evidence in support of this model can be sought in the gamelan music of the 'anthropological present' on the island of Bali (i.e. between 1900 and 1930). As a people, the Balinese have greatly stratified social roles. It is a grave cultural misdemeanour to forget one's place in the social hierarchy, and competition for social position is unknown. Gregory Bateson offers evidence that, even on their small island, they find themselves lost without a clear geographical point of orientation (Bateson 1973: 89). This state of affairs finds a concrete equivalent in the musical structures of the 'gamelan' (the generic term for Indonesian orchestras). Each player, and each musical strand, has a pre-determined role in the whole, from which it, and thus he, is not allowed to stray. Thus, this all-encompassing musical structure does not merely reflect, but *is* part of a fundamental cultural norm (to re-quote Nettl from Chapter 1, music expresses 'the relevant central values of culture in abstracted form').

Balinese gamelan is therefore an example of the homological model for the relationship between music and its parent culture. To put it another way, we could say that the homological model suggests that the *inherent* and *delineated* meanings put forward by Green (1988) are in a causal relationship with one another, that a musical style creates, and is created by, a social identity. Anything less is merely a relationship 'by association', an arbitrary association, suggesting that the style 'reflects' the parent culture. This may be hard for students of language to accept, for it refuses to assert the arbitrariness of the sign. Ever since the work of Saussure, it has generally come to be accepted that the relationship between a linguistic sign (e.g. the word 'dog') and the object it denotes (the 'dog') is arbitrary. It is vital, however, to confuse neither the nature of linguistic and musical signs, nor the nature of linguistic and cultural signs. Non-linguistic sign systems do not necessarily use wholly arbitrary signs. Culler (1976: 98–9) surveys some of these sign systems, while convincing cases for the equivalent musical signs are put forward by Coker (1972) and Shepherd (1991). I shall return to this matter below.

Paul Willis (1978) most notably introduced the notion of homologies into the study of popular culture,[12] but the clearest statement is perhaps that of Dick Hebdige (1985). His reading of punk maintains that:

> There was a homological relation between the trashy cut-up clothes and spiky hair, the pogo and amphetamines, the spitting, the vomiting, the format of the fanzines, the insurrectionary poses and the 'soulless', frantically driven music. . . . They produced Noise in the calmly orchestrated Crisis of everyday life in the late 1970s – a noise which made (no)sense in exactly the same way and to exactly the same extent as a piece of *avant garde* music . . . more concisely: the forbidden is permitted.
>
> (Hebdige 1985: 114–15)

As I implied in Chapter 4, it would be difficult to see how this is borne out by the music. The latter reference seems intended to suggest that the rules of construction for punk (or, as is often mistakenly supposed, their absence) are as hidden as those of avant-garde music, that both styles require a deal of learning. But this is clearly not the case with punk, for it was able blatantly to make its point. Despite the contrary assertions of the musically sophisticated Shepherd (1987a: 170–1; 1990: 141), as I have shown, punk's musical rules have a great deal in common with those of rock.

The Sex Pistols' 'Anarchy in the UK' provides a ready example, wherein its music displays an attitude which is clearly at odds with its lyrical content and visual performance practice. Metrically, it falls throughout into groups of four strong beats, with the verse consisting of eight such groups. This, as Chapter 2 has suggested, is the most normative organizational pattern in rock. Harmonically, the verse uses a simple riff based around the major chords of C–F–E. This reaches G half-way through the verse before returning to C; the second half-verse thus answers the first, exactly as might be expected. (The same pattern appears in Thin Lizzy's 'Killer on the Loose', and a close relative in the refrain to Abba's 'Take a Chance on Me'. In neither case is any link with punk made or even implied.) Melodically, the refrain emphasizes each note of the downward scale in turn, from G through to C, a pattern so basic in its organization that its connotations could not be further from 'anarchy'. Formally, the song uses a standard verse/bridge structure, while in terms of performance and arrangement it is clearly polished, rehearsed and precisely coordinated: it includes a typical rock guitar solo, and all instruments fulfil established rock functions. Even the song's noise-laden timbres, which contrast so strongly with the timbres used contemporaneously in disco and some progressive, 'stadium' rock of the Barclay James Harvest variety, were a regular part of rock guitar technique, from Pete Townshend through to Robert Fripp. What is musically 'forbidden' in rock, chiefly, is metric irregularity and avoidance of conventional chord structures and progressions. (The verse of Neneh Cherry's 'Manchild' provides an excellent example of the latter.)

Musically, 'Anarchy in the UK' does not remotely qualify as a 'reassembly of appropriated objects', to use Hebdige's description of punk culture. This being a not untypical example of the style, punk music cannot be said to embody a homological relation with punk culture, for it gathers its meaning by association.[13] Indeed, the use of strict homological arguments has been criticized on grounds similar to these by Middleton (1985a), who acknowledges their arbitrary nature and instead supports a kind of *qualified homology*, for 'it seems likely that some signifying structures are more *easily* articulated to the interests of one group than are some others' (Middleton 1985a: 7). Therefore, although causative homologies are a theoretical possibility, and although at least one exists in practice (the case of the Balinese gamelan can be pursued to quite a deep level), the temptation to find them underlying every stylistic practice needs to be avoided. Indeed, Middleton's notion of 'qualified homologies' is equivalent at the level of style practices to Gibson's notion of 'affordance', which I have used throughout. Because inherent and delineated meanings do not, in practice, enter into causal relationships, it cannot be asserted that a particular musical style *must* create, or be created by, a particular social identity: neither are meanings irretrievably fixed, nor are they entirely arbitrary.

Meaning and style

In the wake of this ambiguity, and in conjunction with the argument that individual songs cannot be viewed as a means for musicians to communicate an unambiguous expression to listeners, it must be asked: what sort of meanings can the music have?[14] That it does have some import is self-evident. Some cultural theorists suggest that meaning resides *only* in the music's cultural/social setting (see Cutler 1984), while others suggest that the music not so much 'has', but 'generates' meaning. Sean Cubitt argues that 'since it is not referential, we cannot say that the song has meaning, but rather that it means, that it produces meaning' (Cubitt 1984: 215). It seems to me that one place at which such meaning is produced is in the friction between a song and the style that it is engaged in constituting, as I shall explore below. Indeed, Green suggests that we could hardly place a higher value on this concept:

> Style is the medium by virtue of which we experience music, and without which we could have no music at all. No piece of music is ever stylistically autonomous. Whether particular individuals hear all music in terms of either the pop or the classical styles alone, or whether they make finer distinctions between late Haydn and early Beethoven, Tamla Motown and Disco, whether such activity is self-conscious or intuitive, it cannot be avoided. This is not only because musical delineations so forcefully and ubiquitously divide styles of music into categories with appropriately related listeners, but also because *we must have some knowledge of the style of a piece of music in order to experience inherent meanings as distinct from non-musically meaningful sound, at all*. . . . Such knowledge is by no means acquired only through study, but is learnt through repeated experience of music, an experience granted more readily than ever before by the media and the music industry, and is gained, to varying degrees, by every normal member of society.
>
> (Green 1988: 33–4)

Thus, we may take it as axiomatic that listeners make their own distinctions between styles, and that with increasing exposure listeners' powers of discrimination increase, such that what were initially considered monolithic styles are recognized to contain separate styles, down to the level at which the individual style of an individual item can be recognized. Middleton (1990: 174) offers a list, implying that levels of style operate in a strict hierarchy, which I think may not be too helpful: to distinguish between style and idiolect (the particular 'fingerprints' of an individual musician), as both he and Stefani (1987) do, may not be too valuable for rock, in which the production of music is not an individual matter. Moreover, his hierarchy suggests a static situation, taking insufficient account of the permanent state of change of style even with a constant group of performers.

Recognition of style on the part of the listener is predicated upon the notion of competence for that particular style. This may be approached by way of the notion of linguistic competence. To retrieve my citation of Lincicome (Chapter 1), as when listening to a strange tongue, with music one can be captivated by the sheer sound, without any syntactical involvement, i.e. without understanding the relationships between the perceived sounds. But listening is an active process. If competence within a given style is acquired, that understanding is necessarily increased. The plainest example is the use of the 'dominant seventh chord'. In a standard rock blues, such as Led Zeppelin's 'Since I've Been Loving You', the appearance of dominant seventh chords helps to define the style, but they have no greater intrinsic meaning. However, in a standard pop song such as Phil Collins's 'Don't Let Him Steal Your Heart Away', the appearance of I^7 heralds IV, exactly as it might within European common-practice tonality – it therefore carries a different sort of inherent meaning. Misunderstanding the function of this chord within these two different styles may lead to unwarranted expectations.

Stefani suggests that we distinguish between two essential competences, which he unfortunately terms 'high' and 'popular' competences. These are approached through five levels of semiotic code, moving from the general to the particular.[15] 'Popular' competence tends to privilege the more general levels of this schema, while 'high' competence tends to privilege particulars. The benefit of this distinction is that it asserts (rightly) that, just because particular listeners may not be able to conceptualize their understanding, this does not necessarily mean that they lack a competence. What Stefani fails to emphasize is that each competence must be defined in relation to a style: competence (of either kind) in listening to Led Zeppelin does not automatically mean one has the equivalent, or any, competence regarding Phil Collins. Thus, I would prefer not to use Stefani's loaded 'high' and 'popular', but to suggest that *recognition* of a style, and of a song that exemplifies it, must be distinguished from *explanation* of it. I believe that this distinction between recognition and explanation (both of which are measures of competence) is, perhaps, more helpful than that between popular and high competence.

The notion of *competence* comes to music from the study of language, where it is seen in relation to *performance*. This distinction refers to the language available to the speaker/hearer (competence) and the language actually used (performance). In linguistics, the distinction between Stefani's competences is not maintained,[16] although a more important difference is that, in linguistics, 'competence' refers both to speaking and hearing, but in music, it is the latter that has far greater pertinence: this is frequently overlooked. The supposed parallels between linguistic and musical competences can lead us into further problems.

Middleton (1990: 192) suggests that linguistic competence 'relates to a power of *abstraction* and an understanding of *function* rather than just learning particular syntagmatic combinations and their meanings,' with which I agree. But he continues: 'Applied to music, this approach would imply a conception of structure as comprising not just paradigmatic choices and syntagmatic sequences but also a *functional hierarchy* lying "behind" what is heard,' and he continues to equate this 'structure' with pitches and the order in which they appear. This is also the established musicological approach (although as Moore (1990) has shown, even recent 'classical' music does not necessarily derive its structure from its pitch component). I have argued throughout that 'pitch' is not the primary domain in rock, and that we shall need to find some way to equate 'structure' with, perhaps, texture (or at least things in relation to texture);[17] here Middleton's *general* argument may prove to be applicable, although the necessary research has yet to be undertaken.

Middleton (1990: 173) further suggests that not only competence is an important consideration, but also pertinence; that is, finding the levels of code that actually signify. Rock signifies at the level of style for 'general competence'. Not only does it signify at closer, near-idiolectal levels for those with more developed competences for that style, but individual examples will signify for those with a general competence. Green (1988: 26–31) explores this, concluding that

> Delineated meanings are both conventional and individual. Mendelssohn's 'Wedding march' will delineate a (church) marriage to most British people, but it may also hold private delineations for individuals – memories of a particular event, association with certain activities or emotions, and so forth. Hence, although some delineated meanings maintain themselves only by virtue of collective definition, delineated meaning is, to individuals, whatever they make it.
>
> (Green 1988: 31)

We should, therefore, not expect to be able to 'translate' into words the meaning of the music of an individual style, much less that of an individual song. But this does not mean that we have to assume that such meaning cannot be discussed: indeed, it is necessary to discuss it. For example, the renewed commitment to the guitar in the wake of punk, as a way of embodying 'meaningfulness', has its detractors:

> The rock discourse does operate like an organized religion; it channels the mystical impulses of rock fans into orderly, doctrinal adherence. As adepts of the renegade tradition, we preferred the single moment of awe.... Our search was for a new, more credible seriousness, as against the discredited sanctimoniousness of those – U2, Simple Minds – who still believed rock could save the world.
>
> (Reynolds 1990: 13)

In decrying this desire to recapture meaning, Reynolds is praising those who return to the vision of rock as, in some senses, simply celebratory (even of the unlovely), arguing that we are most excited when the tried and tested formulae break down, when what he terms stylistic *disruption* occurs. While I have some time for this view, I am left with the nagging doubt that in refusing to define what it is that is being disrupted, in describing the effect rather than searching for how the object affords that effect, we are somehow missing the point, and are in danger of self-delusion, of imposing what we would like to be there without reference to what actually is there. In order to demonstrate, I would like to suggest how three songs seem to capture meaning by departing from, or creating friction against, the simple textural norms of rock.

The most stable instrumental relationship in rock has always been that between the kit and the bass. Where this relationship is sundered, it can produce just this friction. Having reached a climax towards the end of the Boomtown Rats' 'I Never Loved Eva Braun', the kit breaks into a militaristic snare drum pattern while the bass starts to mark only the beginning of each bar, with a mellow, open fifth chord. This is accompanied by an abrupt change of speed (from 'normal' to 'slow'), which has previously occurred once in the song. As the bass moves from its normal, rhythmically active role, the effect of the again-slower tempo is intensified, especially as this becomes overlain with contrapuntal lines in the vocalization, piano and whistling. Extending the amount of time taken to retrieve the original tempo gives the impression that something has actually been achieved.

A similar effect is found in Nik Kershaw's 'The Riddle'. Here, the sundering of the kit–bass relationship is accompanied by an abrupt change of key, and a clear evocation of marching pipe and drum bands (lacking any bass register). The coincidence of changes of texture and key produces an effect not unlike a change of film shot, with close camera-work suddenly panning out and making the viewer aware that there is a great deal more to the subject than the simple shot.

Elvis Costello's 'Lipstick Vogue' uses the same device, but to a different end. The speed of the drumming from the outset seems close to hysterical. This is intensified after the climax, when not only are all instruments bar voice, kit and (minimal) piano lost, but the kit moves solely over to the less resonant tomtoms – the effect is almost of gasping for air, rounded off with the words 'sometimes I almost feel just like a human being . . .'.

The notion of stylistic disruption to which Reynolds refers, and which goes further than these simple examples, suggests that the search for style has become conscious. Frith (1990: 91) bemoans the present situation, where the history of rock only has import as a source for pastiche. This is not the negative situation Frith believes, and it deserves to be explored in some detail.

Parody, pastiche and performance

Styles of music do not have an autonomous existence apart from the individual exemplars from which they are constituted. Styles are thus *formed through* those exemplars, those individual songs, and the concept of style is properly a grouping together of the common pertinent features of like songs, rather than an 'abstraction of the essence' of them: style is a virtual quality, which has no material existence except in the minds of listeners.

I shall describe the process of *forming* a style *through* the invention of songs as the *performance* of that style: hitherto, almost all discussion of style in this book has been situated within this process for each style. Thus, styles are *referred to* as part of a process of accretion. Styles can, however, be referred to in another way, which is akin to quotation. A song can *pastiche* a style that other songs have previously constituted, by making explicit reference to that style, which process may possibly take on qualities of homage. Beyond this, a constituted style can be referred to with irony or cynicism, in the process of *parody*. Jameson (1983) has called attention to both these latter forms of reference. He draws his examples largely from poetry and the visual arts and, indeed, both pastiche and parody have been used by European composers since the renaissance. None the less, their widespread use in rock may provide further evidence for those concerned to establish links between rock and other contemporary cultural practices. That they are so widely used suggests that listeners in general are assumed by musicians to have a high degree of competence with constituted styles. I shall investigate both techniques in the work of David Bowie and Elvis Costello, in turn.

Bowie has been recording for twenty-five years, Costello for fifteen, and both have amassed sufficient work to indicate that parody and pastiche are integral to their working practices (most artists use the techniques in a far more *ad hoc* manner). *Performance* can involve conscious consideration of the style concerned, but this is by no means necessary. Both *parody* and *pastiche*, however, require understanding of the style to be alluded to. Both Bowie and Costello exhibit a virtuosic command of style, but they use it in different ways: whereas for many years Costello retained a different style referent for each entire album, Bowie tends to work on both larger (exceeding the individual album) and smaller (within an individual song) levels, although in practice these levels cannot be rigorously maintained.

Bowie's work forces a concrete distinction between explicit 'persona' and musical 'style'. As one of the earliest exponents of 'glam rock', Bowie forced attention upon the notion that a performer can inhabit a persona, rather than that persona being an aspect of the performer. The idea finally coalesces for him in the creation of Ziggy Stardust in 1972, continuing through Aladdin Sane and the Diamond Dogs concept to the Thin White Duke (associated with *Young Americans* and *Station to Station*). These were not distinct creations: the material associated with Ziggy was not written as a coherent exploration, some of it also remaining in Bowie's live set through to *Diamond Dogs*, while the latter coincided with part of the 'funk' styled *Young Americans*.

For all the changes of style commentators are keen to find, Bowie's dominant voice is nearer to hard rock than anything else. *The Man Who Sold the World* (1971) is a consistent rock album, while the later and better-known trio *The Rise and Fall of Ziggy Stardust and the Spiders from Mars*, *Aladdin Sane* and *Diamond Dogs* (1972–4) firmly establish his style, which is defined best in terms of instrumentation and structures. Kit and bass are supplemented by strummed acoustic guitar (particularly on *Ziggy Stardust*), with electric guitar ornamental arpeggiated or power chord riffs and occasional solo passages. Bowie consistently employs, and often mixes, both open-ended and periodic structures: the standard example of the latter is probably 'Life on Mars' (1971), whose piano-dominated sequences are inventive in their modulations. 'Ziggy Stardust' itself combines a standard gentle periodic structure for the verse with a power chord open-ended refrain structure, 'Five Years' makes use of an open-ended repetitive sequence (ionian $I-VI-II^{\#3}-IV$), but instead of allowing the song to remain on one level, Bowie uses it to generate tension by, in the first verse, allowing the vocal range to get ever higher, and in the second thickening the texture.[18]

It is not until *Lodger* (1979) and *Scary Monsters* (1980) that Bowie returns to rock as a stylistic basis, but from that point to the present it remains the dominant feature. Laing (1985: 24–6) argues that Bowie's influence on punk was formative: the influence is reflexive. Although neither punk's urgency nor its desire for disruption are present, songs on *Lodger* tend towards unchanging textures, themselves denser than his earlier rock forays. This density is formed by all the arrangements being constrictingly tight, with straight rhythms and a preference for simple sequences, each chord tending to last two bars, not being rounded out to four- or eight-bar phrases. This avoidance of rock's normative grouping prevents a clear sense of orientation. 'Fantastic Voyage', with its lydian $I-II-\#V$, is representative. Only the voice syncopates, and the opposition between voice and frenetic backing (which had arisen between *Diamond Dogs* and *Lodger*) remains strong, as on 'Look Back in Anger'.

On *Scary Monsters*, the bass-heavy textures and Robert Fripp's distorted (and often dissonant) guitar are to the fore. Four-bar groupings return: 'Up the Hill Backwards' alternates conventional ionian $I-IV-V-I$ and $I-VI-V-IV$ patterns, using held organ chords and strummed acoustic guitar – almost a return to the textures of *Ziggy Stardust*. More monolithic groupings also appear. The refrain to 'Because You're Young' begins with a mixolydian $I-IV$; $II-VI$ repeated, slides in a strange $III-I$, then repeats $IV-V^{\#3}$ to the end: this seems to be a cross between the two types of grouping.

Tin Machine (1989) again employs an updated version of the hard rock of *Ziggy Stardust*, complete with riff ('Heaven's in Here'), strummed second guitar (normally electric, but acoustic on 'Amazing'), hook refrain ('Prisoner of Love') and numerous guitar solos. The eight-bar breaks of 'Heaven's in Here' are underpinned by kit patterns in which the second beat of each odd-numbered bar is attacked on all drums, building up to the next such beat through a roll. The pattern was common twenty years ago, being used by Led Zeppelin (e.g. 'Whole Lotta Love'), Cream and Deep Purple. This exemplifies the difficulty of ascertaining whether the style is present just in pastiche or actually in performance: to argue the latter would be to maintain that this hard rock style is still in the historical process of constitution.

Beyond this stylistic basis, Bowie's local stylistic referents are wide, and they normally appear with a strong sense of irony. This is most explicit in

'Ashes to Ashes', his reworking of 'Space Oddity', in which his jaundiced view of earlier success is made apparent. On the *Ziggy–Aladdin–Diamond* trio, the most thoroughgoing reference is to the 'strut rock' reminiscent of the Rolling Stones (suggested by intermittent absence of bass, use of cowbell and minimal riff or boogie pattern on guitar) of 'Rebel Rebel' or 'Watch that Man'. The glitter rock style of the Sweet or Gary Glitter receives a sideswipe in 'Star', with its characteristic repeated piano chords, tempo and backing voices, while 'The Prettiest Star', previously released as a single in the guise of a rather tender love-song, appears here in parody as rock 'n' roll, complete with honking sax, repeated chord piano and doo-wop vocals. Pastiche is widely present. 'Starman' focuses on acoustic guitar but breaks into a boogie bridge from refrain to verse; a boogie pattern also underpins the strange chromatic sequence used to characterize the 'Cracked Actor'. 'Moonage Daydream' combines acoustic guitar with a power chord riff (still a common texture in the late 1980s), but leading into a full string backing in the latter part of the song, while the power riff of 'Panic in Detroit' leads into an overplayed solo play-out over the hackneyed aeolian I–VI–VII pattern. The strangest reference seems to be to modern jazz: Mike Garson's large arpeggios and clusters recall perhaps Keith Tippett's playing, while the searing guitar work on 'Candidate' points in a similar direction. That the latter recalls Robert Fripp, who was to play with Bowie later, and also that Tippett worked with King Crimson, may not be entirely unworthy of note. That such stylistic variety does not sound messy seems a result of the consistent presence of Bowie's remarkable voice (which begins to assume its later, heavily mannered delivery on, for example, 'Sweet Thing') and of a set instrumentation, with roles that are clearly fixed.

Pastiche is rare on *Lodger*, while parody returns on *Scary Monsters*: on 'Ashes to Ashes', ionian I–VI–IV–V and I–III–IV patterns are in evidence, which, when combined with a voice and sub-boogie piano owing much to Bryan Ferry, seems to point further to Ferry's own tongue-in-cheek versions of doo-wop. The beautifully sinister 'Teenage Wildlife' is similar, based on ionian I–IV with a hackneyed riff, and appearing almost as a hard rock pastiche of so many soft rock ballads. 'Fashion', on the other hand, nods back towards Bowie's funk stylings (for which see below), particularly in the bass line, the spaces in the texture formed by Fripp's guitar, an undistorted funk guitar line and the long play-out reminiscent of moments on *Young Americans*.

With *Tin Machine*, pastiches are a little more particular, ranging from the Troggs' 'Wild Thing' in Bowie's 'Crack City' (sharing the I–IV structure, with identical rhythmic articulation and very similar tone) and the Beatles' 'When I Get Home' on Bowie's 'Bus Stop' (again, the same V–I structure and articulation). Irony finds a place in the contradiction between layers:

'Baby Can Dance' features under a smooth,

unsyncopated voice, and 'Pretty Thing' superimposes a very fast kit standard rock beat on a slow-moving aeolian I–II$^{\sharp 5}$–III pattern, each chord stretching over four bars.

On *Low* (1977), Bowie discovered the synthesizer, an instrument that remained central to his music until *Tin Machine*. This discovery has led to claims that he laid some of the foundations for 'synthesizer rock'. Although there are parallels, both obvious and more hidden, they are only partial. *Low* clearly epitomizes three characteristics of 'synthesizer rock' specified in Chapter 4: the 'cleanness' of the synthesized timbres, the rather expressionless voice and the layering of the vocal over pre-existing instrumental tracks, without any sense of interplay.[19] In addition, synthesizers are used to different effect. Brian Eno's strong influence is apparent in the generally thick textures.[20] There is also a concentration on 'sound effects'. Each side of *Low* differs from synthesizer rock in important respects. Side 1 uses conventional rock textures, over which synthesizer lines are sometimes placed, thus retaining the rhythm guitar that is generally absent in synthesizer rock. Side 2, which is dominated by the synthesizer, contains no kit (this being a standard feature in synthesizer rock), thus suggesting strong affinities with 'mood music'. The stylistic allusions that were lost in Bowie's 'plastic soul' phase begin to re-appear. These range from Steve Reich's marimba writing on 'Weeping Wall', through to the dense, slow-moving synthesizer textures and chanting in an unrecognizable tongue (Bowie and Eno's 'Warszawa'), later to be used on *Peter Gabriel IV*, and even to Latin rhythms and Mantovani-like (synthesized) strings on 'Sound and Vision'.

The subsequent *"Heroes"* (1977) has a similar distinction between sides 1 and 2, the second side's 'Sense of Doubt', 'Moss Garden' and 'Neuköln' epitomizing what is sometimes termed 'textural' music, i.e. a series of slowly changing harmonies, no vocals, and no harmonic patterns, conventional melodies or beat-supplying kit. The dense, static textures of these three tracks pervade the entire album (and are a norm for Bowie at this time), with Robert Fripp's guitar laying down ever-present distorted guitar lines, low in the mix, paralleling the use of synthesizer.

Bowie's *Young Americans* (1975) appeared as a complete *volte face*, a rejection of rock in favour of disco ('plastic soul' in Bowie's words). As the dance referents of this album continued through *Let's Dance* (1983), *Tonight* (1984) and *Never Let Me Down* (1987), Bowie effected something of a rapprochement between rock and dance, a movement brought to a temporary close by *Tin Machine* (1989). Bowie is on record as suggesting that the distance between *Diamond Dogs* and his first 'disco/soul' experiments on *Young Americans* was short (Lynch 1984: 103). Indeed, the trend is present earlier. 'Soul Love' (from *Ziggy Stardust*) superimposes on the acoustic guitar a sax riff (later solo) whose style clearly presages 'Young Americans'. On *Diamond Dogs*, 'Candidate' has similar elements, in the use of sax, open-ended sequence and a voice less concerned with line and syntax. Different soul styles are also approached: after opening with a reminiscence of the Beatles' 'Let It Be', the organ of 'Rock 'n' Roll with Me' nods in the direction of 'blue-eyed soul' (Clarke 1989), in the sense of Eric Clapton's eponymous album, while '1984' is an effective post-Motown pastiche, incorporating hihat semiquavers, wah-wah guitar and strings.

Young Americans does represent a large-scale stylistic shift. It was recorded at Gamble and Huff's Philadelphia studios, so influential in the rise of disco, and made use of some in-house musicians. But rather than the massed strings and smooth, parallel vocal harmonies of this style, *Young Americans* is far closer to the funk experiments of James Brown and George Clinton, evinced by the tone and precision of Bowie's backing singers, honking sax, congas, wah wah (especially on 'Fascination') and cut strumming guitar.[21] Textures have become rather looser, instruments tending not to sustain throughout the time of their presence, while short, open-ended patterns have become the structural norm. These are no longer used to increase the tension, but as repeated patterns over which vocal improvisations take place. Bowie's new voice seems to become this style's most characteristic feature: the long play-out to 'Young Americans' gives him room to suggest the physical effort involved in singing while moving (dancing), with syntax split into two and three-word, often repeated, snatches forming a minimal line centring on a single pitch (especially on 'Right'), which surely derives from James Brown. The effort is further conveyed by the sounds being punched out from the diaphragm. The importance of this approach is shown by his turning the Beatles' 'Across the Universe' into a platform for the repeated assertion that 'nothin's gonna (change my world)'.

Both *Let's Dance* and *Never Let Me Down* retain a rock basis, within which references to dance styles appear. The instrumental norm is heavy rock drums, occasional lead guitar breaks ('Cat People', 'China Girl' with its evocative open fourths, 'Let's Dance' and 'Criminal World') and sometimes a chord-sustaining organ. Overt funk references on the former album are legion.[22] Additionally, Bowie makes use of dance mixing procedures on 'Let's Dance', where items from one or more tracks are excised. This track has much production work invested in it, such as the bouncing from side to side of the cut-strum guitar and kit bass drum. On the latter album, although the most detectable pastiches relate to soul,[23] other pastiches are more interesting. 'Shining Star' verges on parody, with the voices clearly referring to the pop ballad as sung by Cliff Richard, but commented on with irony by the jerky bass and kit, which has a 'dirty' tone. The song's sweetness is also an ironic commentary on the lyrics. 'Time Will Crawl' suggests that the stylistic basis remains close to that of *Ziggy Stardust*, complete with acoustic guitar strums, but a harder version of the same. 'Never Let Me Down' refers to a 1960s pop ballad style. Its repeated progression (ionian $I-I^{\#5}-VI/I-I^{\flat 7}$) recalls songs like the Crickets' 'Don't Ever Change' (and, looking back further, many songs of the Ink Spots). This is intensified by its articulation: it appears in the bridge section, with the guitarist slowly drawing the plectrum across the strings once for each chord, while the 'soft' blues harp also refers to 1960s pop; but this is superimposed on a soft funk guitar and 1980s Cliff Richard style, vibrato-heavy backing harmonies. Most rich in reference is 'Zeroes', whose narrative recalls 'Ziggy Stardust' itself, with an extended chord sequence absent from Bowie's repertoire since 'Life on Mars', and a generalized evocation of parts of *Sgt Pepper's* . . . , through instrumentation (sitar and tabla), production, backing voices, melodic turns of phrase and isolated chord successions. 'Beat of Your Drum' refers to earlier Bowie, with its crooning voice (generally missing from the album) and unpredictable use of synthesized textures, while the layered synthesizer opening of 'Glass Spider' looks back to *Low*.

This survey of much of David Bowie's work should make plain how intrinsic a feature of his approach the techniques of pastiche and parody are. As I have said above, we should not expect to be able to translate into words the meaning of the musical syntax, but it appears to me that Bowie provides listeners with a rich ground for appropriating meaning by his constant calling-to-mind of other, familiar styles. Although Elvis Costello seems to provide a similarly rich ground, his different approaches to these techniques are notable.

Paradoxically, although Costello's music does not have such a firm stylistic basis as that of Bowie, Costello's vocal technique and sound do remain a constant feature. He tends to sing in a comfortable middle register, rarely reaching for extremes of pitch. He uses no resonance or vibrato and employs a rather nasal tone, almost as if he is speaking at pitch. He squeezes words into place: there may sometimes be a sense that they fit into the tunes rather than vice versa, although I think this misunderstands him (the influence here is surely early Springsteen). This characterization is important, because despite the excellence of Costello's stylistic pastiches, his distinctive voice remains a constant factor. Additionally, for Gouldstone (1989), he consistently returns to a small group of topics: women, particularly the misuse of them by men; the passing of time; political matters, particularly those of imperialism; and his favoured puns, not all of which work, but which lend his lyrics a particular irony.

There is a characteristic texture to his early albums (as far as *Goodbye Cruel World* of 1984). Their instrumentation develops from 1960s mod/soul bands, with a dominant but idiosyncratic organ sound (Steve Nieve was a classically trained pianist without a pop background), an understated guitar and a full texture. Costello tends to employ conventional verse/refrain structures, without open-ended patterns. However, line and verse lengths are highly variable, to accommodate his verbal flights. This is nowhere more apparent than on 'There's No Action'. The speed is fast, with four straight beats to the bar. Two-bar units are the norm, but extra half-bars are common. These match changes from lines where the first syllable is stressed, to lines with five or six initial unstressed syllables. In this grouping diagram, italicized words *end* each rhythmic group. The second lines of both the verse and the refrain are extended (developed) on repetition.

Verse 1:
2 bars (unaccompanied, *touch*) + 2;   2 (*much*) + $2\frac{1}{2}$;
2 + $1\frac{1}{2}$ + 2 (*friends*); $2\frac{1}{2}$ + 2 (*hands*);
Total: 4 + $4\frac{1}{2}$; $5\frac{1}{2}$ + $4\frac{1}{2}$.

Refrain:
2 + 2 + 2;

2 + 2;
Total: 6 + 4.

Verse 2:
2 (*kingdom*) + 2; 2 (*bring them*) + $2\frac{1}{2}$;
2 + 2;   2 + 2;   2 + 2;   3;
Total: 4 + $4\frac{1}{2}$;   8 + 7.

Refrain:
2 + 2 + 2;
2 + 2;   2 + 2;
2 + 2 + 2;
2 + 2;
Total: 6 + 8;   6 + 4.

This sort of pattern – regular in principle but with local irregularities – can be found throughout Costello's output.

Although Costello was a part of the 'pub rock' scene contemporaneous with the rise of punk, most of his early albums were elegant style pastiches. Thus, *My Aim Is True*, while reminiscent of Graham Parker, refers strongly to country music through its use of country musicians (the vehement 'I'm Not Angry' contains an effective bridge straight out of western swing). *Almost Blue* pastiches a more laid back country style, while *Punch the Clock* has an updated Stax soul style. I shall consider how pastiches on two albums, *Get Happy!!*, with its particular references to soul, and *King of America*, which refers to folk and cajun, are effected.

Get Happy!! was released in 1980, marketed as a pastiche of a scruffy, well-used 1960s soul album, down to the garish green and orange cover with Costello in dance pose, and with built-in blemishes on the cover that would normally take months of constant love and use to produce. 'Secondary Modern' immediately evokes 'soul' through its introductory texture and guitar rhythm and contour (see example 5.1) and their similarity to Marvin Gaye's 'I Heard It through the Grapevine' (see example 5.2). In terms of instrumentation, however, the sound of Costello's guitar is some way from the broody electric piano on 'Grapevine', which the alteration from dorian (Gaye) to ionian (Costello) modes further emphasizes. In this, 'Secondary Modern' is far closer to Creedence Clearwater Revival's guitar version of 'Grapevine', this latter being far from a soul treatment. So, although the allusion is clear, it may not pay to delve too far. The second example is Costello's 'Love for Tender', whose basic kit rhythm sounds as if it is a paradigm for soul (see example 5.3). But almost all 1960s soul has the third beat filled, with the first quite prominent; in 'Love for Tender', they are rather absent. The Supremes' 'You Can't Hurry Love' has a pattern that is very close (see example 5.4), although Motown is a much more commercial style than Costello's commentators (such as St Michael 1986) suggest he is referring to. Even here, Phil Collins's 1982 cover of 'You Can't Hurry Love' gets closest to 'Love for Tender' (see example 5.5). Although my search has been limited by my knowledge of soul, this

Example 5.1 Elvis Costello: 'Secondary Modern'

Example 5.2 Marvin Gaye: 'I Heard It through the Grapevine'

Example 5.3 Elvis Costello: 'Love for Tender' (simplified single kit line)

Example 5.4 Supremes: 'You Can't Hurry Love' (simplified single kit line)

Example 5.5 Phil Collins: 'You Can't Hurry Love' (simplified single kit line)

leaves the interesting possibility that the clearest allusory feature of 'Love for Tender' may not be present in any actual example.

King of America, released in 1986, was largely backed by musicians from the Southern USA, which helps to account for the cajun influence. It contains one overt political track, 'Little Palaces', which concerns slum tower blocks, and which is accompanied only by Costello on strummed acoustic guitar, highlighted at important points by mandolin. Here, it is the means of performance that seems important, allying the song with similar offerings by singers such as Martin Carthy (Leon Rosselson's song 'Palaces of Gold', for example), Dick Gaughan, or even Billy Bragg, thereby alluding to the 'folk protest' style, where articulatory simplicity has to be dominant. Indeed, this album served to enable Costello's appropriation by the vanguard of the folk/roots movement – as evinced by his appearance in the pages of *Folk Roots* magazine, including an interview with him – which recent changes of style *away from* this album have done little to diminish. This is a further illustration that style carries ideological baggage.

More recently, Costello has tended to pursue pastiche in individual songs on albums, rather than throughout whole albums. Thus on *Spike*, for example, 'Veronica' alludes to numerous songs by the Move in its arrangement, vocal tone and harmonic sequences, particularly at the beginning of the refrain, while 'Miss Macbeth' evokes Madness through its instrumentation, and 'Any King's Shilling' pastiches Irish bands like Clannad or the Chieftains, with its characteristic use of Uillean pipes and harp, but with serious intent. Again, on *Mighty as a Rose*, 'Harpies Bizarre' refers to the rather glittery late 1960s 'arty' pop (groups such as Harpers Bizarre or Honeybus) in the way a wind quintet is used as accompaniment and in the style of instrumental interludes, while on 'So Like Candy', co-authored with Paul McCartney, not only does the use of the mellotron recall 'Strawberry Fields Forever', but the 'Hard Day's Night' chord (a ringing minor eleventh) is also prominent. I noted above that techniques of pastiche and parody are an intrinsic feature of the work of David Bowie: the same is clearly true of the work of Elvis Costello. It remains to suggest what effect the use of these techniques may have.

Throughout this discussion, I have noted very few examples of direct quotation, and I believe a clear distinction has to be drawn between pastiche and parody on the one hand, and borrowing (or even theft?) on the other. I cannot accept the notion of 'ownership' of such things as a particular combination of instruments, a manner of vocal delivery, a given rhythmic pattern or a certain harmonic sequence: one could hardly copyright these, after all. 'Borrowing' suggests, to me, that the concept of 'ownership' of particular features is accepted, while 'wholesale borrowing', perhaps with the intention of passing the copy off as the original, would presumably count as 'forgery'. Pastiche and parody are never quite so precise and are dependent, in any case, on the *explicit* recognition of prior instances. The effect of the use of parody in rock is perhaps fairly self-evident: it permits a degree of irony to enter the song that is difficult to achieve in other ways, and that reinforces the ideology of some writers of commenting on events from something of a distance. (Apart from Costello and Bowie, Ray Davies and Paul McCartney come immediately to mind.) Pastiche probably occurs more widely, although it seems to receive less attention: its effect is more difficult to determine. Certainly it marks an important position in the debate over 'authenticity', since explicit reference to, and virtuosic display of, pre-existent styles is necessarily a denial of the notion of unmediated expression. It also strengthens the sense of rock's continuing tradition. For Frith (1990: 91), this tradition seems to be nearing its end *because* it is used, more and more, as a source for pastiche. On the contrary, the friction produced in the music of Bowie and Costello seems to me to have an enriching effect: rock's performers have constructed a music that, in its self-reference, has senses both of its history and of its own identity.

Stylistic development

At the beginning of Chapter 3, I suggested that new styles have related to established styles by way of a number of subtly different approaches:

formation, reconciliation, development, opposition, regression, innovation and consolidation. Here, I want to pursue that question in relation to specific examples, in order to focus on the issue that stylistic development, and hence growing maturity, is the accepted norm for (at least) rock musicians. For these case studies, I have chosen three bands and one solo artist. Genesis were a popular progressive band whose personnel changes have had their effect on style: they are now a straight rock band. Gentle Giant had a devout if limited following: after a series of progressive albums they relocated to the USA to join the AOR market, after which they disbanded. Status Quo were never really a progressive band, and indeed have acquired a name among their detractors for a highly inbred brand of formula rock. Finally, Paul McCartney's post-Beatle career has been highly varied, but he remains a well-respected writer. For each study, I shall report the detailed comparison of a single recent album with a single earlier one. Ideally, a larger spread of detail in each case should be discussed, but pressure of space prevents such detail here. None the less, the results point to an important conclusion.

Both *Foxtrot* (1972) and *Invisible Touch* (1986) achieved popularity and chart success. Without the necessary audience research, it is not possible to assert whether the tastes of Genesis's original audience changed or they acquired a wholly new audience, although I have cause to doubt the latter. The style of neither album is so limited that it can be described in full briefly, but the chief differences can be pinpointed in terms of the later album. Most audible is the constant presence on *Invisible Touch* of the standard rock beat, overlaid with many frills. This means that the metric irregularities of earlier albums, including *Foxtrot*, have all been ironed out. Perhaps as a consequence of this, verse structures are far clearer, while harmonic sequences repeat in shorter blocks. 'Land of Confusion' illustrates this most clearly, but it is also present in the less mainstream 'The Brazilian' (which would not have been out of place on *Peter Gabriel IV*). Related to this, the sense of harmonic arrival that ends the introduction to 'Watcher of the Skies' is missing on the later album. The textural balance on *Invisible Touch* has altered such that the kit is fore-grounded, as is Phil Collins's straighter delivery, although in places this textural change (textures on the whole are far denser) means that the instrumentation is rather more integrated than of old.[24]

There are, however, certain stylistic features that remain. The chromatic harmonies of the verse of 'The Last Domino' are similar to those of the earlier 'Watcher of the Skies', although the ever-present and much maligned mellotron has now disappeared. The electric guitar tends to hide within the texture, rather than appearing as a soloist, while the keyboard appears in a quasi-solo role but playing accompanimental patterns.[25]

Perhaps the subtle differences are of greatest interest. On 'Tonight Tonight Tonight', both the keyboard break and the harmonies of the extended bridge are straight out of the earlier style, but the bass, constantly anticipating the beat, is a new (soul-influenced) feature. Again, the gentle but extended bridge in 'The Last Domino' could have appeared on earlier albums on many of the longer songs, but the thickening of texture with slight percussion is not present in the earlier style. The final point of difference, which is most marked, is that on the later album, most of the lyrics can be interpreted immediately by the listener, as if they were drawn from direct personal experience, rather than assuming allegorical or fantastical poses. In the wake of critical disdain regarding the pomposity of the lyrics of progressive rock, this may be viewed as exemplifying growing maturity, although it is hard to state the criteria according to which a similar view could reasonably be propounded for the musical style.

A similar problem is apparent in consideration of the change of style undergone by Gentle Giant. Although their *Civilian* (1980) is commonly identified as far less complex than earlier efforts (see e.g. Clarke 1989), the differences between it and *Octopus* (1972) are not as great as they initially appear. The basic change in stylistic direction is not dissimilar to that posited above for Genesis, but it is achieved in a different way. Most notable on *Civilian* are normal verse/refrain structures and constant use of a standard rock beat, even down to the quaver hihat strokes on 'Number One'. Although it is not immediately apparent, this aspect of their style is present on almost all tracks on *Octopus*: 'Knots' uses it for the refrain, while 'A Cry for Everyone' and 'River' place it beneath unorthodox harmonic patterns with stresses in unexpected places. This latter track also employs a standard guitar break.

What marks out the initial style most clearly is that all but the love ballad 'Think of Me with Kindness' manage to combine standard rock passages with a variety of distant stylistic allusions, in which linear textures are ubiquitous. 'The Boys in the Band' illustrates this well, where the long unison 'jazz fusion' upbeat settles down into a rock passage. 'Raconteur Troubadour', with its alternation of $\frac{5}{8}$ and $\frac{6}{8}$, seems to suggest a medieval pastiche (which it is not), breaking into an anthemic break that, as everywhere else, is clearly 'composed'. Metric/rhythmic irregularity is also a common feature: 'The River' opens with four bars of $\frac{8}{8}$, perfectly standard, but with highly unusual stresses (see example 5.6). This level of intricacy is entirely missing from *Civilian*.

Timbrally, *Octopus* is highly varied: trumpet, trombone, xylophone and violin (played by members of the band) are treated soloistically, in addition to the standard ensemble. These former are lacking on *Civilian*. Texturally, *Octopus* is unusually dense for 1972, deriving from the overlaying of one linear part with others. This linearity, which derives from both modern jazz and the baroque styles, remains as a vestige on *Civilian*: half the tracks are based on guitar riffs, over either drones or stepwise basses, these riffs remaining throughout, but overlain with other material. Harmonically, however, *Civilian* is by comparison unadventurous. Both 'All Through the Night' and 'Inside Out' move constantly at two chords per bar (nothing could be more con-

Example 5.6 Gentle Giant: 'The River' (pattern of stresses)

Example 5.7 Guitar 'boogie' pattern (can appear with either shuffle or straight beats)

Example 5.8 Guitar 'driving' pattern (can appear with either shuffle or straight beats)

ventional), whereas on *Octopus* harmonies have to be inferred by ear from the contrapuntal lines. Comparing the two, the later album is far less stylistically adventurous.[26]

Status Quo's style is often considered to be represented by an early single such as 'Down the Dustpipe'. Rhythmically this employs a shuffle standard rock beat, with a 'boogie' accompanimental pattern (see example 5.7), while formally and harmonically it is a twelve-bar blues. One of the stylistic requirements for the employment of either a boogie or a driving pattern (also used by Status Quo: see example 5.8), is speed: at anything less than about 160 beats to the minute, such a pattern becomes laboured and will normally be replaced by a pattern admitting rests.

A comparison of *Quo* (1974) with *Perfect Remedy* (1989) suggests that Status Quo have become stylistically able. Of eight tracks on the earlier album, only three are actually twelve-bar sequences, although seven make use of either boogie or driving patterns (and only four make use of shuffle rhythms). Riffs are correspondingly rare (indeed, functionally speaking, both boogie and driving patterns can be considered minimal riffs), only 'Just Take Me' making use of a power chord riff. Open-ended sequences predominate: only 'Fine Fine Fine' has something approaching a non-twelve-bar periodic structure.

On the later album, shuffle rhythms are more common (seven from twelve), although twelve-bar sequences are wholly absent, and at least five songs have clear periodic structures. On only five songs are clear driving patterns used, with a quasi-boogie pattern under the break on 'Man Overboard'. There have been replaced by power chord sequences and, in three clear cases, power riffs. The range of stylistic referents has also increased greatly,[27] while harmonically, Status Quo have ventured further on the later album, being no longer restricted to the primary (i.e. I, IV and V) triadic sequences of *Quo*.

By 1970, Paul McCartney was an experienced songwriter. Thus, a comparison between that year's *McCartney* and *Flowers in the Dirt*, from 1989, will suggest the extent to which his style changed after achieving stability. As he is an individual songwriter, discussion will necessarily be at a more local level than hitherto, since details of arrangement are far more varied than with bands, and therefore these cannot usefully be compared.

The outstanding feature on both albums is the high degree of regular eight-bar groupings: the latter's 'We Got Married' is standard, with an 8 + 8 verse answered by an 8 ($\times$ 2) refrain. Certain rhythmic patterns also predominate,

particularly ♩ ♪♩ ♪♩ , familiar from Beatles songs: here it underpins

both 'Every Night' (1970) and 'This One' (1989). The refrain of this latter song also seems to recall McCartney's earliest love song sequences. Particularly clear 'genre' items return: the acoustic guitar figurations of 'Blackbird', from the *White Album*, equally underpin both 'Junk' and, nineteen years later, 'Put It There'. The memorable ionian VI–III$^{\#3}$–I–IV–I pattern of 'Junk', with its chromatically descending bass line (itself a McCartney fingerprint) returns in the link to 'My Brave Face', the opening track of *Flowers in the Dirt*. Other typical McCartney gestures can be found: the occasional lopsided groupings,[28] the use of piano and organ on 'That Day Is Done', to strengthen the gospel evocations of 'Let It Be' (particularly when both end the refrain with ionian IV–I cadences, modified through the mode having particularly fluid sixth and seventh scale-degrees), and the use particularly of clarinet and strings to evoke a certain nostalgia: thus 'When I'm Sixty-four' and 'Eleanor Rigby' are recalled again in 'Distractions'.

In all, and notwithstanding the explicit influence of Elvis Costello on the production of the later album, the style of the two is remarkably similar, and both retain very definite traits from earlier McCartney songs. Thus, in this case, his musical style cannot be said to have moved on in twenty years. The problem is that this is likely to be construed as a criticism.

With the exception of McCartney, these studies clearly point to changes of style, and, with Genesis and Gentle Giant, away from features that seemed to betoken a strong measure of originality. This is not to suggest that all bands move in this direction, but it may well be the case that the greater wealth invested in the USA market, and the corresponding corporate liking for a homogenized market, may at least begin to account for this directional change. The greater accessibility gained by Genesis and Gentle Giant could be construed as maturing (in terms of their becoming less 'obscure' and thus more 'relevant') but could equally be seen as a loss of vitality and settling for the easy way out.

In 1975, Graham Vulliamy argued that rock (as opposed to pop) was 'in the process of legitimation' as a result of striking parallels between the views of those involved in rock and those defending a 'high culture' position. One of the most telling of these parallels is the gradual assumption of maturity. Vulliamy quotes Hopkins to the effect that:

> One of the many things the Beatles would give rock was the concept that groups should evolve and grow – developing musically – rather than stand in place and merely continue to issue dozens of records that sounded like those that preceded them.
>
> (Hopkins 1970, quoted in Vulliamy 1975: 137)

There is, of course, an immediate problem here, in that evolution (with its connotation of 'progress') and simple change are equated, but I shall leave that to one side for now.

In terms of lyrics, it is not hard to see how maturity can be shown. Presumably, the longer any (good) writer lives, and hence the greater experience that writer acquires, the more insight will be gained into things that matter, and this insight should find its way into the writer's songs. As far as the accompanying music is concerned, it is hard to see how maturity might be shown in this context. For art music composers, maturity is shown by a composer's growing control over musical material, over setting (technical) objectives and knowing how to achieve them. This is close to the notion that the language of music itself progresses, and that a mature composer will expand the possibilities inherent within it. This model is difficult to apply to rock. Evolution of the harmonic/melodic language must, of necessity, remove it from its modal roots, whereby it would arguably lose at least its audience. It may be that this evolution should therefore be sought within other domains, for instance the employment of studio and other technology, but this is frequently out of the direct control of musicians. It is my impression that, whenever the notion of maturity is invoked by commentators, it refers only to lyrics, and not to the rest of the music (notwithstanding the Beatles: the style of 'Get Back' certainly does not represent an evolution from 'Penny Lane', nor that of 'Let It Be' from 'If I Fell').

Within a static language, and the harmonic/melodic/rhythmic materials of rock must now be construed as such, the issue hinges on the extent to which stylistic 'progress' is achievable. Christopher Small insists that, by definition, it is not:

> The notion of 'progress' may have some meaning in regard to science, which is concerned with the accumulation of abstract and objective knowledge divorced from personality, but is impossible to sustain in the arts, based as they are on experience, which is unique to the individual and must be renewed with each succeeding generation.
>
> (Small 1977: 9)

I suggested earlier that the language of rock progressed from its blues roots, via the appropriation of elements of diverse stylistic practices, until the 1970s, at which point it seemed to reach an impasse, which has been overcome by various returns to simplicity, combined with greater sophistication in the less determinate domains, particularly texture and timbre. If this explanation is adequate, a style can only 'progress' to the point at which it has all the possible materials available for use. Thereafter, these elements can only be juggled with to produce new, different, but not 'better' styles. After this point, styles change, but do not develop.

The difficulty with the notion of development is that it implies a teleology: we develop *from* something inchoate *to* something more fully formed, and hence, better, which is perhaps a supreme arrogance. There do not seem to me to be *any* universally valid criteria for the determination of value in respect to *any* music: as soon as we propose such criteria, we re-trace the arguments for aesthetic autonomy long associated with the classical tradition. No sooner do we suggest that a music is 'better', than we have to ask 'better at what?' and 'for whom?' Thus, to return to the argument I proposed in Chapter 1, any criteria for the evaluation of rock must be made against a background of the function that a particular music is being made to perform at the place and time of its being heard and about which we know, in detail, very little. The extreme relativism that this implies is both unavoidable and to be embraced, for it asserts that not only music's meaning, but its values too, are the preserves of listeners.

Conclusion

Although 'rock' is not a monolithic style, although there are no 'essential features' which distinguish rock from other musical practices, there are internal consistencies of practice which make it both possible and useful to view rock as a relatively bounded musical discourse. It has been my main aim to demonstrate the consistencies of this stylistic practice, and also some of its boundaries, by developing a body of coherent techniques and testing these against the music, coming thereby to something of an understanding of what 'rock' is. Other commentators may seek to establish other consistencies and limits, and this issue is open to debate but must be argued, at least in part, on the basis of what is present in the music. I have pointed out at a number of places in the text that rock scholarship has, until now, largely been a creature of cultural and sociological reductionism, and that much of the blame for this must be laid at the door of those musicologists who have ignored massive regions of the 'total musical field'. In my desire to redress the balance, some readers will have cause to criticize what may appear as 'musicological reductionism', the impression I may have given that 'musical meaning' is all, and that the *cultural* effects of styles are illusory. My emphasis on the ways open to listeners to construe sounds, rather than on the intentions of musicians and producers, should give indication that I do not consider such a reductionist position valid. Neither do I believe that 'musical meaning' is all, nor that a musicological enquiry is in any way self-sufficient. I am, however, certain that its techniques have been too long ignored. To quote from the conclusion to Tagg's study of 'Fernando':

> any discussion of mass culture or mass society in general will need to include analyses of musical meaning, for it is in the non-verbal forms of symbolic representation that emotional levels of social, cultural, political and ideological meaning are to be found . . . if cultural theorists, sociologists, linguists, etc. are not prepared to take music into consideration in their discussion of symbolic production in contemporary society and if musicians and musicologists are not prepared to shoulder the responsibility this lays on them to demystify their art and its hieroglyphics, we will be left with little or no viable cultural theory of our own times.

> (Tagg 1991: 144)

This process of demystification is vital, for the unease many listeners encounter when determining the import of musical sounds results in their treating them either as magical, or as insignificant. They are neither. It is only through developing an adequate theory of rock stylistic processes that I have arrived at a position from where various rock myths, particularly those of 'authenticity' and 'unmediated expression', can be approached critically. As such, I have not produced a 'complete' view of rock, nor have I tried to do so. But, I believe that by opening up the debate, and suggesting techniques for the explicit treatment of the sounds themselves, the ground is better prepared for a more completely interdisciplinary understanding of the practices which form such a large part of many peoples' lives.

So, what remains to be done? Throughout the text I have indicated various avenues for further research. I shall cite here only those that I perceive as being the most urgent. They fall into three distinct groups. Firstly, a great deal of work remains to be done amongst rock's listening publics. It has been possible for me to informally test some of my relevant conclusions amongst acquaintances, friends and students, but the notion of 'affordance' indicates, in part, that we do not know precisely why listeners interpret particular things in particular ways, nor according to what critera. Although such reception tests would seem to be totally unmanageable due to their necessary breadth and depth, can we afford to do without them? The audience research I have in mind needs to proceed both from the particular and the general, and I give three examples. To what *extent* does the semantic significance of lyrics matter, with respect to different styles and audiences? To what extent are the findings of psychologists with regard to listeners' models of the structures of concert musics relevant to listeners' models of the structures of rock? We know that differences of style are recognized by listeners, and that these differences form the basis of matters of taste. We do not know the details as to *how* these differences are recognized.

Secondly, there is much scope for work from musicologists. This study is by no means exhaustive with respect to rock styles. There are many more consistently 'mainstream' UK artists I have barely mentioned (Queen, Elton John, Dire Straits, the Rolling Stones), while questions remain of the music contemporary with progressive rock. For example, was its consistency and distinctiveness of timbre an important factor in the reception of 'teenybop', as I surmise? Alternatively, what were the stylistic features of reggae which enabled its appropriation by skinheads? Moreover, the similarities and differences between styles in the USA and UK need to be investigated, and not only because the 'world market' perceived by the industry hides a multitude of varying social practices. This can be particularly investigated with respect to US artists whose styles seem to have no direct equivalent in the UK: Lynyrd Skynyrd, the Grateful Dead, Frank Zappa and R.E.M. come to mind. Aside from this work with style, there is room for more precisely analytical and theoretical investigation. Is it possible to develop a generative harmonic theory for rock, or will we need one which is more particularly style-specific? Is it possible to develop a theory of 'deep structures' which is not pitch-based, but which is founded on matters of texture? Is it possible to develop a semiotic 'lexicon' of musical attitudinal stances to lyrical content and, if so, by what processes and over what time scales would it change? In addition to these, the deficiencies which readers may discover in the concepts I have developed here will suggest further lines of enquiry.

The third area of research is more directly interdisciplinary. I have traced in some detail the existence of style change. What are the mechanics of style change? Styles are socially grounded: does style change, which is much more the preserve of musicians than listeners, function with greater autonomy? Do style distinctions have total material reality other than as (shared) constructs inside listeners' memories? Whether or not they do, to what extent do cultural practices differ with respect to styles? How can contradictory tendencies co-exist within the same listening publics (for example, the consolidatory and innovatory tendencies towards tradition cited in Chapter 3), and how do listeners deal with these contradictions?

As you will see from this list, rock scholarship is still at an early stage. Many of these questions relate to the 'total musical field', i.e. musical practices of which rock only forms a part and, if I have managed to bring rock within the orbit of established musicological enquiry, I will regard that as a valuable achievement. More importantly, only by accepting musicological approaches as indispensable techniques, among others, can we, as a community, come to a greater understanding of our role within the practices which constitute rock music.

Notes

Introduction

1 For example, the Beatles' singing of 'Twist and Shout', Elvis Costello's singing of 'Mystery Dance', Elton John's singing of 'Crocodile Rock' or Slade's singing of 'Get Down and Get with It'. A note on attributions. Throughout, my emphasis is on the heard text, the sounds themselves as listeners receive them. Therefore, I refer throughout to songs *as performed by* certain people rather than *as written by* them, since the differences between different performances are material and must be acknowledged. This does not mean that I generally regard the act of writing, and songwriters, as inconsequential, but for the purposes of this book, citation of authors of songs would only confuse. Therefore, in referring to Martin Carthy's 'Palaces of Gold', for example (note 4, below), I do not intend to denigrate Leon Rosselson, the song's author, but in effect I refer to Martin Carthy's *singing of* 'Palaces of Gold'. This should always be understood, throughout this book.
2 For example, Jeff Beck's 'Hi-ho Silver Lining', Rod Stewart's 'Sailing', Sheila Walsh's 'Hope for the Hopeless' or the Edgar Broughton Band's 'Out Demons Out'.
3 For example, the Beatles' 'And I Love Her', Elvis Costello's 'Alison', Elton John's 'Your Song' or Slade's 'Everyday'.
4 For example, Bob Dylan's 'The Times They Are A-changing', Martin Carthy's 'Palaces of Gold' or Elvis Costello's 'Little Palaces'.
5 Although Gibson's work is specifically related to the visual environment, recent research (as yet unpublished), by Eric F. Clarke in particular, suggests that it is equally applicable to the perception of auditory phenomena.

Chapter 1

1 Further reasons are offered by McClary and Walser (1990).
2 See Wolff (1987) and Willis (n.d.: 2–5) for refutations of the ideology of autonomy in music.
3 See the Glossary for an explanation of these and similar terms.

4 This is how it looks from the perspective of 1990. When the book first appeared, it seemed to legitimize for (some) music undergraduates a music they were being (professionally) encouraged to despise.

5 For those readers who are interested, the best succinct account of Schenkerian analytical theory in English is given in Dunsby and Whittall (1988: 29–61); Schenker's own writings can be pretty inaccessible even to the musically literate. In their terms, Mellers's method owes most to the English writer Donald Tovey (see Dunsby and Whittall 1988: 62–73).

6 For criticisms of this theory from opposing ends of the political spectrum, see Andersen (1988) and Sampson (1980).

7 See the Glossary entry 'Roman numerals'.

8 For such an attempt with reggae, see Ehrlich (1983); for the same on the classicism of Mozart and Haydn, see Ford (1991).

9 And also to the linguistic/semiotic 'morpheme', for discussion of which see Middleton (1990: 269–86).

10 It should also be noted that isolated instances of interesting work have come out of British undergraduate music studies in recent years (I am personally aware of work emanating from the music departments of the City University and Thames Valley University). For instance, John Quirke's explanation of the factors contributing to Eric Clapton's wholesale rethinking of guitar technique is a worthy model for any similar investigation (Quirke 1987). Should such students join the professional community, the prospects for serious discussion of rock will improve greatly.

11 My thanks to Richard Middleton for pointing this out.

12 I would direct any reader who feels that I am reifying music to Green's excellent argument for the material existence and objectivity of music (see Green 1988: 12–16).

13 Spelling taken from a recent undergraduate essay.

14 Their existence affirmed by Lucy Green: private communication.

15 See also Gammon (1982: 23–7) and Green (1988: 130–1, 156–7) for refutations of Shepherd's encoding of Western industrial ideology in European classical music.

16 Chester cites The Band in this context because of its use in the article to which Chester's own forms a rejoinder.

17 The last movement of Schubert's quartet *Death and the Maiden*, recorded by the Allegri Quartet, illustrates this perfectly.

18 For a parallel argument from a very different viewpoint, see Molino (1990: II.2, especially 141–2).

19 In this discussion of Adorno, I am relying heavily on Bradley (n.d.).

20 Her 'delineated' does rather more work than my 'analogue', but the differences are not material here. Shepherd (1977b) also addresses these matters.

Chapter 2

1 Arguments against the use of notation *per se* have been well rehearsed in a number of texts in recent years, most particularly those of Small (1977) and parts of Shepherd *et al.* (1977), and, from a different standpoint, McLean (1981–2).

2 The viol family was the immediate ancestor of the violin family.

3 This rider is necessary since, until the development during the last decade of detailed guitar transcriptions in professional and semi-professional magazines (both in the UK, such as *Guitarist*, and in the USA, such as *Guitar for the Practicing Musician*), rock sheet music has been notoriously inaccurate as a coded version of

the sounds heard (and in many cases it remains so). These inaccuracies refer not only to melodies and rhythms, which do not always fall into the precise determinations notation requires, but also to harmonies, which can be described precisely.

4   I am sceptical of the 'great person' theory of culture, but in this case I am convinced that Clapton did indeed redefine the notion of guitar solo (see Quirke 1987).

5   Established theory makes use of different hierarchical levels of hypermetre (see Lerdahl and Jackendoff 1985: 18–25), but to pursue the relatively short formal lengths found in rock, one single level will be sufficient here.

6   The same pattern will be found in the Searchers' 'When You Walk in the Room', the verse of King Crimson's 'Court of the Crimson King', and the refrain of Derek and the Dominos' 'Layla'.

7   Other examples include immediately preceding the verse in Clapton's 'Let It Grow', the Beatles' 'Ticket to Ride', or the Mamas and the Papas' 'Creeque Alley'.

8   'Formants' are the constituents of a sound that give it its particular tone-qualities. They can be isolated and their relative presences analysed by means of an oscilloscope.

9   Roland Gift (of Fine Young Cannibals) and Jimmy Somerville provide clear examples.

10   Spandau Ballet were considered to be at the forefront of the 'new romantic' movement.

11   Honeybus's 'I Can't Let Maggie Go' is a rare example taken from the pop repertoire. This formal proportion is widely used in the songs of Tin Pan Alley, and many of the 1930s standards used for jazz improvisation. It is also fairly widely used in music hall songs.

12   Employing a modal (or even a tonal) system for the discussion of harmony requires that some harmonies assume the status of tonic. Sheet music treats all chords as functionally equivalent, by specifying their names rather than their relationships. This should not deafen us to the fact that those relationships are none the less present (this is fully argued in Moore 1992).

13   To give three examples: the tonal ♭II major is often part of a simple phrygian succession (e.g. the Moody Blues' 'Nights in White Satin', I–VII$^{\sharp3}$–VI–III–II–I; and Slade's 'Coz I Luv You', IV–I–II–I); tritone-prominent patterns are often part of simple locrian successions (e.g. David Bowie's 'The Bewlay Brothers', I$^{\sharp5}$–II–V–I$^{\sharp5}$; and Van Halen's 'Intruder', I$^{\sharp5}$–V); and the more common II major often belongs to a simple lydian succession (e.g. Fleetwood Mac's 'Dreams', I–II; Blondie's 'Atomic', I–V–VI–II; and Deep Purple's 'Flight of the Rat', I–V–II).

14   See Glossary.

15   The way this drone is articulated differs greatly between studio and live recorded performances.

16   For example, from A to C; that is, two steps, involving three letter-names.

17   For example, the solos in Jimi Hendrix's 'Voodoo Chile', the Doors' 'Riders on the Storm', Eric Clapton's 'Tell the Truth' (as Derek and the Dominos) or Fleetwood Mac's 'Gold Dust Woman'.

18   Fine Young Cannibals' 'As Hard as It Is' represents an extreme, being based on an ionian I–VII$^{\sharp5}$–VI–V–IV–III–II–V.

19   Abba's 'Gimme Gimme Gimme' uses aeolian I–III–V.

20   Abba's 'Voulez-vous' and Neil Young's 'Southern Man' both make use of aeolian I–VI–IV, Peter Gabriel's 'Solsbury Hill' extends this sequence to ionian I–VI–IV–II$^{\sharp3}$–V, and also to ionian I–VI–IV–V.

21   Among many other examples: Abba's 'Mama Mia', Beautiful South's 'Song for

Whoever', Orchestral Manoeuvres in the Dark's 'Enola Gay', Queen's 'Somebody to Love' and Simon and Garfunkel's 'Mrs Robinson'.

22 Respectively aeolian alternating $I^{\#3}$–VI, and dorian alternating I–VI$^{\#5/7}$.

23 Mixolydian I–IV–VII–V$^{\#3}$ in Elvis Costello's 'Alison' and, for the same in dorian, Procol Harum's 'Conquistador'.

24 Ionian as used in Abba's 'Fernando' or Gerry and the Pacemakers' 'How Do You Do It'.

25 Ionian as used in Transvision Vamp's 'Landslide of Love' or Bonnie Tyler's 'Lost in France'.

26 For example, the Beatles' 'Can't Buy Me Love', Big Country's 'Eiledon' and Elvis Costello's 'Living in Paradise.'

27 Jimi Hendrix's 'Hey Joe' and Siouxsie and the Banshees' 'Love in a Void' are the only examples of this sequence of which I am aware.

28 Taking examples from a wide range of styles: Abba's 'Take a Chance on Me' (refrain), the Animals' 'House of the Rising Sun' (verse), Big Country's 'The Sailor', the Electric Light Orchestra's 'Wild West Hero', John Lennon's 'Mother', Queen's 'Save Me', the Rolling Stones' 'Honky Tonk Women' and Cliff Richard's 'Please Don't Tease' (and many other late 1950s rock and roll songs) all make use of this basic structure.

29 For example, Freddie and the Dreamers' 'I'm Telling You', the Kinks' 'Till the End of the Day', Chris Rea's 'The Road to Hell' and Bonnie Tyler's 'Lost in France'.

30 For example, Bon Jovi's 'Born to Be My Baby', Eric Clapton's 'After Midnight', Creedence Clearwater Revival's 'Down on the Corner', Manfred Mann's 'Semi-detached Suburban Mr James', Nazareth's 'Broken Down Angel' and Procol Harum's 'Homburg'.

31 David Bowie's 'Changes' and the Move's 'Fire Brigade' end each phrase on V, although the Kinks' 'Waterloo Sunset' uses IV, while the Jam's 'Town Called Malice' uses the pairing II; V. All available pairings would seem potentially usable, and there seems little value in enumerating examples of each.

32 Variants stretch from the ionian I–IV–I–I–IV–IV–I–I–V–IV–{I–IV}–{I–V} of Derek and the Dominos' 'Have You Ever Loved a Woman' (where the braces indicate a change of chord within a bar) and the aeolian I–IV–I–I–IV–IV–I–I–V–{VI–IV}–{I–III}–{II$^{\#3}$–♭II$^{\#3}$} of Led Zeppelin's 'Since I've Been Loving You' at one (minimally changing) extreme to Jimi Hendrix's 'Little Miss Lover' (aeolian I–I–I–I–III$^{♭3}$–III$^{♭3}$–I–I–V–VII–I–I) at a second, and the Electric Light Orchestra's ionian I–I–I–III$^{\#3}$–VI–II$^{\#3}$–VII$^{♭3}$–III$^{\#3}$–IV–V–I–V of 'Mr Blue Sky' at a third.

33 As in Elvis Costello's 'Waiting for the End of the World' and Jimi Hendrix's 'She's So Fine'.

Chapter 3

1 For example, Gillett (1983: 375–99), Chambers (1985: 84–112), Cutler (1985: 181–90), Wicke (1990: 91–114).

2 They also beg an immense number of questions: in what sense 'classic'?; does 'melodic rock' have a monopoly on melodies?; to whom is non-adult-oriented rock oriented?; what is 'inauthentic' rock?; etc. These questions merely reinforce the inadequacy of the terminology bequeathed us.

3 Such a *comparison* is beyond the scope of this book.

4　The contradictions inherent in listeners' acceptance of both the consolidatory and innovatory tendencies cannot simply be argued away. It may be indicative of different functions the music has for listeners at different times, or it may be indicative of entirely different listening publics. This can only be ascertained through further research.

5　Although drummers like John Bonham and Phil Collins often come close to this sense of internal movement.

6　Haralambos (1974) explores the growing disaffection among black audiences in the USA for the accommodatory message of the blues, and their take-up of the protestant ethic, as found in soul, from the late 1950s on.

7　Paradoxically, the *vocal* aspect of blues singers had far less effect on progressive rock than the intensional structure of the form. This is not to say that there were not British singers who actually wanted to sing the blues (Jo-Anne Kelly, John Mayall, etc.), but they took no part in progressive rock.

8　Nick Dow traces such tunings in the UK back to Davy Graham in the early 1960s. They differ from the open tunings used by bottleneck blues players in that the strings are not tuned to the notes of a triad: the tuning D, A, D, G, A, D is perhaps the commonest. See Dow (1991).

9　The album is known under various names, *Led Zeppelin IV* and *Zoso* being the other common ones.

10　I would surmise that the norms of voice-leading in rock are not dissimilar to those familiar to students of Schenker, with the exception that in rock, added-note chords are normally perfectly stable entities.

11　See Sorrell and Narayan (1980). Indian improvisation theory has a long history, and a detailed comparison of the techniques used there with those invented by rock musicians would probably be highly instructive, but is beyond both the scope of this book and of my current competence.

12　Among the more notable examples here are Van Der Graaf Generator's 'A Plague of Lighthouse Keepers', the Beatles' 'Revolution No. 9', Yes's Brahms arrangement on *Fragile*, Keith Emerson's arrangements of Bartok, Moussorgsky and Janaček, Eno's work with Roxy Music and others, and albums by both Queen and Emerson, Lake and Palmer entitled *The Works*, which seem designed to 'legitimise' the product.

13　Denselow (1990) explores the ambiguities of Lennon's professed position, both at this time and later.

14　I am grateful to Charlie Ford for pointing these out to me.

15　I am grateful to Richard Middleton for reminding me of this point.

16　I actually have grave doubts as to whether even hippies failed to hear the reprise of 'Spoonful' as just that, but this is because I have little faith in the reality of 'hippy consciousness'.

17　Further examples are the long dominant preparation at the beginning of Yes's 'Close to the Edge', which 'correctly' resolves into the song proper (i.e. from chord V to chord I), and the gradual passing from harmonies with ambiguous tonics to a clear point of arrival in this song, 'Supper's Ready' and 'The Lamb Lies Down on Broadway', both by Genesis.

18　Bennett (1986) examines the stylistic development of music hall songs.

19　It remains a journalistic truism that there is a sound somehow quintessential to England: reviewing Blur's *Leisure* in *Q*, no. 61, Paul Davies tells us that they 'have arrived at a distinctly English sound', which he tries to specify, chiefly in terms of texture. None the less, I think this epithet is used to describe a sound world that tends to proceed from English studios, rather than a sound world that has 'English' characteristics, whatever these might be.

20 Examples are 'Heavy Horses' from the album of the same name, and 'Dark Ages' from *Stormwatch*. 'Seal Driver' (from *Broadsword and the Beast*) takes on some of these characteristics, while 'Whaler's Dues', the focal song on *Rock Island*, has the familiar slow tempo and free tempo introduction of 'Dark Ages' and 'Cap in Hand'. These songs might almost form a genre of their own.

21 As Harker (1985) points out, this material was as much the invention of collectors as it was of those from whom they collected. None the less, the *belief* that one was singing hallowed material was a powerful motivating factor.

22 Another early use is in Yes's 'Astral Traveller'. Since the device does not appear elsewhere in their repertoire (as far as I am aware), its possible connotation here (with reference to the song's title and ensuing subject matter) becomes highly significant.

23 Tamm (1991) identifies Robert Fripp, the leader of King Crimson, as the architect of this 'testing', a view I would endorse.

Chapter 4

1 This section is a slightly expanded version of Moore (1991).

2 Chambers (1985: 109–11) does briefly acknowledge its importance, but does not raise the question of its impact on listening practices.

3 A loose, generic term for devices that allow sound to be distorted and changed in various ways, to add precise forms of echo and reverberation, and even to construct previously unplayable concatenations of sound.

4 I acknowledge Alistair Cunningham's accidental coining of this term.

5 The samisen and koto are the most familiar of Japanese string instruments. Both are plucked instruments: the former has a small, treble range, while the latter is larger and more resonant.

6 Rogan (1982: 16) suggests that Ferry's keyboard skills were largely self-taught, with some assistance from Graham Simpson, bassist on the first album.

7 I am at odds with Laing's subsequent suggestion that the rhythmic monad 'is a state of entropy (or perfection) to which much of punk seems constantly aiming' (Laing 1985: 61). As Campbell (1984) notes, 'entropy' is a buzz-word with a wide range of used meanings, some of them contradictory, but among them the most sure is that of entropy as a measure of uncertainty. Perhaps Laing is suggesting that we have to balance the notion that 'when [entropy] rises to a maximum in any isolated system, that system is incapable of doing anything interesting, novel, or useful' (Campbell 1984: 33), which while close to Laing's meaning is not that close, and the idea that entropy measures the disorderliness, i.e. lack of predictability, of a system. The predictability of punk's 'monadic' rhythm, however, is at a virtual maximum.

8 Although evidence from psychologists of music seems to me to be of value when discussing rock and other popular musics, it must be noted that all the research widely published so far has been undertaken with respect to classical musics and the results, therefore, must be considered provisional. We still await music psychologists willing to work with popular musics.

9 My thanks to Charlie Ford for these locations.

10 Thus, 'The Blue-skinned Beast' alternates ionian V–I, 'Rise and Fall' is based on aeolian I–V$^{\#3}$–VI–III, 'The March of the Gherkins' uses the standard ionian I–V–IV–V and 'Samantha' uses the equally widespread aeolian I$^{\#3}$–VII–VI.

11 In 'In the City', Weller has learnt from Townshend the combination of rhythm and

occasional lead guitar within the same part. In 'All around the World', the Jam learn from the vocal interchanges often utilized by Townshend and Daltrey. Many songs recall Townshend's actual guitar work, particularly the angry 'slide' (dissonant glissando from high to low pitch on one or more strings), which is clear in 'News of the World', where it forms a conventional representation of chaos, and 'Eton Rifles', a song describing social warfare.

12 'Away from the Numbers', with its characteristic ionian I–II–IV–V and backing vocals, seems particularly evocative.

13 For example, on *Psonic Psunspot*.

14 Throughout this discussion, I shall tend to underestimate the extent to which these styles have changed over the past twenty years. A detailed survey of these changes awaits further research.

15 Nazareth's 'This Flight Tonight' illustrates a potential problem with any firm categorization of speed. It begins at a 'laid back' pace, but the kit subsequently doubles the speed of its beats, immediately increasing the subjective speed of the whole song.

16 The alternation between E in the bass and B♭ power chord seems unusually common in thrash metal. In Renaissance theory, this relationship connoted the works of the devil: considering the overt references of much thrash metal, it may well carry a similar connotation here.

17 And the increasingly common strained female voice, as per Lita Ford and Alannah Myles. The register of these voices tends to be lower than that of their male counterparts.

18 Examples of this abound: Def Leppard's 'Pour Some Sugar on Me', Whitesnake's 'Slip of the Tongue', Magnum's 'Start Talking Love' and Robert Plant's 'Ship of Fools' might be cited.

19 These factors taken in conjunction (and particularly this last comment) seem to me to serve to differentiate hard rock from contemporary r&b, such as Chris Rea's *Road to Hell*, Dire Straits' *Making Movies*, Eric Clapton's *Another Ticket*, the Rolling Stones' *Steel Wheels* and even Status Quo, for whom see the next chapter.

20 Confirmation of this awaits further research.

21 I am grateful to Peter Grimm for pointing out that Metallica construct their songs *during* soundchecks, out of riffs that may have been invented at other times.

22 Clyde Stubblefield's playing on the original issue of this single is normally considered to have originated the kit patterns on which so much of the 'indie dance' style is said to be dependent. Close listening reveals little more than similar semiquaver hihat patterns.

23 These are exemplified, respectively, in 'Right Here, Right Now' and 'Nothing to Hold Me', both from *Trust*.

24 That is, the electronic music of Stockhausen, Berio, Nono, Harvey, etc. See Griffiths (1979).

25 Moore (1990) explores the basis of such a theory with respect to the 'classical' repertoire, but the comments there have little relevance to rock.

26 Technically, all instruments are 'acoustic', because all produce sound. Because the 'lay' use of 'acoustic', to refer to instruments that do not rely on electronic means of amplification, has such great currency and is less unwieldy than any 'technically correct' term, I adopt it here.

27 I am grateful to Charlie Ford for pointing out the paradox that Dylan, that 'often most obscure and tangential of lyricists', and often very stroppy and unhelpful personality, has become so associated with 'honesty'.

28 The best example is, perhaps the *Symphonies of Wind Instruments*, written in memory of Debussy, and described as 'an austere ceremony unfolding in short litanies' (Boucourechliev 1987: 145).

29 The genre of *piobaireachd* (or pibroch) is the extended, slow, Highland lament for cultural heroes.

30 The technique is also known as playing 'chics' (see Ihde 1981: 11). It has been in widespread use at least since the mid-1960s, employed by Jimi Hendrix and various guitarists working with James Brown and Isaac Hayes.

31 I have observed this connotation in informal studies, although in wide open spaces sounds actually die rather quickly, for there is nothing for them to bounce back from. I wish to put forward no theory to account for this paradox.

32 My thanks to Charlie Ford for pointing this out.

33 This arrangement notably recalls the Band's similarly stark 'Tears of Rage'.

34 European music has a long history of African influence, which can be traced back at least to the late sixteenth-century Flemish composer Orlando di Lasso.

35 On BBC Radio 4's *Today* programme, broadcast on 15 October 1990, Stern's African record shop, the leading London retailer, reported that sales of 'Afro-pop' had rocketed since the release of *Graceland*.

36 It should be noted that this is only a recent development of technique for both Bush and Gabriel. Both were originally involved in more harmonically complex music. Genesis's *Foxtrot* is briefly discussed in Chapter 5, section 6, while Bush's early songs often evaded strict modal interpretations: 'Wuthering Heights', for example, is based on the ionian pattern $I-\flat VI(major)-V-III^{\#3}$.

37 'Blistering' and the similar 'searing' are terms often used to describe a solo of great virtuosity and speed, where the timbre has a rich overtone structure created by fuzz boxes and similar devices. It thus relates to the physical effect on the fingers – blisters caused by great friction – and also seems to evoke the sound of friction itself. It is, therefore, a most apt term. Although work by Hendrix and Fripp is taken to connote this most clearly, to my mind the best examples of the *timbre* of friction appear in Phil Manzanera's work on Quiet Sun's *Mainstream*.

38 A number of revivalist songs attempt to explore their singers' world-view through a device strongly related to the riddle, whereby successive verses follow a centripetal, rather than a narrative structure. Thus, 'We Sing Hallelujah' suggests 'A man is like . . .' in successive verses; in 'Scarborough Fair', the subject successively asks the go-between to 'Tell her to . . .'; at the climax of the ballad 'Tam Lin', the subject is changed in turn into a serpent, a lion, a white-hot bar of iron, etc. This construction also frequently occurs in children's rhymes.

39 Even here there are exceptions, such as the Javanese *degong* style, which develops from the popularization of features of Javanese traditional music, without the incorporation of European techniques.

Chapter 5

1 Techniques of semiology have been used in markedly different ways by musicologists in recent years. For three very different surveys, see Cook (1987: 151–82), Middleton (1990: 172–236) and Monelle (1992).

2 In much the same way that spittle would be ejected at gigs (see Laing 1985: 85).

3 Further points of disagreement have been raised by others. For example, Durant (1984: 10–13) rightly argues that Cooke's theory totally ignores the historical construction of style and the changing social relationships between composer and audience.

4 This approach may make it appear that I consider the effects of the music industry to be transparent. On the contrary, only by focusing on them in this way can we see that their effects are supremely important.

5 Laing (1985: 19) argues that recording musicians occupy this position at one remove: 'The customary position of musicians in the production process of the record industry is an unusual one. . . . Musicians are involved at the stage which in other industries would be called *design*: the preparation of a prototype [the 'master tape'] from which mass production can begin.' While recognition of this is vital, it represents something of a side-issue here.

6 Even King Crimson, a highly experienced band, had no veto regarding a single song on *Three of a Perfect Pair* (see Tamm 1991: 139). It is remarkable in this context that there have been so few successful musician-owned labels (see Wright 1988: 292).

7 With some other style groups, such as soul, the roles of the writers and producers are often given greater primacy than that of the artist (cf. the situation that obtains with composers of concert music).

8 His claim that most rock musicians never had that shared viewpoint is unsubstantiated, although his point that success brings freedom from the routine, uniformity and constraints of the factory is well made. Yet this is also to argue a reverse discrimination in favour of the requirements of 'working-class teenagers'.

9 Stokes (1976) argues persuasively for the lack of influence musicians have over the destination and form of their product.

10 See, for example, Peter Everett (1986).

11 See Rowell (1983) and the notion of paradigm change introduced in Kuhn (1970). In contrast, Leonard Meyer has argued that this art music tradition has now entered a period of stasis, so that no single style and set of values can be considered predominant (Meyer 1967: 89–232).

12 Willis has used 'integral' as a level of cultural relation in the way I am using 'homological' (and at a deeper level than his own use of the latter term). I am not worried by this, since no two writers seem to mean exactly the same thing by the term 'homology'. See Willis (n.d.).

13 John Shepherd also criticizes Willis's earlier notion of homology. The length to which he goes to argue for a strict homology seems to be the root cause for his position with regard to the pop–classical split cited in Chapter 1. See Shepherd (1977c, 1985).

14 This discussion ignores the semantic sense of the lyrics.

15 Note that what Stefani calls 'semiotic codes' are not the codes of 'translation' suggested by Whiteley (1990), for instance. His full definition is as follows. *General codes* (GC): perceptual and mental schemes, anthropological attitudes and motivations, basic conventions through which we perceive or construct or interpret every experience (and therefore every sound experience). *Social practices* (SP): projects and modes of both material and symbolic production within a certain society; in other words, cultural institutions such as language, religion, industrial work, technology, sciences, etc., including musical practices (concert, ballet, opera, criticism). *Musical techniques* (MT): theories, methods and devices that are more or less specific and exclusive to musical practices, such as instrumental techniques, scales, composition forms, etc. *Styles* (St): historical periods, cultural movements, authors or groups of works; that is, the particular ways in which MT, SP and GC are concretely realized. *Opus* (Op): single musical works or events in their concrete individuality (Stefani 1987: 9). His distinction between high and popular competence has found experimental support. Rita Wolpert (1990) reports the results of experiments which suggest that 'untrained listeners' (that is, those without formal theory or instrumental training) recognize examples of music primarily through instrumentation and texture, while 'trained musicians' make use of features such as harmony. Although she is unwilling to state whether or not different cognitive processes are involved (or simply whether the same processes are

involved at different levels of precision), Howard Gardner (1985) posits, as one of his multiple intelligences, an intelligence he explicitly terms 'musical'. Although he fails to make it style-specific (in fact he relates it purely to the western classical tradition), he describes the acquisition of 'musical competence', drawing on research by Jeanne Bamberger, a developmental psychologist, who distinguishes between *figural* and *formal* modes of processing music, a distinction clearly similar to the high/popular competence distinction, although arrived at empirically.

16 Andersen (1988: 30) calls attention to Chomsky's conception of linguistic competence, which is an individual attribute, to be uncovered by reference to the 'ideal speaker–hearer's intuitions', this person normally being the linguist!

17 It seems to me likely that the extent to which my previous discussions may seem to have privileged harmonic patterns at the expense of other domains owes more to the residues of my conventional training than to the music itself. But, it must also be said that, judging by the evidence offered both by player's magazines, and by musicians conversing together, harmonic patterns and ways of articulating them are preoccupations that many musicians themselves share (heavy metal is only the most obvious example: see the evidence gathered in Walser 1992). Whether most listeners share these preoccupations I doubt.

18 Again, he had already used the technique, but in a looser form, in the rambling 'Cygnet Committee' (1969).

19 Compare, respectively, 'A New Career in a New Town' with the work of Ultravox, 'Breaking Glass' with Gary Numan's vocal delivery and 'Sound and Vision' with anything by Orchestral Manoeuvres in the Dark.

20 Eno was working with a monophonic synthesizer, building textures part by part, without sticking to the melody/chords/bass textural norm.

21 Treble strums on off-beats with no sustain, 'cutting' the sound.

22 They include the bass of 'Shake It', the voice of the same (singing in snatches, but without the audible energy of 'Young Americans'), horns (on 'Let's Dance' and most notably on 'Ricochet', where the riff seems to imitate salsa, which relates to the Spanish vocal interjections), the funk guitar from 'Fashion' (in 'Criminal World'), the long play-out with vocal phrases ('Cat People', where Bowie has two phrases, but little improvisation as per the earlier style), the textural space into which upper instruments are slotted ('Modern Love', 'Shake It') and the pyramid harmonies on 'Let's Dance' (like, for example, those on the Isley Brothers' 'Twist and Shout').

23 'Day in – Day out' and 'New York's in Love' retrieve something of his earlier vocal energy: the former also has soul-style female backing voices.

24 For example, on 'Anything She Does'.

25 Compare 'Tonight Tonight Tonight' (from *Invisible Touch*) with 'Can-Utility and the Coastliners' (from *Foxtrot*). Some timbres also remain: compare 'In the Glow of the Night' (*Invisible Touch*) with much of 'Supper's Ready' (*Foxtrot*).

26 In 1972, the rising bass of 'It's Not Imagination' would have been transposed up a fourth to provide a dramatic twist, as happens before the bridge of 'Think of Me with Kindness'.

27 These range from Toto (on 'Heart on Hold'), Queen (on 'Man Overboard') and middle-of-the-road (MOR) pop (three songs) to the hard rock anthem ('The Power of Rock'), and on to the inclusion of organ, piano and synthesizer ('Throw Her a Line' is remarkable for both its synthesizer hook and its combination of a clear period structure with a driving pattern).

28 The verse of 'Every Night' groups 3 + 3; 4 + (4 + 2), 'Maybe I'm Amazed' has a verse of 8 + (8 + 2), and a refrain of 4 + 4; (4 + 2) + 4, while 'Distractions' (from *Flowers in the Dirt*) has a verse of 8 + 8, with a refrain of 3 + 4 (+2).

Glossary of Musicological Terms

acciaccatura	a very short, accented melodic note (usually not part of the underlying harmony) which immediately resolves to a longer note.
accompaniment	the part of the musical fabric that appears subsidiary to any main melody.
added note chord	a triad with the addition of another note (normally the sixth or seventh) from the parent mode.
additive rhythm	a rhythm built from the smallest possible unit, adding together an unspecified number of these to produce a series of beats, which will generally be of uneven lengths. See divisive rhythm.
arpeggiate	to play the constituent notes of a chord consecutively rather than simultaneously.
auxiliary note	in a melody, a note that is one step away from those of the accompanying triad in force at that point. See passing note.
backbeat	beats 2 and 4 of every four-beat bar.
bar	a group of (in rock, normally) four beats.
barre	on the guitar, a chord formed after placing the index finger across all six strings, that finger acting as a temporary capo.
bass	in terms of register, the lowest part of the musical fabric.
beats	accents formed from the perception of a (regular) pulse within the music's rhythm. See rhythm.
boogie	see example 5.7, p. 182.
bridge	an intermediate section of a song, which will normally be heard only once.
capo	on the guitar, a device placed across all six strings, effectively tuning the whole instrument higher in pitch.
coda	a final, rounding-off section of some songs (often synonymous with the fade-out).
contour	the shape formed by the notes of a melody. See example 2.1 (p. 35) for an example of clear contour repetition.
contrapuntal	the practice of proceeding via independent, concurrent melodies rather than by block harmonies.

cycle of fifths	a harmonic pattern wherein the chords' roots move by the interval of a fifth (five steps), i.e. I–IV–VII–III–VI–II–V–I.
diatonic	strictly, using only the notes of the mode.
divisive rhythm	a rhythm formed from the successive division of a temporal unit into equal portions, yielding a series of equal-length beats. See additive rhythm.
domain	the virtual categories into which music is analysed, i.e. pitch, duration, timbre, dynamics, etc.
dynamics	the domain formed by the loudness of notes.
elaboration	the decoration of a structure with ornamental (e.g. auxiliary and passing) notes.
flatten	to lower a pitch by a semitone.
harmony	the simultaneous sounding of two or more notes.
interval	the distance between two pitches, described either by a count of semitones or in terms of the number of letter-names involved.
key	every piece of tonal music is *in* one of the twenty-four keys, each of which can be theoretically represented by the scale of the same name. A key is normally established by unambiguous emphasis on chords I, IV and V in close proximity.
major third	the interval of four semitones (e.g. C to E).
melisma	the stretching of a sung syllable across two or more notes of melody.
melody	the gestalt formed by a succession of pitches.
minor third	the interval of three semitones (e.g. E to G).
mix	the disposition of sounds in the stereo image. The 'height' of a sound in a mix normally corresponds to the level of perceived loudness of that sound.
mode	a theoretical construct: a disposition of five tones and two semitones in a particular order. See scale.
modulation	change from one key or mode to another.
motif	a short sequence of notes used as the basis of a song or a section of one; a musical idea. See riff.
musique concrète	avant-garde tape music of the 1940s and 1950s which *avoided* electronically generated sounds.
open position	the disposition of the notes of a triad with relatively wide registral spacing.
overtones	the constituents of a note which, in their degree of presence, give it its timbre. In vibrating at a particular frequency, a medium (column of air, string etc.) will also vibrate less strongly at other, subsidiary frequencies, which are in whole-number ratios to the particular, *fundamental* frequency. These subsidiary frequencies are the overtones.
passing note	in a melody, a non-triadic note passing between two of the notes of the triad in force at that point. See auxiliary note.
pentatonic	a five-note scale: conventionally, that formed by C, D, E, G, A and any transposition of this.
phrase	a segment of melody formed from one or more motifs, its end normally coinciding with the taking of breath (whether actual or nominal).

pitch	that aspect of a single heard note remaining after removing its duration, timbre and dynamic level. Conventionally identified by means of letter names.
pyramid harmony	the practice of attacking the notes of a harmony in succession, holding each one until all are present in the musical fabric.
range	a portion of musical pitch space delimited by the upper and lower notes of a voice, song, melody, etc.
recitative	a style of singing in which rhythms tend to follow speech rhythms rather than a strict beat, and pitches follow speech inflections as much as a tempered scale.
refrain	the portion of a song that follows a verse. On repetition, its lyrics will normally recur.
register	an imprecise descriptor of range. Registers tend to be relatively high, middle or low.
relative major	major key whose tonic is a minor third higher than the relative minor key (e.g. C major is the relative major of A minor).
rhythm	the actual pattern of individual durations through which a pulse will be perceived.
riff	a simple (normally repeated) musical idea.
Roman numerals	a system of identifying the seven triads available in any mode, numbering these successively from the triad built on the first note through to the triad built on the seventh note. Thus, for the aeolian mode beginning on D (i.e. D, E, F, G, A, B♭, C, D), triad I will contain D, F, A; triad II will contain E, G, B♭; through to triad VII, which will contain C, E, G.
root	for any triad, that note of the mode on which the triad is built. Thus, for the aeolian mode beginning on D, the root of chord II will be E.
scale	an actual disposition of seven intervals. Thus, the major scale is constituted by tone, tone, semitone, tone, tone, semitone. The (harmonic) minor scale is constituted by tone, semitone, tone, tone, semitone, minor third, semitone. See mode.
semitone	the interval between adjacent notes on the keyboard, or a single fret on the fretboard.
sequence	the transposition of a melodic segment, normally by one tone up or down.
sharpen	to raise a pitch by a semitone.
shuffle	division of beats into uneven (i.e. ♩ ♪ ♩ ♪ etc.) notes.
straight	division of beats into even (i.e. ♫ ♫ etc.) notes.
tempered pitch	a note *exactly* in tune with an in-tune piano. It is a necessary prerequisite for all music that employs the concept of modulation. In rock, tempered pitch is normal for bass and rhythm guitars and for keyboards, but is frequently treated by voices, lead guitars and other solo instruments with some disdain.
tessitura	the most frequently used part of a range.

texture	the presence of, and types of relationships between, identifiable strands of sound.
timbre	a note's tone colour, formed by the precise mix of overtones present in its sounding.
tonal system	an elaborate and rich system of note relationships underlying Western 'classical' music. All notes are interrelated hierarchically, and are fundamentally related to the tonic of the piece's parent key (i.e. the key-note).
tone	the interval of two semitones.
tonic	the note of a mode that has conceptual priority: the note of a mode from which that mode's other notes are calculated.
transposition	the moving of an entire pitch unit by any given interval. Thus, transposing C, E, G, by a major third yields E, G♯, B.
treble	in terms of register, the upper part of the musical fabric.
triad	three-note chord built from alternate notes of the parent mode. See Roman numerals.
upbeat	the subsidiary beat belonging to, and immediately preceding, the downbeat (the first beat of a bar).
verse	the portion of a song that precedes a refrain. On repetition, its lyrics are unlikely to recur.
vocal tone	the timbral qualities of a particular voice, often described in terms of the voice's degree of richness.

Bibliography

Adorno, Theodor (1976) *Introduction to the Sociology of Music*, New York: Seabury Press.

Andersen, Roger (1988) *The Power and the Word*, London: Paladin.

Barnard, Stephen (1989) *On the Radio*, Milton Keynes: Open University Press.

Barnes, Ken (1990) 'A fragment of the imagination', in S. Frith (ed.) *Facing the Music*, London: Mandarin.

Barthes, Roland (1979) *Image – Music – Text*, trans. Stephen Heath, London: Fontana.

Bateson, Gregory (1973) *Steps to an Ecology of Mind*, London: Paladin.

Beardsley, Monroe (1981) 'Understanding music', in K. Price (ed.) *On Criticizing Music*, Baltimore, MD: Johns Hopkins University Press.

Bennett, Anthony (1986) 'Music in the halls', in J.S. Bratton (ed.) *Music Hall: Performance and Style*, Milton Keynes: Open University Press.

Bent, Ian (1987) *Analysis*, London: Macmillan.

Bergman, Billy (1985) *African Pop: Goodtime Kings*, London: Blandford.

Berry, Wallace (1987) *Structural Functions in Music*, New York: Dover.

Bjornberg, Alf (1985) 'On aeolian harmony in contemporary popular music', unpublished paper cited in Middleton (1990).

Blacking, John (1987) *A Common Sense View of All Music*, Cambridge: Cambridge University Press.

Bohlman, Philip V. (1988) *The Study of Folk Music in the Modern World*, Bloomington: Indiana University Press.

Boucourechliev, Andre (1987) *Stravinsky*, London: Gollancz.

Bradley, Dick (n.d.) *The Cultural Study of Music*, Birmingham: Centre for Contemporary Cultural Studies, paper SP 61.

Bradley, Dick (1992) *Understanding Rock 'n' Roll: Popular Music in Britain 1955–1964*, Buckingham: Open University Press.

Braun, Michael, Eckford, Richard and Stimpson, Peter (eds) (1970) *Jesus Christ Superstar: the Authorised Version*, London: Pan.

Bright, Spencer (1988) *Peter Gabriel: an Authorized Biography*, London: Sidgwick & Jackson.

Brown, Ashley (ed.) (1990) *Encyclopedia of Popular Music*, London: Marshall Cavendish.

Brown, Keith (1984) *Linguistics Today*, London: Fontana.

Brunning, Bob (1986) *Blues: the British Connection*, London: Blandford.

Burns, Gary (1987) 'A typology of "hooks" in popular records', *Popular Music*, 6, 1–20.

Byrnside, Ronald (1975) 'The formation of a musical style: early rock', in C. Hamm. B. Nettl and R. Byrnside (eds) *Contemporary Music and Music Cultures*, Englewood Cliffs, NJ: Prentice-Hall.

Campbell, Jeremy (1984) *Grammatical Man*, Harmondsworth: Pelican.

Chambers, Iain (1985) *Urban Rhythms*, London: Macmillan.

Chandler, Russell (1988) *Understanding the New Age*, Milton Keynes: Word.

Chapple, Steve and Garofalo, Reebee (1977) *Rock 'n' Roll is Here to Pay: The History and Politics of the Music Industry*, Chicago: Nelson-Hall.

Charters, Samuel (1982) *The Roots of the Blues*, London: Quartet.

Chester, Andrew (1970) 'Second thoughts on a rock aesthetic: The Band', *New Left Review*, 62, 75–82, partially reprinted in Frith and Goodwin (1990).

Childs, Barney (1977) 'Time and music: a composer's view', *Perspectives of New Music*, 15, 194–219.

Clarke, Donald (ed.) (1989) *Penguin Encyclopedia of Popular Music*, Harmondsworth: Penguin.

Clifton, Thomas (1969) 'Training in music theory: process and product', *Journal of music theory*, 13, 38–65.

Cohen, Sara (1991) *Rock Culture in Liverpool: Popular Music in the Making*, Oxford: Clarendon Press.

Cohn, Nik (1970) *A WopBopaLooBopALopBamBoom*, London: Paladin.

Coker, Wilson (1972) *Music and Meaning*, New York: Free Press.

Collins, John (1985) *African Pop Roots*, London: Foulsham.

Cone, Edward (1974) *The Composer's Voice*, Berkeley: California University Press.

Cook, Nicholas (1987) *A Guide to Musical Analysis*, London: Dent.

Cook, Nicholas (1990) *Music, Imagination & Culture*, Oxford: Clarendon Press.

Cooke, Deryck (1959) *The Language of Music*, Oxford: Oxford University Press.

Cooper, Grosvenor and Meyer, Leonard (1960) *The Rhythmic Structure of Music*, Chicago: Chicago University Press.

Cooper, Mark (1989) 'The resurrection shuffle', *Q*, 39, 38–65.

Cott, Jonathan (1974) *Stockhausen: Conversations with the Composer*, London: Picador.

Covach, John (1992) 'Yes' 'Close to the Edge' and the Boundaries of Rock', paper given at the Conference *Popular Music: the Primary Text*, Thames Valley University, July.

Crocker, Richard L. (1986) *A History of Musical Style*, New York: Dover.

Cubitt, Sean (1984) 'Maybellene': meaning and the listening subject', *Popular music*, 2, 207–24.

Culler, Jonathan (1976) *Saussure*, London: Fontana.

Cutler, Chris (1984) 'Technology, politics and contemporary music: necessity and choice in musical forms', *Popular music*, 2, 279–300.

Cutler, Chris (1985) *File under Popular*, London.

Davies, John Booth (1980) *The Psychology of Music*, London: Hutchinson.

Deevoy, Adrian (1989) 'The last gang in town', *Q*, 37, 74–84.

Denselow, Robin (1975) 'The roots of tradition', in D. Laing *et al.*, *The Electric Muse*, London: Methuen.

Denselow, Robin (1990) *When the Music's Over*, London: Faber.

Dick, Kay (1977) *They*, Harmondsworth: Penguin.

Dow, Nick (1991) 'Guitar angles', *Folk Roots*, 94, 28–9.

Dowling, W. Jay (1978) 'Scale and contour: two components of a theory of memory for melodies', *The Psychological Review*, 85, 341–54.

Dunsby, Jonathan and Whittall, Arnold (1988) *Music Analysis in Theory and Practice*, London: Faber.

Duran, Lucy (1989) 'Djely Musso – woman of Mali', *Folk Roots*, 75, 34–9.

Durant, Alan (1984) *Conditions of Music*, London: Macmillan.

Edworthy, Judy (1985) 'Interval and contour in melody processing', *Music perception*, 2, 375–88.

Ehrlich, Luke (1983) 'The reggae arrangements', in S. Davis and P. Simon (eds) *Reggae International*, London: Thames & Hudson.

Eisen, Jonathan (ed.) (1969) *The Age of Rock*, New York: Vintage.

Eisenberg, Evan (1988) *The Recording Angel*, London: Picador.

Emmerson, Simon (1986) 'The relation of language to materials', in S. Emmerson (ed.) *The Language of Electroacoustic Music*, London: Macmillan.

Everett, Peter (1986) *You'll Never Be 16 Again*, London: BBC.

Everett, Walter (1985) 'Text-painting in the foreground and middleground of Paul McCartney's Beatle song "She's leaving home": a musical study of psychological conflict', *In Theory Only*, 9, 5–13.

Everett, Walter (1986) 'Fantastic remembrance in John Lennon's "Strawberry fields forever" and "Julia"', *Musical Quarterly*, 72, 360–85.

Fabbri, Franco (1982) 'What kind of music?', *Popular Music*, 2, 131–43.

Feldstein, Sandy (1978) *Drum-set Club Date Dictionary*, USA: Alfred.

Finkelstein, Mike (1979) *Teach Yourself Rock Drums*, New York: Amsco.

Ford, Charles (1991) *Cosi?: Sexual Politics in Mozart's Operas*, Manchester: Manchester University Press.

Frame, Pete (1983) *Rock Family Trees, Volumes 1 and 2*, London: Omnibus.

Frith, Simon (1983) *Sound Effects*, London: Constable.

Frith, Simon (1987) 'Towards an aesthetic of popular music', in R. Leppert and S. McClary (eds) *Music and Society*, Cambridge: Cambridge University Press.

Frith, Simon (1988a) *Music for Pleasure*, Cambridge: Polity Press.

Frith, Simon (1988b) 'Popular music 1950–1980', in G. Martin (ed.) *Making Music*, London: Barrie & Jenkins.

Frith, Simon (1989) 'Why do songs have words?', *Contemporary music review*, 5, 77–96.

Frith, Simon (ed.) (1990) *Facing the Music*, London: Mandarin.

Frith, Simon and Goodwin, Andrew (eds) (1990) *On Record*, London: Routledge.

Frith, Simon and Horne, Howard (1987) *Art into Pop*, London: Methuen.

Frith, Simon and McRobbie, Angela (1978) 'Rock and sexuality', in S. Frith and A. Goodwin (eds) *On Record*, London: Routledge.

Gambaccini, Paul (1982) *Masters of Rock*, London: BBC/Omnibus.

Gambaccini, Paul, Rice, Tim and Rice, Jo (1988) *British Hit Albums*, London: Guinness.

Gammon, Vic (1982) 'Problems of method in the historical study of popular music' in D. Horn and P. Tagg (eds) Popular Music Perspectives, Exeter: IASPM.

Gardner, Howard (1985) *Frames of Mind: the Theory of Multiple Intelligences*, Cambridge, MA: Harvard University Press.

Gibson, James J. (1979) *The Ecological Approach to Visual Perception*, London: Lawrence Erlbaum.

Gillett, Charlie (1975) *Making Tracks*, London: Panther.

Gillett, Charlie (1983) *Sound of the City*, London: Souvenir.

Goldstein, Richard (1969) *The Poetry of Rock*, New York: Bantam.

Gouldstone, David (1989) *Elvis Costello: a Man Out of Time*, London: Sidgwick & Jackson.

Green, Lucy (1988) *Music on Deaf Ears*, Manchester: Manchester University Press.

Griffiths, Paul (1979) *A Guide to Electronic Music*, London: Thames & Hudson.

Grossberg, Lawrence (1985) 'Another boring day in paradise: rock 'n' roll and the empowerment of everyday life', *Popular music*, 4, 225–58.

Haralambos, Michael (1974) *Right On: from Blues to Soul in Black America*, London: Eddison.

Harker, Dave (1980) *One for the Money*, London: Hutchinson.

Harker, Dave (1985) *Fakesong*, Milton Keynes: Open University Press.
Hatch, David and Millward, Stephen (1987) *From Blues to Rock*, Manchester: Manchester University Press.
Hebdige, Dick (1985) *Subculture*, London: Methuen.
Hennion, Antoine (1983) 'The production of success: an anti-musicology of the pop song', *Popular Music*, 3, 32–40.
Hill, Dave (1986) *Designer Boys and Material Girls*, Poole: Blandford.
Hopkins, J (1970) *The Rock Story*, London: Signet.
Horn, David (ed.) (1985) *Popular Music Perspectives 2*, Exeter: International Association for the Study of Popular Music.
Horn, David and Tagg, Philip (eds) (1982) *Popular Music Perspectives*, Exeter: International Association for the Study of Popular Music.
Hoskyns, Barney (1991) *From a Whisper to a Scream*, Hammersmith: Fontana.
Ihde, Mike (1981) *Rock Guitar Styles*, Milwaukee: Berklee.
Jakubowski, Franz (1976) *Ideology and Superstructure in Historical Materialism*, London: Allison and Busby (originally 1936).
Jameson, Fredric (1983) 'Postmodernism and consumer society', in H. Foster (ed.) *The Anti-aesthetic*, San Francisco: Bay Press.
Jones, Trevor (1980) 'The traditional music of the Australian Aborigines', in E. May (ed.) *Musics of Many Cultures*, Berkeley: University of California Press.
Juby, Kerry (1988) *Kate Bush: the Whole Story*, London: Sidgwick & Jackson.
Karolyi, Otto (1965) *Understanding Music*, Harmondsworth: Penguin.
Keil, Charles (1966) *Urban Blues*, Chicago: Chicago University Press.
Kramer, Jonathan (1988) *The Time of Music*, New York: Schirmer.
Kuhn, Thomas (1970) *The Structure of Scientific Revolutions*, Chicago: Chicago University Press.
Laing, Dave (1975) 'Troubadours and stars', in D. Laing *et al.* (eds) *The Electric Muse*, London: Methuen.
Laing, Dave (1985) *One Chord Wonders*, Milton Keynes: Open University Press.
Laing, Dave, Dallas, Karl, Denselow, Robin and Shelton, Robert (1975) *The Electric Muse*, London: Methuen.
Laing, R.D. (1970) *Knots*, Harmondsworth: Penguin.
Langer, Susanne K. (1942) *Philosophy in a New Key*, Cambridge, MA: Harvard University Press.
LaRue, Jan (1970) *Guidelines for Style Analysis*, New York: Norton.
Lent, Chris (ed.) (1984) *Rockschool*, London: BBC.
Leppert, Richard and McClary, Susan (eds) (1987) *Music and Society*, Cambridge: Cambridge University Press.
Lerdahl, Fred and Jackendoff, Ray (1985) *A Generative Theory of Tonal Music*, Cambridge, MA: Massachusetts Institute of Technology Press.
Levy, Janet (1987) 'Covert and casual values in recent writings about music', *Journal of Musicology*, 5, 3–27.
Ligeti, Gyorgy (1958) 'Pierre Boulez', *Die Reihe*, 4, 36–62.
Lincicome, David (1972) 'Iterational systems', *Journal of Music Theory*, 16, 168–205.
Lippmann, Edward (1977) *A Humanistic Philosophy of Music*, New York: New York University Press.
List, George (1985) 'Hopi melodic concepts', *Journal of the American Musicological Society*, 38, 143–52.
Loewenthal, Sandy (1988) 'Instruments in combination', in G. Martin (ed.) *Making Music*, London: Barrie & Jenkins.
Logan, Nick and Wooffinden, Bob (1982) *The Illustrated Encyclopedia of Rock*, London: Salamander.
Lynch, Kate (1984) *David Bowie: a Rock 'n' Roll Odyssey*, London: Proteus.

Mackay, Andy (1981) *Electronic music*, London: Phaidon.

McClary, Susan and Walser, Robert (1990) 'Start making sense! Musicology wrestles with rock', in S. Frith and A. Goodwin (eds) *On Record*, London: Routledge.

McLean, Barton (1981–2) 'Symbolic extension and its corruption of music', *Perspectives of New Music*, 19, 331–56.

MacNeill, Seamus and Richardson, Frank (1987) *Piobaireachd and Its Interpretation*, Edinburgh: John Donald.

Manning, Peter (1985) *Electronic and Computer Music*, Oxford: Clarendon Press.

Marten, Neville (1987) 'Interview with Martin Barre', *Guitarist*, September, 46–9.

Martin, George (ed.) (1988a) *Making Music*, London: Barrie & Jenkins.

Martin, George (1988b) 'Record production' in G. Martin (ed.) *Making Music*, London: Barrie & Jenkins.

May, John (1985) *Big Country: a Certain Chemistry*, London: Omnibus.

Mellers, Wilfrid (1968) *Caliban Reborn: Renewal in Twentieth-century Music*, London: Gollancz.

Mellers, Wilfrid (1973) *Twilight of the Gods: the Beatles in Retrospect*, London: Faber.

Mellers, Wilfrid (1980) *Bach and the Dance of God*, London: Faber.

Melly, George (1970) *Revolt into Style*, Harmondsworth: Penguin.

Merriam, Alan (1964) *The Anthropology of Music*, Chicago: Northwestern University Press.

Meyer, Leonard (1956) *Emotion and Meaning in Music*, Chicago: Chicago University Press.

Meyer, Leonard (1967) *Music, the Arts, and Ideas*, Chicago: Chicago University Press.

Michaels, Mark (1990) *The Billboard Book of Rock Arranging*, New York: Billboard.

Middleton, Richard (1972) *Pop Music and the Blues*, London: Gollancz.

Middleton, Richard (1985a) 'Articulating musical meaning/re-constructing musical history/locating the "popular"', *Popular Music*, 5, 5–43.

Middleton, Richard (1985b) 'Popular music, class conflict and the music-historical field', in D. Horn (ed.) *Popular Music Perspectives 2*, Exeter: IASPM.

Middleton, Richard (1990) *Studying Popular Music*, Milton Keynes: Open University Press.

Miller, George (1956) 'The magical number seven, plus or minus two: some limits on our capacity for processing information', *The Psychological Review*, 63, 81–97.

Molino, Jean (1990) 'Musical fact and the semiology of music', *Music Analysis*, 9, 113–56.

Monelle, Raymond (1992) *Linguistics and Semiotics in Music*, Chur: Harwood.

Moore, Allan (1990) *On the Late Chamber Works of Roberto Gerhard*, PhD thesis, University of Southampton.

Moore, Allan (1991) 'The textures of rock', paper given at the Second European Conference on Music Analysis, Trento, October.

Moore, Allan (1992) 'Patterns of harmony', *Popular Music*, 11, 73–106.

Morley, Paul (1981) 'The very dream of smartness', in T. Stewart (ed.) *Cool Cats*, London: Eel Pie.

Music Master (1989) *Record Catalogue*, 16th edition, London: Humphries.

Narmour, Eugene (1977) *Beyond Schenkerism – the Need for Alternatives in Music Analysis*, Chicago: Chicago University Press.

Nattiez, Jean-Jacques (1990) *Music and Discourse: Toward a Semiology of Music*, Princeton: Princeton University Press.

Neisser, Ulrich (1967) *Cognitive Psychology*, New York: Appleton-Century-Crofts.

Nettl, Bruno (1983) *The Study of Ethnomusicology*, Indianapolis: Indiana University Press.

Nettl, Bruno (1985) *The Western Impact on World Music*, New York: Schirmer.

Oakley, Giles (1976) *The Devil's Music*, London: BBC Books.

Oliver, Paul (1969) *The Story of the Blues*, Harmondsworth: Penguin.

Palmer, Tony (1977) *All You Need Is Love*, London: Futura.

Peel, John (1986) Untitled interview, *Sunday Express* magazine, 16 November.

Perlman, Alan and Greenblatt, Daniel (1981) 'Miles Davis meets Noam Chomsky: some observations on jazz improvisation and language structure', in W. Steiner (ed.) *The Sign in Music and Literature*, Austin: Texas University Press.

Porter, Lewis (1985) 'John Coltrane's "A love supreme": jazz improvisation as composition', *Journal of the American Musicological Society*, 38, 593–621.

Prato, Paolo (1985) 'Musical kitsch: close encounters between pops and classics', in D. Horn (ed.) *Popular Music Perspectives 2*, Exeter: IASPM.

Priasky, Lorraine E. and Rosenbaum, Jill (1987) ' "Leer-ics" or lyrics: teenage impressions of rock 'n' roll', *Youth and Society*, 18, 384–97.

Quirke, John (1987) *Eric Clapton: a Seminal Figure in English Guitar Playing*, BA dissertation, Polytechnic of West London.

Rees, Dafydd and Crampton, Luke (eds) (1989) *The Guinness Book of Rock Stars*, London: Guinness.

Reynolds, Simon (1990) *Blissed Out*, London: Serpent's Tail.

Rimmer, Dave (1985) *Like Punk Never Happened*, London: Faber.

Rogan, Johnny (1982) *Roxy Music*, London: Star.

Rorem, Ned (1969) 'The music of the Beatles', in J. Eisen (ed.) *The Age of Rock*, New York: Vintage.

Rowell, Lewis (1983) *Thinking about Music*, Amherst: University of Massachusetts Press.

Ryback, Timothy W. (1990) *Rock Around the Bloc*, New York: Oxford University Press.

Sachs, Curt (1962) *The Wellsprings of Music*, New York: Da Capo.

St Michael, Mick (1986) *Elvis Costello*, London: Omnibus.

Sampson, Geoffrey (1980) *Making Sense*, Oxford: Oxford University Press.

Sandall, Robert (1990) 'The solo artist: interview with Eric Clapton', *Q*, 40, 82–8.

Sanders, Rick (1976) *The Pink Floyd*, London: Futura.

Schenker, Heinrich (1979) *Der freie Satz*, trans. Ernst Oster, Harlow: Longman.

Schoenberg, Arnold (1967) *Fundamentals of Musical Composition*, London: Faber.

Scott, Derek (1989) *The Singing Bourgeois*, Milton Keynes: Open University Press.

Shaar Murray, Charles (1989a) *Crosstown Traffic*, London: Faber.

Shaar Murray, Charles (1989b) 'Rock on, Tommy', *Q*, 38, 66–72.

Shapiro, Harry (1990) *Waiting for the Man*, London: Mandarin.

Shepherd, John (1976) ' "Serious music" – an a-social phenomenon?', *Contact*, 14, 3–10.

Shepherd, John (1977a) 'Media, social process and music', in J. Shepherd *et al.*, *Whose Music?*, London: Latimer.

Shepherd, John (1977b) 'The "meaning" of music' in J. Shepherd *et al.*, *Whose Music?*, London: Latimer.

Shepherd, John (1977c) 'The musical coding of ideologies', in J. Shepherd *et al.*, *Whose Music?*, London: Latimer.

Shepherd, John (1982) 'A theoretical model for the sociomusicological analysis of popular musics', *Popular Music*, 2, 145–77.

Shepherd, John (1985) 'Definition as mystification: a consideration of labels as a hindrance to understanding significance in music', in D. Horn (ed.) *Popular Music Perspectives 2*, Exeter: IASPM.

Shepherd, John (1987a) 'Towards a sociology of musical styles', in A.L. White (ed.) *Lost in Music*, London: Routledge & Kegan Paul.

Shepherd, John (1987b) 'Music and male hegemony', in R. Leppert and S. McClary (eds) *Music and Society*, Cambridge: Cambridge University Press.

Shepherd, John (1991) *Music as Social Text*, Cambridge: Polity Press.
Shepherd, John, Virden, Phil, Vulliamy, Graham and Wishart, Trevor (1977) *Whose Music?*, London: Latimer.
Sloboda, John (1987) *The Musical Mind*, Oxford: Oxford University Press.
Small, Christopher (1977) *Music – Society – Education*, London: John Calder.
Small, Christopher (1987) *Music of the Common Tongue*, London: John Calder.
Sorrell, Neil and Narayan, Ram (1980) *Indian Music in Performance*, Manchester: Manchester University Press.
Stapleton, Chris and May, Chris (1989) *African All-stars*, London: Paladin.
Steedman, Mark (1984) 'A generative grammar for jazz chord sequences', *Music Perception*, 2, 52–77.
Stefani, Gino (1987) 'A theory of musical competence', *Semiotica*, 66, 7–22.
Stokes, Geoffrey (1976) *Star-making Machinery*, Indianapolis: Bobbs-Merrill.
Street, Alan (1989) 'Superior myths, dogmatic allegories', *Music Analysis*, 8, 77–123.
Street, John (1986) *Rebel Rock: The Politics of Popular Music*, Oxford: Blackwell.
Stroppa, Marco (1984) 'The analysis of electronic music', *Contemporary Music Review*, 1, 175–80.
Struthers, Stephen (1987) 'Technology in the art of recording', in A.L. White (ed.) *Lost in Music*, London: Routledge & Kegan Paul.
Sutcliffe, Phil (1989a) 'Tears for Fears: the sequel', *Q*, 36, 60–66.
Sutcliffe, Phil (1989b) 'Mission improbable', *Q*, 38, 96–102.
Tagg, Philip (1979) *Kojak – Fifty Seconds of Television Music: Towards the Analysis of Affect in Popular Music*, PhD thesis, University of Gothenburg.
Tagg, Philip (1982) 'Analysing popular music: theory, method and practice', *Popular Music*, 2, 37–67.
Tagg, Philip (1989) ' "Black music", "Afro-American music" and "European music" ', *Popular Music*, 8, 285–98.
Tagg, Philip (1991) *Fernando the Flute*, unpublished research report from University of Liverpool Institute of Popular Music.
Tamm, Eric (1991) *Robert Fripp*, London: Faber.
Taylor, Derek (1987) *It Was Twenty Years Ago Today*, New York: Bantam.
Tegen, Martin (1985) 'Changing concepts of western popular music before and after 1900', in D. Horn (ed.) *Popular Music Perspectives 2*, Exeter: IASPM.
Trudgill, Peter (1983) *On Dialect*, Oxford: Blackwell.
Turner, Steve (1988) *Hungry for Heaven*, London: Virgin.
van der Merwe, Peter (1989) *Origins of the Popular Style*, Oxford: Oxford University Press.
Virden, Phil and Wishart, Trevor (1977) 'Some observations on the social stratification of twentieth-century music' in J. Shepherd *et al.*, *Whose Music?*, London: Latimer.
Volosinov, V.N. (1973) *Marxism and the Philosophy of Language*, Moscow: Seminar (originally 1923).
Vos, P.G. (1973) 'Pattern perception in metrical tone sequences', *Psychological Laboratory Report*, *73*, University of Nijmegen.
Vulliamy, Graham (1975) 'A re-assessment of the "mass culture" controversy: the case of rock music', *Popular Music and Society*, 4, 130–55.
Vulliamy, Graham (1977) 'Music and the mass culture debate', in J. Shepherd *et al.*, *Whose Music?*, London: Latimer.
Wallis, Roger and Malm, Krister (1984) *Big Sounds from Small Peoples*, London: Constable.
Walser, Robert (1992) 'Eruptions: heavy metal appropriations of classical virtuosity', *Popular Music* 11(3). (forthcoming).
Ward, Ed, Stokes, Geoffrey and Tucker, Ken (1987) *Rock of Ages*, Harmondsworth: Penguin.

Weller, Paul (1981) 'The total look', in T. Stewart (ed.) *Cool Cats*, London: Eel Pie.

White, Avron Levine (ed.) (1987) *Lost in Music: Culture, Style and the Musical Event*, London: Routledge & Kegan Paul.

Whiteley, Sheila (1990) 'Progressive rock and psychedelic coding in the work of Jimi Hendrix', *Popular Music*, 9, 37–60.

Whiteley, Sheila (1992) *The Space between the Notes*, London: Routledge.

Whittall, Arnold (1988) *Music Since the First World War*, London: Dent.

Wicke, Peter (1990) *Rock Music*, Cambridge: Cambridge University Press.

Williams, Raymond (1981a) *Culture*, London: Fontana.

Williams, Raymond (1981b) *Keywords*, London: Flamingo.

Willis, Paul (n.d.) *Symbolism and Practice: a Theory for the Social Meaning of Pop Music*, Birmingham: Centre for Contemporary Cultural Studies, paper SP 13.

Willis, Paul (1978) *Profane Culture*, London: Routledge & Kegan Paul.

Winckel, Fritz (1967) *Music, Sound and Sensation*, New York: Dover.

Winkler, Peter (1978) 'Toward a theory of pop harmony', *In Theory Only*, 4, 3–26.

Wolff, Janet (1987) 'The ideology of autonomous art', in R. Leppert and S. McClary (eds) *Music and Society*, Cambridge: Cambridge University Press.

Wolpert, Rita S. (1990) 'Recognition of melody, harmonic accompaniment and instrumentation: musicians vs nonmusicians', *Music perception*, 8, 95–105.

Wright, Chris (1988) 'The record industry', in G. Martin (ed.) *Making Music*, London: Barrie & Jenkins.

Discography

I have cited here only albums, not individual album tracks. I have also cited, where at all possible, compilations rather than original seven-inch singles.

Abba (1988) *Absolute Abba*, Telstar.
Allman Brothers Band (1988) *Nightriding*, Knight.
Anderson, Bruford, Wakeman and Howe (1989) *Anderson, Bruford, Wakeman and Howe*, Arista.
Animals (1988) *EP Collection*, See for Miles.
Frankie Armstrong *et al.* (1985) *Tam Lin*, Plant Life.
Billy Boy Arnold (1982) *Blow the Back Off It*, Red Lightnin'.
Asia (1982) *Asia*, Geffen.
Band (1968) *Music from Big Pink*, Capitol.
Beatles (1963) *With the Beatles*, Parlophone.
Beatles (1964) *A Hard Day's Night*, Parlophone.
Beatles (1965) *Help!*, Parlophone.
Beatles (1965) *Rubber Soul*, Parlophone.
Beatles (1966) *Revolver*, Parlophone.
Beatles (1967) *Sgt. Pepper's Lonely Hearts Club Band*, Parlophone.
Beatles (1968) *Magical Mystery Tour*, Parlophone.
Beatles (1968) *White Album*, Apple.
Beatles (1969) *Abbey Road*, Apple.
Beatles (1970) *Let it Be*, Apple.
Beatles (1973) *1962–1966*, Parlophone.
Beatles (1980) *Rock 'n' Roll Music, Vol. 1*, MFP.
Beatles (1987) *Decca Sessions 1.1.62*, Topline.
Beautiful South (1989) *Welcome to the Beautiful South*, Go! Discs.
Jeff Beck (1968) *Truth*, EMI.
Chuck Berry (1983) *Chess Masters*, Chess.
Big Country (1983) *The Crossing*, Mercury.
Big Country (1984) *Steeltown*, Mercury.
Big Country (1986) *The Seer*, Mercury.
Black Sabbath (1970) *Paranoid*, Vertigo.
Blondie (1979) *Eat to the Beat*, Chrysalis.

Blur (1991) *Leisure*, Food.
Bon Jovi (1986) *Slippery when Wet*, Vertigo.
Bon Jovi (1988) *New Jersey*, Vertigo.
Boomtown Rats (1978) *Tonic for the Troops*, Ensign.
Boston (1978) *Don't Look Back*, Epic.
David Bowie (1972) *Hunky Dory*, RCA.
David Bowie (1972) *The Man who Sold the World*, RCA.
David Bowie (1972) *The Rise and Fall of Ziggy Stardust and the Spiders from Mars*, RCA.
David Bowie (1972) *Space Oddity*, RCA.
David Bowie (1973) *Aladdin Sane*, RCA.
David Bowie (1974) *Diamond Dogs*, RCA.
David Bowie (1975) *Young Americans*, RCA Victor.
David Bowie (1976) *Station to Station*, RCA.
David Bowie (1977) *'Heroes'*, RCA.
David Bowie (1977) *Low*, RCA.
David Bowie (1979) *Lodger*, RCA.
David Bowie (1980) *Scary Monsters and Super Creeps*, RCA.
David Bowie (1983) *Let's Dance*, EMI.
David Bowie (1984) *Tonight*, EMI.
David Bowie (1987) *Never Let me Down*, EMI.
Billy Bragg (1986) *Talking with the Taxman about Poetry*, Go! Discs.
Edgar Broughton Band (1986) *Out Demons Out*, Harvest.
James Brown (1986) *In the Jungle Groove*, Polydor.
Bill Bruford (1987) *Earthworks*, EG.
Burundi Steiphenson Black (1971) *'Burundi Black'*, Barclay.
Kate Bush (1980) *Never for Ever*, EMI.
Kate Bush (1982) *The Dreaming*, EMI.
Kate Bush (1989) *The Sensual World*, EMI.
Cameo (1986) *Word Up*, Club.
Martin Carthy (1981) *Crown of Horn*, Topic.
Casuals (1968) *'Jesamine'*, Decca.
Neneh Cherry (1989) *'Manchild'*, Virgin.
Eric Clapton (1970) *Eric Clapton*, Polydor.
Eric Clapton (1974) *461 Ocean Boulevard*, RSO.
Eric Clapton (1981) *Another Ticket*, RSO.
Dave Clark Five (1978) *25 Thumping Great Hits*, Polydor.
Clash (1979) *London Calling*, CBS.
Clash (1980) *Sandinista!*, CBS.
Phil Collins (1982) *Hello! I Must be Going*, Virgin.
John Coltrane (1964) *Love Supreme*, Impulse.
John Coltrane (1965) *Ascension*, Impulse.
Elvis Costello (1977) *My Aim is True*, Stiff.
Elvis Costello (1978) *This Year's Model*, Radar.
Elvis Costello (1980) *Get Happy*, F-Beat.
Elvis Costello (1982) *Almost Blue*, F-Beat.
Elvis Costello (1983) *Punch the Clock*, F-Beat.
Elvis Costello (1984) *Goodbye Cruel World*, F-Beat.
Elvis Costello (1986) *King of America*, F-Beat.
Elvis Costello (1989) *Spike*, Warner Bros.
Elvis Costello (1991) *Mighty Like a Rose*, Warner Bros.
Cream (1969) *Best of Cream*, Polydor.
Cream (1969) *Fresh Cream*, Reaction.

Cream (1969) *Wheels of Fire*, Polydor.
Creedence Clearwater Revival (1970) *Bayou Country*, Liberty.
Creedence Clearwater Revival (1970) *Willy and the Poorboys*, Liberty.
Crickets (1989) *Rock 'n' Roll Masters*, Liberty.
Cuff Links (1969) 'Tracy', MCA.
Damned (1981) *Best of the Damned*, Chiswick.
Damned (1985) *Phantasmagoria*, MCA.
Miles Davis (1970) *Bitches Brew*, CBS.
Spencer Davis Group (1965) 'Keep on Running', Fontana.
Spencer Davis Group (1966) 'Somebody Help Me Now', Fontana.
Deep Purple (1970) *Concerto for Group and Orchestra*, Harvest.
Deep Purple (1970) *Deep Purple in Rock*, Harvest.
Deep Purple (1972) *Machine Head*, Purple.
Deep Purple (1973) *Made in Japan*, Purple.
Def Leppard (1987) *Hysteria*, Bludgeon Riffola.
Derek and the Dominos (1970) *Layla and Other Assorted Love Songs*, Polydor.
Doors (1971) *Doors*, Elektra.
Doors (1971) *L.A. Woman*, Elektra.
Drifters (1988) *The Drifters*, Europe.
Dukes of Stratosphear (1987) *Psonic Psunspot*, Virgin.
Simon Dupree and the Big Sound (1986) *Amen*, See for Miles.
Bob Dylan (1964) *The Times they are A-changin'*, CBS.
Bob Dylan (1974) *Planet Waves*, Island.
Echo and the Bunnymen (1983) *Porcupine*, Korova.
Electric Light Orchestra (1977) *Out of the Blue*, United Artists.
Emerson, Lake and Palmer (1971) *Pictures at an Exhibition*, Island.
Emerson, Lake and Palmer (1977) *The Works*, Atlantic.
Eurythmics (1983) *Touch*, RCA.
Fairport Convention (1970) *Liege and Lief*, Island.
Fall (1985) *This Nation's Saving Grace*, Beggars Banquet.
Fine Young Cannibals (1989) *The Raw and the Cooked*, London.
Fleetwood Mac (1968) *Mr Wonderful*, Blue Horizon.
Fleetwood Mac (1977) *Rumours*, Warner Bros.
Fleetwood Mac (1987) *Tango in the Night*, Warner Bros.
Flying Lizards (1980) *Flying Lizards*, Virgin.
Focus (1972) *Focus 3*, Polydor.
Freddie and the Dreamers (1983) *Best of Freddie and the Dreamers*, EMI.
Funkadelic (1978) *One Nation under a Groove*, Warner Bros.
Peter Gabriel (1977) *Peter Gabriel*, Charisma.
Peter Gabriel (1980) *Peter Gabriel*, Charisma (aka Peter Gabriel III).
Peter Gabriel (1982) *Peter Gabriel*, Charisma (aka Peter Gabriel IV).
Gang of Four (1979) *Entertainment!*, EMI.
Dick Gaughan (1988) *Handful of Earth*, Topic.
Marvin Gaye (1981) *Best of Marvin Gaye*, Motown.
Genesis (1970) *Trespass*, Charisma.
Genesis (1972) *Foxtrot*, Charisma.
Genesis (1974) *The Lamb Lies Down on Broadway*, Charisma.
Genesis (1986) *Invisible Touch*, Charisma.
Gentle Giant (1972) *Octopus*, Vertigo.
Gentle Giant (1973) *In a Glass House*, WWA.
Gentle Giant (1980) *Civilian*, Chrysalis.
Gerry and the Pacemakers (1986) *Hit Singles Album*, EMI.

Grateful Dead (1973) *Live/Dead*, Warner Bros.
Hawkwind (1987) *British Tribal Music*, Start.
Heart (1987) *Bad Animals*, Capitol.
Jimi Hendrix (1967) *Are you Experienced*, Track.
Jimi Hendrix (1967) *Axis: Bold as Love*, Track.
Jimi Hendrix (1968) *Electric Ladyland*, Track.
Jimi Hendrix (1981) *Essential Jimi Hendrix. Vol. 2*, Polydor.
Buddy Holly (1985) *Golden Greats*, MCA.
Honeybus (1989) *At their Best*, See for Miles.
Howlin' Wolf (1985) *Collection*, Deja Vu.
Human League (1981) *Dare*, Virgin.
Icicle Works (1987) *If you Want to Defeat your Enemy Sing his Song*, Beggars Banquet.
Incredible String Band (1967) *5000 Spirits or the Layers of the Onion*, Elektra.
Incredible String Band (1968) *The Hangman's Beautiful Daughter*, Elektra.
Ink Spots (1982) *Best of the Ink Spots*, Coral.
Iron Maiden (1981) *Killers*, EMI.
Isley Brothers (1983) *20 Golden Pieces of the Isley Brothers*, Bulldog.
Jam (1977) *In the City*, Polydor.
Jam (1978) *All Mod Cons*, Polydor.
Jam (1979) *Setting Sons*, Polydor.
Jam (1982) *The Gift*, Polydor.
Jam (1983) *Snap!*, Polydor.
James (1990) *Gold Mother*, Fontana.
Jesus Jones (1990) *Doubt*, Food.
Jethro Tull (1969) *Stand Up*, Island.
Jethro Tull (1970) *Benefit*, Island.
Jethro Tull (1971) *Aqualung*, Island.
Jethro Tull (1972) *Thick as a Brick*, Chrysalis.
Jethro Tull (1973) *A Passion Play*, Chrysalis.
Jethro Tull (1975) *Minstrel in the Gallery*, Chrysalis.
Jethro Tull (1976) *Too Old to Rock 'n' Roll too Young to Die*, Chrysalis.
Jethro Tull (1977) *Songs from the Wood*, Chrysalis.
Jethro Tull (1978) *Heavy Horses*, Chrysalis.
Jethro Tull (1979) *Stormwatch*, Chrysalis.
Jethro Tull (1980) *A*, Chrysalis.
Jethro Tull (1982) *Broadsword and the Beast*, Chrysalis.
Jethro Tull (1984) *Under Wraps*, Chrysalis.
Jethro Tull (1989) *Rock Island*, Chrysalis.
Elton John (1970) *Elton John*, DJM.
Elton John (1973) *Don't Shoot Me I'm only the Piano Player*, DJM.
Robert Johnson (1985) *King of the Delta Blues*, CBS.
Janis Joplin (1980) *Anthology*, CBS.
Salif Keita (1984) *Mandjou*, Celluloid.
Nik Kershaw (1984) *The Riddle*, RCA.
Ben E. King (1987) *Stand by Me*, Atlantic.
King Crimson (1969) *In the Court of the Crimson King*, Island.
King Crimson (1972) *Islands*, Island.
King Grimson (1973) *Larks' Tongues in Aspic*, Island.
King Crimson (1974) *Red*, Island.
King Crimson (1974) *Starless and Bible-black*, Island.
King Crimson (1984) *Three of a Perfect Pair*, EG.
Kinks (1967) *Something Else*, Pye.

Kinks (1968) *Village Green Preservation Society*, Pye.
Kinks (1983) *Dead End Street: Greatest Hits*, PRT.
Led Zeppelin (1969) *Led Zeppelin*, Atlantic.
Led Zeppelin (1969) *Led Zeppelin II*, Atlantic.
Led Zeppelin (1970) *Led Zeppelin III*, Atlantic.
Led Zeppelin (1971) *Four Symbols*, Atlantic.
Led Zeppelin (1973) *Houses of the Holy*, Atlantic.
Led Zeppelin (1975) *Physical Graffiti*, Swan Song.
Led Zeppelin (1976) *Presence*, Swan Song.
John Lennon (1975) *Shaved Fish*, Apple.
Madness (1980) *Absolutely*, Stiff.
Madness (1982) *Complete Madness*, Stiff.
Madness (1982) *Rise and Fall*, Stiff.
Madness (1984) *Keep Moving*, Stiff.
Magnum (1988) *Wings of Heaven*, Polydor.
Mahavishnu Orchestra (1973) *Between Nothingness and Eternity*, CBS.
Mahavishnu Orchestra (1973) *Birds of Fire*, CBS.
Mamas and Papas (1967) *Elliott, Phillips, Gilliam, Docherty*, RCA.
Manfred Mann (1979) *Semi-detached Suburban*, EMI.
Yngwie J. Malmsteen's Rising Force (1984) *Yngwie J. Malmsteen's Rising Force*, Polydor.
Marillion (1983) *Script for a Jester's Tear*, EMI.
Marvelettes (1987) *Compact Command Performances*, Motown.
John Mayall's Blues Breakers (1966) *John Mayall's Blues Breakers*, Decca.
John Mayall's Blues Breakers (1967) *Hard Road*, Decca.
Paul McCartney (1970) *McCartney*, Apple.
Paul McCartney (1989) *Flowers in the Dirt*, Parlophone.
Malcolm McLaren (1989) 'Waltz Darling', Epic.
Metallica (1988) *And Justice for All*, Vertigo.
Mission (1986) *God's own Medicine*, Mercury.
Mission (1988) *Children*, Mercury.
Joni Mitchell (1975) *Hissing of Summer Lawns*, Asylum.
Moody Blues (1968) *Days of Future Passed*, Deram.
Gary Moore (1984) *Dirty Fingers*, Jet.
Gary Moore (1984) *Victims of the Future*, Virgin.
Van Morrison (1968) *Astral Weeks*, Warner Bros.
Motorhead (1979) *Overkill*, Bronze.
Move (1970) *Fire Brigade*, MFP.
Nazareth (1975) *Greatest Hits*, Mountain.
Gary Numan (1982) *New Man Numan*, TV.
Orchestral Manoeuvres in the Dark (1988) *Best of O.M.D.*, Virgin.
Osibisa (1972) *Woyaya*, MCA.
Ozzy Osbourne (1980) *Blizzard of Ozz*, CBS.
Graham Parker and the Rumour (1977) *Stick to Me*, Vertigo.
Pink Floyd (1967) *Piper at the Gates of Dawn*, Columbia.
Pink Floyd (1968) *Saucerful of Secrets*, Columbia.
Pink Floyd (1970) *Atom Heart Mother*, Harvest.
Pink Floyd (1972) *Obscured by Clouds*, Harvest.
Pink Floyd (1973) *Dark Side of the Moon*, Harvest.
Pink Floyd (1979) *The Wall*, Harvest.
Robert Plant (1988) *Now and Zen*, Atlantic.
Pogues (1985) *Rum, Sodomy and the Lash*, Stiff.
Elvis Presley (1975) *40 Greatest Hits*, Arcade.
Prince Buster (1980) *Fabulous Hits*, Melodisc.

Procol Harum (1969) *A Salty Dog*, Regal Zonophone.
Public Image Ltd (1981) *Flowers of Romance*, Virgin.
Queen (1976) *A Day at the Races*, EMI.
Queen (1980) *The Game*, EMI.
Queen (1984) *The Works*, EMI.
Quiet Sun (1975) *Mainstream*, EG.
Chris Rea (1989) *The Road to Hell*, WEA.
Otis Redding (1968) *Dock of the Bay*, Stax.
Cliff Richard (1977) *40 Golden Greats*, EMI.
Smokey Robinson (1987) *Compact Command Performances*, Motown.
Rolling Stones (1964) *12 × 5*, Decca.
Rolling Stones (1965) *Out of our Heads*, Decca.
Rolling Stones (1982) *Story of the Stones*, K-Tel.
Rolling Stones (1989) *Steel Wheels*, CBS.
Roxy Music (1972) *Roxy Music*, Island.
Roxy Music (1973) *For your Pleasure*, Island.
Roxy Music (1982) *Avalon*, EG.
Rush (1989) *Presto*, Atlantic.
Saxon (1983) *Power and the Glory*, Carrere.
Searchers (1974) *Golden Hour: The Searchers*, Golden Hour.
Sex Pistols (1977) *Never Mind the Bollocks Here's the Sex Pistols*, Virgin.
Shadows (1989) *Shadows in the 60s*, MFP.
Paul Simon (1986) *Graceland*, Warner Bros.
Simon and Garfunkel (1968) *The Graduate*, CBS.
Siouxsie and the Banshees (1981) *Once Upon a Time*, Polydor.
Slade (1984) *Slade's Greats*, Polydor.
Slits (1979) *Cut*, Island.
Small Faces (1968) *Ogden's Nut Gone Flake*, Immediate.
Smiths (1984) *The Smiths*, Rough Trade.
Soft Machine (1990) *Peel Sessions*, Strange Fruit.
Spandau Ballet (1983) *True*, Reformation.
Bruce Springsteen (1975) *Born to Run*, CBS.
Squeeze (1982) *Singles – 45s and Under*, A & M.
Status Quo (1974) *Quo*, Vertigo.
Status Quo (1983) *Works*, PRT.
Status Quo (1989) *Perfect Remedy*, Phonogram.
Rod Stewart (1976) *Atlantic Crossing*, Riva.
Style Council (1985) *Our Favourite Shop*, Polydor.
T. Rex (1987) *Singles Collection – 1*, Marc on Wax.
Tears for Fears (1989) *Seeds of Love*, Phonogram.
Thin Lizzy (1980) *Chinatown*, Vertigo.
Richard and Linda Thompson (1974) *I Want to See the Bright Lights Tonight*, Island.
Richard and Linda Thompson (1986) *Shoot Out the Lights*, Hannibal.
Tin Machine (1989) *Tin Machine*, EMI.
Toto (1979) *Toto*, CBS.
Transvision Vamp (1989) *Velveteen*, MCA.
Tina Turner (1989) *Foreign Affair*, Capitol.
Bonnie Tyler (1981) *Very Best of Bonnie Tyler*, RCA.
Tyrannosaurus Rex (1968) *My People were Fair and had Sky in their Hair but now they're Content to Wear Stars on their Brows*, Regal Zonophone.
Tyrannosaurus Rex (1968) *Prophets, Seers and Sages, the Angels of the Ages*, Regal Zonophone.
Tyrannosaurus Rex (1970) *Beard of Stars*, Regal Zonophone.

UFO (1974) *Phenomenon*, Chrysalis.
Ultravox (1980) *Vienna*, Chrysalis.
Uriah Heep (1970) *Very 'eavy Very 'umble*, Island.
Uriah Heep (1972) *Demons and Wizards*, Bronze.
U2 (1981) *Boy*, Island.
U2 (1983) *War*, Island.
U2 (1984) *The Unforgettable Fire*, Island.
U2 (1987) *The Joshua Tree*, Island.
U2 (1988) *Rattle and Hum*, Island.
Van der Graaf Generator (1971) *Pawn Hearts*, Charisma.
Van Halen (1982) *Diver Down*, Warner Bros.
Van Halen (1984) *1984*, Warner Bros.
Various (1975) *African Journey: A Search for the Roots of the Blues Volume 1*, Sonet.
Various (1986) *Rock 'n' Roll Greats Volume 1*, MFP.
Various (1986) *Rock 'n' Roll Greats Volume 2*, MFP.
Bobby Vee (1980) *Singles Album*, United Artists.
Sheila Walsh (1987) *Say So*, Myrrh.
Muddy Waters (1985) *On Chess, Vol. 1*, Vogue.
Wedding Present (1987) *George Best*, Reception.
Whitesnake (1980) *Live in the Heart of the City*, United Artists.
Whitesnake (1989) *Slip of the Tongue*, EMI.
Who (1969) *Tommy*, Track.
Who (1971) *Meaty, Beaty, Big and Bouncy*, Track.
Wishbone Ash (1972) *Argus*, MCA.
XTC (1982) *English Settlement*, Virgin.
XTC (1982) *Waxworks*, Virgin.
XTC (1986) *Skylarking*, Virgin.
Yardbirds (1983) *Our Own Sound*, Charly.
Yes (1970) *Time and a Word*, Atlantic.
Yes (1971) *Fragile*, Atlantic.
Yes (1972) *Close to the Edge*, Atlantic.
Neil Young (1970) *After the Gold Rush*, Reprise.

Appendix: Sources of
Music Examples

'A Day in the Life' (Lennon/McCartney) © Northern Songs Ltd.
'Alive and Well and Living in' (Anderson) © Ian Anderson Music Ltd.
'Aqualung' (Anderson/Anderson) © Ian Anderson Music Ltd/Chrysalis Music Ltd.
'Being for the Benefit of Mr Kite' (Lennon/McCartney) © Northern Songs Ltd.
'Bike' (Barrett) © Essex Music International.
'Blueberry Hill' (Lewis/Stock/Rose) © Victoria Music Publishing Ltd/Redwood
 Music Ltd.
'Cold Wind to Valhalla' (Anderson) © Five Star Publishing Ltd.
'David Watts' (Davies) © Davray Music Ltd.
'Deserted Cities of the Heart' (Bruce/Brown) © Dratleaf Music.
'Fixing a Hole' (Lennon/McCartney) © Northern Songs Ltd.
'Flame of the West' (Adamson/Brzezicki/Watson/Butler) © 10 Music Ltd.
'Glad All Over' (Clark/Smith) © Ivy Music Ltd.
'Harvester of Sorrow' (Hetfield/Ulrich) © Creeping Death Music.
'Heartbreak Hotel' (Axton/Durden/Presley) © Tree Publishing Co. Inc.
'Holidays in the Sun' (Rotten/Vicious/Cook/Jones) Copyright Control.
'I Heard It through the Grapevine' (Whitfield/Strong) © Jobete Music Ltd.
'I Looked Away' (Clapton/Whitlock) © Throat Music/Delbon.
'In the Country' (Marvin/Welch/Bennett/Rostill) © Shadows Music Ltd.
'Kashmir' (Bonham/Page/Plant) © Joaneline Music Inc.
'Larks' tongues in Aspic (Part II)' (Fripp) © EG Music Ltd.
'Life on Mars' (Bowie) © Chrysalis Music Ltd/Titanic Music Ltd.
'Love for Tender' (Costello) © Plangent Visions Music Ltd.
'Lucy in the Sky with Diamonds' (Lennon/McCartney) © Northern Songs Ltd.
'Passing the Time' (Baker/Taylor) © Dratleaf Music.
'Rock around the Clock' (deKnight/Freedman) © E. Kassner Music.
'Secondary Modern' (Costello) © Plangent Visions Music Ltd.
'Seconds' (Callis/Oakey/Wright) © Sound Diagrams/Virgin Music Publishers Ltd/
 Dinsong Ltd.
'Shadow of Fear' (Barson/McPherson) © Nutty Sounds/Warner Bros Music Ltd.
'Sole Survivor' (Wetton/Downes) © Warner Bros Music Ltd/Island Music Ltd.
'Songs from the Wood' (Anderson) © Salamander and Son Music Ltd.

Index